# Constructive Vision and Visionary Deconstruction

# Constructive Vision and Visionary Deconstruction

## Los, Eternity, and the Productions of Time in the Later Poetry of William Blake

PETER OTTO

CLARENDON PRESS · OXFORD
1991

*This book has been printed digitally and produced in a standard design in order to ensure its continuing availability*

# OXFORD
UNIVERSITY PRESS

Great Clarendon Street, Oxford OX2 6DP

Oxford University Press is a department of the University of Oxford.
It furthers the University's objective of excellence in research, scholarship,
and education by publishing worldwide in

Oxford New York

Athens Auckland Bangkok Bogotá Buenos Aires Cape Town
Chennai Dar es Salaam Delhi Florence Hong Kong Istanbul Karachi
Kolkata Kuala Lumpur Madrid Melbourne Mexico City Mumbai Nairobi
Paris São Paulo Shanghai Singapore Taipei Tokyo Toronto Warsaw

with associated companies in Berlin Ibadan

Oxford is a registered trade mark of Oxford University Press
in the UK and in certain other countries

Published in the United States
by Oxford University Press Inc., New York

© Peter Otto 1991

The moral rights of the author have been asserted
Database right Oxford University Press (maker)

Reprinted 2001

All rights reserved. No part of this publication may be reproduced,
stored in a retrieval system, or transmitted, in any form or by any means,
without the prior permission in writing of Oxford University Press,
or as expressly permitted by law, or under terms agreed with the appropriate
reprographics rights organization. Enquiries concerning reproduction
outside the scope of the above should be sent to the Rights Department,
Oxford University Press, at the address above

You must not circulate this book in any other binding or cover
and you must impose this same condition on any acquirer

ISBN 0-19-811751-5

*Jacket illustration: Milton, plate 10,'Satan,
Palamabron, and Rintrah' by William Blake. The
Trustees of the British Museum.*

*For*
*Gai Wilson*

# Acknowledgements

I would first like to thank Dr Michael J. Tolley for his careful reading and perceptive criticism of my argument in each of its many stages of evolution. A special debt of gratitude is also due to Dr Mary Lynn Grant and Professor John E. Grant (University of Iowa, Iowa), who provided an invaluable forum for testing and refining the ideas presented here.

Friends and colleagues who have contributed substantially to the ideas and presentation of this essay in the course of its evolution include: Wendy Abbott-Young, William and Barbara Clements, David Dodwell (Hawthorn CAE, Melbourne), Robin Eaden (University of Adelaide), Professor Morris Eaves (University of Rochester), Diane Fahey, Dr Margaret Hood, Max Hicks (Swinburne CAE, Melbourne), Kevin Magarey (University of Adelaide), Dr Russell McDougall (University of Adelaide), Professor Ken Ruthven (University of Melbourne), and Gai Wilson.

Mention should also be made of the friends and family without whose support, ideas, and conversation this book would not have been finished: Jim Barbour, Julie Coulls, Jeremy Hurley, Elizabeth Kriewaldt, Margaret Magarey, Max and Dawn Otto, Philip and Sharon Sluczanowski, and John and Win Wilson. Much more than thanks are due to Gai Wilson and my children, Daniel, Gabriel, and Jordan, who have lived with me over the years that it has taken to complete this book.

This book began life as a doctoral dissertation that was made possible by a Post-Graduate Research Award from the Australian Government. A version of Chapter One first appeared in *Philological Quarterly*. It appears here with the permission of the editors.

Peter Otto

*University of Melbourne*
*September 1988*

# Contents

| | |
|---|---|
| *List of Illustrations* | x |
| *Key to References* | xi |
| Introduction | 1 |

## PART I: THE MOMENT OF EMBRACE

| | |
|---|---|
| 1. Visionary Deconstruction | 37 |
| 2. 'To bathe in the Waters of Life; to wash off the Not Human' | 63 |

## PART II: VISIONARY CONSTRUCTION

| | |
|---|---|
| 3. Los and *Jerusalem* | 101 |
| 4. Beginning | 137 |
| 5. The Geography of the Present | 158 |
| 6. Winding the Golden String into a Ball | 191 |
| 7. Los and Jesus | 218 |
| *Notes* | 223 |
| *Index* | 241 |

# List of Illustrations

1. Title-page to *Milton*.    39
2. *Milton*, plate 10: 'Satan, Palamabron, and Rintrah'.    59
3. Frontispiece to *Jerusalem*.    103

Photographs are reproduced by permission of the Trustees of the British Museum.

# Key to References

All Blake quotations are from the newly revised edition of *The Complete Poetry and Prose of William Blake*, edited by David V. Erdman, commentary by Harold Bloom (Garden City, NY: Anchor Press–Doubleday, 1982), abbreviated as E.

Citations usually note plate (or page) number, line numbers, and then page numbers in the Erdman edition. All citations of full-plate illustrations in Blake's illuminated poems refer to David V. Erdman, *The Illuminated Blake* (Garden City, NY: Anchor Press–Doubleday, 1974).

In parenthetical documentation, the following abbreviations will be used where the work cited is not clear from the context:

| | |
|---|---|
| BT | *The Book of Thel* |
| BU | *The Book of Urizen* |
| DC | *Descriptive Catalogue* |
| EG | *The Everlasting Gospel* |
| FZ | *The Four Zoas* |
| J | *Jerusalem* |
| M | *Milton* |
| SL | *The Song of Los* |
| VLJ | *[A Vision of the Last Judgment]* |

# Introduction

In working through the wealth of secondary material on Blake one cannot but be struck by the incomprehension with which the major part of Blake's work was greeted during the nineteenth and even the early twentieth centuries. According to this point of view Blake is the writer of exquisite fragments and beautiful short poems who somehow lost his touch in later life. Robert Southey called *Jerusalem* 'a perfectly mad poem'[1] and Allan Cunningham in his *Lives of the Most Eminent British Painters, Sculptors, and Architects* remarked of the same poem that 'The crowning defect is obscurity . . . the whole seems a riddle which no ingenuity can solve.'[2] William Michael Rossetti, in his edition of *The Poetical Works*, described what he called Blake's 'difficult' poetry as balderdash. He added: 'For he must be a "queer fellow" . . . who, being sane, can write the sort of thing which, had it proceeded from a madman, we should recognize all altogether (sic) in character.'[3] As recently as 1956 Margaret Rudd, in her book *Organiz'd Innocence*, was arguing from the point of view that we should 'give what Blake is *saying* a hearing even if we consider that it fails as poetry'.[4] To a certain extent one can feel their sense of Blake's strangeness, but no sooner has one grasped this partial truth than one is taken aback by the more recent development where critics seem to be able to hear Blake speak in a voice which they share and which can be shared with others.

S. Foster Damon clearly set this modern tradition in motion with the publication in 1924 of his *William Blake: His Philosophy and Symbols*, and more recently the comprehensive *A Blake Dictionary*. Both books purport to give us through the medium of encyclopaedic cross-reference and systematic organization a measure of insight into the ideal and organized text of what Blake wrote. The Dictionary in particular is strangely reminiscent of Voltaire's *Philosophical Dictionary* and its belief in a world of unchanging and unchangeable natural laws beneath the flux of experience. Damon offers to give us a voice which will bridge the gap between Blake's voice and our own.

This project of translation does not stop with Damon. In her massive book *Blake and Tradition* Kathleen Raine attempts to

## 2  Introduction

give us a different sort of structure. Blake's voice can be heard through the voice of the Neo-Platonic tradition, which Raine, Yeats, and sundry others happen to share: 'Since Blake never did draw his diagram or provide notes to his Prophetic Books, it has remained for others to do so; for the "symbolic bones" are there, as Yeats was in a position to know.'[5] David Erdman's very different book *Blake: Prophet Against Empire* advances a similar programme. The 'bones' can be uncovered and the text behind the text discovered if one hears in Blake's work the voice of history:

In order to get close to the eye-level at which Blake witnessed the drama of his own times ... I have read the newspapers and looked at the prints and paintings and sampled the debates and pamphlets of Blake's time. As Blake would say, I have 'walked up & down' in the history of that time. And I have learned to read the idiom of current allusion with sufficient familiarity to detect its presence even in Blake's obscurer pages, where workshops are dens of Babylon and royal dragoons are punishing demons and the House of Commons is a windy cave.[6]

Northrop Frye, in a structuralist and Saussurean vein, goes one step further and discovers beneath Blake's pictographs the ideal text beneath all texts, the formative principle of the imagination itself:

According to Bacon the experimenter searches nature for its underlying principles or forms, and Bacon believed it probable that there were comparatively few of these forms, which, when discovered, would be to knowledge what an alphabet is to a language. And, reading imagination for experiment and art for nature, Blake also seems to be striving for an 'alphabet of forms', a Tarot pack of pictorial visions which box the entire compass of the imagination in an orderly sequence.[7]

In the work of each of these critics we find an attempt to delineate an objective field which, they claim, generates their voice and the voice of Blake's poetry.

In drawing attention to the methodology common to the critical work of Raine, Frye, Erdman, and Damon I am not, of course, implying that it is possible to approach the text in some unmediated fashion, nor am I suggesting that the Cartesian and Enlightenment ideal of a subjectivity which is able to free itself from the prejudices of its time and history is possible or desirable. Reading is, as Paul Ricoeur observes, the yoking of the reader's discourse to the discourse of the text.[8] Moreover, it is only through this yoking that the meaning of a text can be articulated. The second term in this articulation is, however, obscured by the minute elaboration of an objective framework which in itself constitutes the poem and the critic. It re-emerges with quite some force as soon as one begins to read Blake's text. Readers encounter within their own voice as they read the words on the page a voice which, despite the wealth of secondary material, stubbornly refuses to become confused with their own.

The contours of this second discourse and this second voice are particularly difficult to delineate with any clarity in an age which is still preoccupied (and necessarily so) with the hermeneutics of suspicion, the mode of interpretation fathered by Nietzsche, Freud, and Marx.[9] Nietzsche writes, for example, in an often quoted passage, that thought is always a reduction of difference to sameness:

> All thought, judgement, perception, as comparison [Gleichnis] has as its precondition a 'positing of equality' [Gleichsetzen], and earlier still a 'making equal' [Gleich-machen]. The process of making equal is the same as the incorporation of appropriated material in the amoeba ... [and] corresponds exactly to that external, mechanical process (which is its symbol) by which protoplasm continually makes what it appropriates equal to itself and arranges it into its own forms and ranks [in seine Reihen und Formen einordnet].[10]

Within a hermeneutics of suspicion the reader's articulation of a text, or the yoking of the reader's discourse to that of the text, involves the translation of the text into the constituted world of the self. To articulate is to translate what is other into the world of the same.[11]

To articulate can, however, also be used to mean the yoking together of two disparate entities in which one gives voice to the other. To articulate means to give voice to what would otherwise remain mute and silent. This is, of course, a translation and, as Derrida's critique of western logocentrism would remind us, not an innocent one. It involves the translation of the voiceless into the syntax of the voiced, of the night into the spaces of the day. Nevertheless, this yoking of one discourse to another introduces within the 'forms and ranks' of the same, the force and the appeal of others. This is suggested by Gadamer who writes that

> the historicity of our existence entails that prejudices, in the literal sense of the word, constitute the initial directedness of our whole ability to experience. Prejudices are biases of our openness to the world. They are simply conditions whereby we experience something— whereby what we encounter says something to us.[12]

This openness is, of course, not unequivocal and it certainly does not offer an unmediated access to the other or to the text. Our prejudices, the world that we consciously and unconsciously constitute around us, are the initial framework of any attempt to reach what has not been constituted by us. At the same time, they are clearly also the ground which hems us in. They are the foundation for a mirror world where we see only what we are able to constitute. Openness and closure are closely intertwined with each other.

Merleau-Ponty discusses a similar dichotomy in *The Prose of the World* and in *Signs*. He distinguishes between sedimented language and speech. 'Sedimented language is the language the reader brings with him, the stock of accepted relations between signs and familiar significations ... It constitutes the language and the literature of the language.' Speech on the other hand 'is the operation through which a certain arrangement of already available signs and significations alters and then transfigures each of them, so that in the end a new signification is secreted.'[13] Sedimented language is an institution and forms the horizon of possible significations; yet this same language has the uncanny capacity to come to sudden and unprecedented life in speech. The central methodological problem is therefore the problem of understanding how one constitutes the meaning-structures of experience and at the same time finds that 'it is always already constituted in terms of meanings we have not bestowed upon it'. Merleau-Ponty speaks of this difficulty in the *Phenomenology of Perception* where he writes that the central problem is to understand how 'I can be open to phenomena which go beyond me, and which nevertheless exist only to the extent I take them up and live them; *how the presence to myself ("Urpräsenz") which defines me and conditions all alien presence is at the same time de-presentation ("Entgegenwärtigung") and throws me outside myself.*'[14]

That the world of the self, the discourses which we use to generate the voice of ourselves and of others, can in fact be opened is without doubt the belief which underlies the major part of Blake's artistic production. In many of his poems and particularly in *The Four Zoas*, *Milton*, and *Jerusalem*, where the apocalypse itself is predicated upon a consolidation and epiphany of Error, we witness a startling transformation of our prejudices and closed world into a radiant perception of the other. The illumination on the sixth plate of *Milton* is a good illustration of this phenomenon. At first glance there is no doubt that the rocking stone on the right-hand side of the plate is a rock; and yet, as one looks more closely at its contours, it can be seen as a ship. In the Rosenwald copy of the poem, this ship seems almost about to set sail in a bluish water-coloured sky in which all of the stars have gathered.[15] We are therefore able to see, traced upon the features of the landscape through which the traveller is passing, the possibility of transcendence. The time and space of the fallen world exist as 'one infinite plane, and not as apparent | To the weak traveller confin'd beneath the moony shade' (15: 32–3, E109).[16] This glimpse of movement and escape does not separate itself unequivocally from the state of closure implied by the stone and the trilithon: the plate seems to oscillate between these two possibilities. Our perception of freedom seems always on the verge of becoming an enclosure. And, of course, from the point of view of the corporeal man this possibility is nothing more than an optical illusion, a '[*most simulative*] Phantom of the over heated brain! shadow of immortality!' (J4: 23–4, E146).

A very different kind of 'opening' can be seen in the poem 'How sweet I roam'd', which Blake included in *Poetical Sketches*.

> How sweet I roam'd from field to field
>     And tasted all the summer's pride,
> 'Till I the prince of love beheld,
>     Who in the sunny beams did glide!
>
> He shew'd me lilies for my hair,
>     And blushing roses for my brow;
> He led me through his garden fair,
>     Where all his golden pleasures grow.
>
> With sweet May dews my wings were wet,
>     And Phoebus fir'd my vocal rage;
> He caught me in his silken net,
>     And shut me in his golden cage.
>
> He loves to sit and hear me sing,
>     Then, laughing, sports and plays with me;
> Then stretches out my golden wing,
>     And mocks my loss of liberty.          (E412–13)

The poem revolves between a world which the speaker reads as part of him/herself and a world that claims him/her as part of itself. In the course of the poem's four stanzas the qualifications to the speaker's freedom move from the background into the foreground. The self discovers itself in the matrix of the other and the last two lines are a disturbing account of the extent to which one's actions can be defined by the world. This poem suggests that our constituted worlds can, under certain conditions, open to disclose the world in which we exist. This can be seen in Blake's use of the words 'sweet' and 'golden'. 'Sweet' changes from an expression directly associated with freedom to a word which describes the bait used to catch the speaker. 'Golden' refers at first to the 'golden pleasures' which simply belong to the prince; in the last stanza it has become a property of the cage itself. A change of comportment changes the content of these words and they are used to qualify radically different nouns.

The complexities of 'How sweet I roam'd' are owing in part to the ambiguities of the relationship between reader and poem. The poem folds back on itself in an unnerving manner. The speaker's misapprehension of the prince of love's intentions and his or her slide from the role of actor to being acted upon mirrors precisely the reader's experience of the poem. In the last stanza the poem's readers could be forgiven if they feel that they have been read by the poem. From a pleasurable beginning in which the poem seemed to take them into its confidence they have fallen into a state where the poem acts on them. The poem seems to de-centre its readers: at first they are subject and the poem is the object of their scrutiny, but at the end this relationship has reversed. We have moved from our sedimented language and constituted world to the mystery of speech. The poem attempts a visionary deconstruction of the reader's assumptions which, as we shall see, is in some respects similar to the Bard's many times more complex visionary deconstruction of his audience in *Milton*. In this later poem the voice of Milton (and of Milton's prophetic endeavour) is such a potent force and inspiration that Blake can feel the presence of others within his own body.

This capacity of Blake's poems to become a voice which exerts a force upon the reader is entirely appropriate for a literary form that is at once prophetic and visionary. The poems attempt to awaken their readers, to make them aware of the confines of the world in which they exist and in this way open their eyes to Eternity. Blake defines his role in *Jerusalem* as an attempt 'To open the Eternal Worlds, to open the immortal Eyes | Of Man inwards into the Worlds of Thought: into Eternity | Ever expanding in the Bosom of God' (5: 18–20, E147). It is, however, this prophetic and visionary dimension of Blake's poetry which is obscured in any attempt to delineate an objective ground which will produce the voice of the poem and of the reader. Blake is not simply concerned to create an '"alphabet of forms", a Tarot pack of pictorial visions which box the entire compass of the imagination in an orderly sequence', but to move his readers to a position from which the confines of the box can be breached. Similarly, there is no doubt that, thanks to the illuminating work of David Erdman, Blake scholars are now able to detect the history of Blake's time 'even in Blake's obscurer pages'. The thrust of Blake's major prophecies is, however, not simply to allude to the history of his time but, by reading that history in the forge of both hope and fear, to open it to Eternity. Damon's dictionary is an important and useful tool, and Raine's Neo-Platonic Blake gives us useful insights into his work, but as prophet and as visionary Blake is concerned to open the worlds held by the Spectres belonging to his readers, not least of which is the world held by the Spectral portion of his critics.

The central problem which arises for Blake studies at this point in its history is how Blake's prophetic visions or visionary prophecies actually work? How does Blake propose to open the linear expanse of time to the corrosive fires of Eternity? In what sense is Eternity in love with the 'productions of time'? And how are we to conceive of this art which insists on opening what is closed, and making problematic what has been taken for granted? In more general philosophical terms, these concerns become the question of the relationship between a hermeneutics of suspicion (Nietzsche, Freud, Marx) and a hermeneutics of belief (Bultmann, Eliade).

Questions such as these have for the most part not been taken up because Blake criticism, particularly since the work of Northrop Frye, has worked within a discourse which tends to erase the very distinction between self and other, and time and Eternity. As a result the question of how our worlds are to be opened, and how we can perceive what is other, does not appear in its full force. This can be seen in the way that key terms such as 'imagination' have been defined by Blake's critics.

Criticism of Romantic poetry has in general worked within a view of the imagination similar to that put forward by Coleridge in the thirteenth chapter of *Biographia Literaria*:

primary IMAGINATION I hold to be the living Power and prime Agent of all human Perception, and as a repetition in the finite mind of the eternal act of creation in the infinite I AM. The secondary I consider as an echo of the former, co-existing with the conscious will, yet still as identical with the primary in the *kind* of its agency, and differing only in *degree*, and in the *mode* of its operation. It dissolves, diffuses,

## 8  Introduction

dissipates, in order to re-create; or where this process is rendered impossible, yet still at all events it struggles to idealize and to unify.[17]

The imagination in this sense is basically the power to create a unified and self-contained form or world. This conception of the imagination has always dominated Blake criticism. In *Fearful Symmetry*, for example, one of the pillars of Frye's account of Blake is the philosophy of Berkeley. A central theme of this philosophy is expressed in the phrase *esse est percipi*: 'to be is to be perceived'. 'Perception' is therefore, in Frye's words, 'not something we do with our senses; it is a mental act'.[18] For Frye the faculty which performs these acts is the human imagination. He writes:

If man perceived is a form or image, man perceiving is a former or imaginer, so that 'imagination' is the regular term used by Blake to denote man as an acting and perceiving being ... To be perceived, therefore, means to be imagined, to be related to an individual's pattern of experience, to become a part of his character.[19]

The idea that 'to be is to be perceived' introduces into Berkeley's philosophy a gap between one's own subjective perceptions and those of everyone else. For this reason Berkeley proposed the idea of God as the perceiver of each entity. This created a ground which linked self and other, but this was achieved only by introducing a new gap, this time between God and man. Frye argues that Blake closes this second gap 'by identifying God with human imagination'.[20]

The contention that the image- or world-forming capacity is at the very centre of the human psyche and can be identified with the human imagination and therefore with God results in a series of quite startling propositions. First, the gap between God and Man/Woman disappears—Frye in fact writes that: 'Man in his creative acts and perceptions is God, and God is Man. God is the eternal Self, and the worship of God is self-development.'[21] There is therefore no longer an attempt to break or disrupt the reasonable or the imaginative (in Frye's sense of the word) world which closes us from others and from God (as Los must learn to do in *The Four Zoas* and in *Milton*); instead the very form of this closure is celebrated. Frye writes that the 'only legitimate compulsion on the artist is the compulsion to clarify the form of his work'[22] and that the 'fact that in the world of vision or art we see what we want to see implies that it is a world of fulfilled desire and unbounded freedom'. In this world 'the fact that imagination creates reality' means that 'as desire is a part of imagination, the world we desire is more real than the world we passively accept'.[23]

What is most disconcerting about the view of the imagination in Frye's criticism is that it leaves no room for relationship or dialogue as constitutive features of that 'faculty' and as a result the other almost disappears. The imaginer in Frye's sense is not very different from Thel or Urizen, for he/she also retreats into the closed world of the self. Frye contends, for example, that 'the world of vision' is a place where there are only creators and their creatures.[24] The prophetic anger which in the Bard's Song attempts to overturn the most fundamental categories of the world that the fallen self both desires and imagines (again in Frye's sense) here becomes yoked to the preservation of an analogous world.

*Fearful Symmetry* is one of those few critical books which can be classified legitimately as a work of art. Its immense erudition, the consistency of its argument, and its tone of passionate conviction make it worth reading even if one disagrees with its premises and its conclusions. It is therefore not at all surprising that it has shaped Blake criticism to a remarkably high degree. Time and time again one reads recensions of Frye's argument which remove the other as a source of concern in Blake's poetry, collapse or radically reduce the gap between time and Eternity, and between the self and the other, and make the fabrication and expression of the world of the individual or collective self of paramount concern. I can perhaps best illustrate the ubiquity of this phenomenon by quoting from this criticism.[25]

For Blake the mental image, the form—the very act which creates the image—is the single reality. The world is a world of mental acts. (Adams)[26]

And sun, and moon, the universe entire, are as we are, that we may be as they are, both of us the human released from every limitation and therefore both of us the divine. Like Keats's intelligences which are atoms of perception, we too know, and we see, and we are god. (Bloom)[27]

What we must do is spread our inside—our interior life—outside so as to make the outside alive with our humanity. (Rose)[28]

Man in his creative acts, as well as in his perceptions, is a god; the world of imagination is one of creators and creatures. But if perception is a godlike act, God Himself cannot be perceived except as He exists in the perceiver. (Gleckner)[29]

## 10  Introduction

A man becomes what he beholds, and 'As man is, So he Sees' . . . These principles operate jointly to fuse subject and object in a cycle of perception that gives the power of creation to the taker. (Eaves)[30]

For Blake, imagination is the supreme fiction, but it is not an absolute because it is conscious of itself as a fictive, fabricating activity, a maker of illusions. (Mitchell)[31]

In the classical space that separates the self from itself are located those 'Realities of Intellect' that are the 'Treasures of Heaven'. (Stempel)[32]

The moment that all men see themselves and each other as gods is the moment when earth becomes heaven, the particular becomes infinite, and time becomes eternity. When all distinctions between the finite and the infinite are merely modes of perception, capable of being reperceived and recreated simultaneously, then such distinctions no longer 'exist' in any meaningful sense. (Mellor)[33]

Neither Blake nor Shelley sees the universe with a vision that divides subject and object, the outer world from the mind which projects it: whatever is projected returns to the beholder and he becomes like it. (Bandy)[34]

Every real poem is . . . a 'heterocosm', not an imitation of nature but itself another nature and to the extent that man achieves such creations, he becomes like God. (James)[35]

In Eternity, the scope of the senses is neither restricted by anatomical deficiencies nor are they dependent on the weakness or intensity of impressions received from an as yet unperceived outside world. The active mind is autonomous and instantaneously fulfils its desires. (Kittel)[36]

Art, to Blake, is the highest and most unitive activity of mind and body, but all life aspires to the condition of art. In Jerusalem Energy and Imagination meet in a new synthesis, the best exemplification of which is the great poem itself—a little world made cunningly, microcosm and object of art, painting, and prophecy—the Emanation of William Blake. (Paley)[37]

For Blake, true or essential humanity is a power of unlimited creative act. (Deen)[38]

The entire universe is humanized in the subjective identification of all creation within Albion . . . There is no longer any separation between self and other, or perceiving subject and objective universe. All appearances and phenomena are reintegrated in one subjective whole since everything outside reflects an inner condition or is shaped by an inner state. (Doskow)[39]

The text participates equally with the reader in their acts of mutual constitution and revision . . . From the perspective of the reader's response, however, the *Four Zoas* narrative and text either come into existence or fail to come into existence only through the reader's imaginative acts and decisions. (Ault)[40]

The capacity to form worlds is quite clearly an important part of imagination, but it is important to recognize that this capacity, by itself, is more closely associated with Los than Jesus. Even in Eternity Los is identified as Urthona (the owner of the earth or the constituted world of each individual), and not as Christ. Yet it is Christ who is the Imagination and not Los.[41] As a result of the self-transformations undergone in *Milton* and *Jerusalem*, Los is seen in the similitude of Christ, but is still not identified with Christ.

Even with regard to Los, any attempt to suggest that Los's work is homologous with that of the world-forming imagination is fraught with difficulty. In *The Book of Urizen*, for example, Los's fabrication of the fallen world is preceded by an attempt to remain open to Urizen-in-withdrawal. It is only when Los turns away in despair from Urizen that the fallen world is 'created'. Up to this time it is not so much a world as a conversation which lacks a partner. In other words, for Los creation is intimately bound up with relationship and friendship in a way which is not suggested by the more or less successfully world-forming imaginations described by humanism, modernism, or post-structuralism.

Moreover, as has been suggested by a number of contemporary critics, in the Lambeth prophecies it is the image- and world-forming capacities of Los that close us off from others.[42] These productions, as the name Los (loss) suggests, result in the final separation of time from Eternity. As Paul de Man writes, the poetic image is 'always constitutive, able to posit regardless of presence but, by the same token, unable to give a foundation to what it posits except as an intent of consciousness'.[43] Los is a figure who is able to constitute a world which stops Albion from falling into nothingness, but he is unable to give this world any other foundation than that offered by loss.

These problems are not eased when we turn to Christ-the-Imagination, who seems to appear at the points at which particular worlds are 'breached' by dialogue and relationship. The distance that separates this figure from a world-forming imagination is implied in the rather provocative words of *A Vision of The Last Judgment*. Blake writes:

If the Spectator could Enter into these Images in his Imagination approaching them on the Fiery Chariot of his contemplative Thought if

## 12   Introduction

he could Enter into Noahs Rainbow or into his bosom or could make a Friend & Companion of one of these Images of wonder which always intreats him to leave mortal things as he must know then would he arise from his Grave then would he meet the Lord in the Air & then he would be happy. (VLJ, E558)

It is true that Blake's poetic productions are an attempt to show collective and individual humanity that we bear our heavens and our earths in our bosoms (J 71: 17–18, E225). However, he does this not in order to celebrate a potential or actual capacity to create worlds, but in order to induce us to move out from these worlds into relationship. In Blake's œuvre the world-forming imagination is itself a portion of the prophetic imagination; the major prophecies are an attempt to describe the way in which the created world, the universe of Los and Enitharmon, can open itself to others.

When one turns to Blake's poems one finds that many of the texts which are used by Frye or those influenced by his criticism to support his case for the redemptive power of the fallen or unfallen world-forming imagination contradict such a claim. The most striking passage cited by Frye in support of his argument is taken from *A Vision of the Last Judgment*:

I assert for My self that I do not behold the Outward Creation & that to me it is hindrance & not Action it is as the Dirt upon my feet No part of Me. What it will be Questiond When the Sun rises do you not see a round Disk of fire somewhat like a Guinea O no no I see an Innumerable company of the Heavenly host crying Holy Holy Holy is the Lord God Almighty I question not my Corporeal or Vegetative Eye any more than I would Question a Window concerning a Sight I look thro it & not with it. (E565–6)

Frye interprets this passage in the following way: 'The Hallelujah-Chorus perception of the sun makes it a far more real sun than the guinea-sun, because more imagination has gone into perceiving it.'[44] This seems to me to miss the point. The perception of the sun as a guinea is tied to the economy of the self. A guinea is something which we can use; it suggests a world that is seen only in terms of its relative usefulness to the self. The vision of the sun as a Hallelujah-Chorus is, however, radically different. It is, of course, still a perception, but now it is one which has been interpenetrated with others. These others can talk, move, sing, and can therefore suffuse the self with a force which cannot be reduced to our perception of them. The world formed by Frye's imagination discovers within its bounds a force and presence which far exceeds its domain.

Similarly, in a letter to Dr Trusler dated 23 August 1799 Blake writes:

> I feel that a Man may be happy in This World. And I know that This World Is a World of Imagination & Vision I see Every thing I paint In This World, but Every body does not see alike. To the Eyes of a Miser a Guinea is more beautiful than the Sun & a bag worn with the use of Money has more beautiful proportions than a Vine filled with Grapes. The tree which moves some to tears of joy is in the Eyes of others only a Green thing that stands in the way. (E702)

Vision is here linked not solely with the ability to form a world, but with the capacity to be moved by things which lie outside of the world formed by the self. It is, of course, true that in the lines immediately preceding the Hallelujah-Chorus passage Blake writes that 'Mental Things are alone Real what is Calld Corporeal Nobody Knows of its Dwelling Place <it> is in Fallacy & its Existence an Imposture Where is the Existence Out of Mind or Thought Where is it but in the Mind of a Fool' (E565). The contention that 'Mental Things are alone Real' and the denial of the existence of the corporeal remind us of Berkeley's denial of the existence of matter and his location of being in the act of perception. Frye in fact uses this passage as a paraphrase of an idealist position.[45] This is, however, a little too pat. First, the meaning of the word 'Mental' in Blake's œuvre cannot be adequately represented by the world-forming imagination. It refers primarily to realities which lie outside of the purview of the constituted world of the self. Second, the very distinction between the world that is formed by the fool (a corporeal and therefore self-enclosing world) and Mental realities gains its force by implicit reference to a reality (such as that exemplified by the Hallelujah-Chorus) which exceeds the limits set by the world-forming imagination. The fool is a fool and his world is corporeal because he cannot open his imagined world to others. Third, and most decisively, these words are followed by others which tell us that creation itself (the entire world forged by Frye's imagination) will be cast off at the Last Judgement: 'Error is Created Truth is Eternal Error or Creation will be Burned Up & then & not till then Truth or Eternity will appear It is Burnt up the Moment Men cease to behold it' (E565). In these lines the world formed by Frye's imagination, creation itself, is associated with Error. It is this which 'is Burnt up the Moment Men cease to behold it', while Truth is not created or imagined in Frye's sense, but is 'Eternal'.

Perhaps the clearest indication of the distance which separates Blake from the view of the imagination held by Frye can be seen in his own account of the creative process. Blake wrote in a letter to Thomas Butts dated the 22 November 1802 that he both sees a vision (that he constitutes it and so gives it form) and that this vision is given to him (and therefore proceeds from a source outside the world of the self): 'Now I a fourfold vision see | And a fourfold vision is given to me' (E722). This intertwining of what is given and what is constituted or imagined (again in Frye's understanding of this word) can be seen in the account at the beginning of *Jerusalem* of that poem's conception:

> Of the Sleep of Ulro! and of the passage through
> Eternal Death! and of the awaking to Eternal life.
>
> This theme calls me in sleep night after night, & ev'ry morn
> Awakes me at sun-rise, then I see the Saviour over me
> Spreading his beams of love, & dictating the words of this mild song.
>
> (4: 1-5, E146)

The theme begins with the Sleep of Ulro. Ulro is a state where one is locked within one's self. In this world there is a complete split between the self and the other. It is therefore characterized as sleep. We next hear of the passage through Eternal Death and 'of the awaking to Eternal Life'. Eternal Life is described as an awaking from sleep and therefore, in the terms of this image, a standing in the presence of things that are other. The theme therefore sets up a movement, as though one were moving through a cave or tunnel. One is asleep, lost in the ground, one passes through Eternal Death and then, like a seed emerging, or the sun dawning, one awakes to Eternal Life. The theme calls Blake and it awakes him at sunrise. It is this contact with what is not constituted by the self that is the condition of Blake's emergence. This parallels the way in which the sun, in waking the solitary dreamer, throws him into a universe of participation.

As a result of this awakening Blake is able to see and hear Christ the Imagination, the Vine of Eternity. In other words, the Imagination is first glimpsed not in the fabrication of a world, but at the point at which our worlds are cast off. It appears not as a faculty which is possessed by the individual, but as an other who calls Blake. In fact, in the introduction to the second chapter of this poem, the poet asks Jesus the Imagination to do the work of creation ('Create my Spirit to thy Love') and to subdue his Spectre. The Imagination, far from generating the world of the self, or underwriting a world of creators and creatures, introduces an unprecedented call into the world of the poet.

The call of Christ can be heard only within the voice of Blake and within the confines of his poem. This necessity does not, however, result in the erasure of that call. In the lines of *Jerusalem* that follow Christ's appearance to Blake we discover that it is within the words of the call of the other (Saviour and theme) that Blake has found his own voice. There is therefore a curious intertwining of the Saviour's call to Blake and Blake's call to the reader:

> Awake! awake O sleeper of the land of shadows, wake! expand!
> I am in you and you in me, mutual in love divine:
> Fibres of love from man to man thro Albions pleasant land.
> In all the dark Atlantic vale down from the hills of Surrey
> A black water accumulates, return Albion! return!
>
> (4: 6-10, E146)

To the extent that a call from what has not been constituted by the self is embraced, it becomes a vocation. In this oscillation between call and response the self escapes from the closed world of Urizen, whom Blake describes as a 'self-contemplating shadow' (*BU* 3: 21, E71), and emerges into a shared world. Jerusalem (the poem, the city, and the woman) emerges within relationship. A world of creators and creatures is here transformed into one in which self and other, God and Man/Woman, time and Eternity, reside in each other's bosoms. Christ (and Blake in Christ) says to his audience: 'I am not a God afar off, I am a brother and friend; | Within your bosoms I reside, and you reside in me' (4: 18-19, E146).

This presence of the other within the self is a reality and, indeed, a ground for the self which is not always recognized. Christ's call in the opening plates of *Jerusalem*, for example, is not heeded by Albion. He has heard his voice, but not his call. Albion

> away turns down the valleys dark;
> [Saying. We are not One: we are Many, thou most simulative]
> Phantom of the over heated brain! shadow of immortality!
> Seeking to keep my soul a victim to thy Love! which binds
> Man the enemy of man into deceitful friendships:
> Jerusalem is not! her daughters are indefinite:
> By demonstration, man alone can live, and not by faith.
> My mountains are my own, and I will keep them to myself!

The Malvern and the Cheviot, the Wolds Plinlimmon & Snowdon
Are mine. here will I build my Laws of Moral Virtue!
Humanity shall be no more: but war & princedom & victory!

(4: 22-32, E146-7)

The Perturbed Man wants to remain within the world of the self. He is willing to believe only if it is demonstrated to him and in this way brought into his frame of reference. He demands that the other be judged and assessed according to the categories of his world, instead of opening his world to the potentially unsettling call of Christ. As a result of this withdrawal the world becomes one in which self is pitted against self, and the Laws and Moral Virtue of one are used to judge another.

Albion is a giant figure who contains all of humanity within his bulk. His withdrawal into the world of the self is, therefore, not simply an action undertaken by an individual, but something in which we all share. In Blake's own time the most conspicuous manifestation of this turn into the world of the self was the metaphysics inaugurated by Bacon, Newton, and Locke. Blake pictures these philosophies as a tremendous force which is pitted against the very possibility of life. He writes in *Jerusalem*, for example, that Bacon and Newton are 'sheathd in dismal steel' and 'their terrors hang | Like iron scourges over Albion' (15: 11-12, E159).

The intensity of Blake's tone in lines such as these can be understood if we remember that these philosophies move the locus of reality to the individual reasoning self. As the being of the whole Man is formed in relationship, they therefore do indeed 'hang | Like iron scourges over Albion'. Locke, for example, makes no apology for confining the object of his inquiry to the understanding of the 'cavern'd man'. He writes:

I pretend not to teach, but to inquire; and therefore cannot but confess here again,—that external and internal sensation are the only passages I can find of knowledge to the understanding. These alone, as far as I can discover, are the windows by which light is let into this *dark room*. For, methinks, the understanding is not much unlike a closet wholly shut from light, with only some little openings left, to let in external visible resemblances, or ideas of things without: [would the pictures coming into such a dark room but stay there], and lie so orderly as to be found upon occasion, it would very much resemble the understanding of a man, in reference to all objects of sight, and the ideas of them.[46]

The ideas which together provide 'all the *materials* of reason and knowledge'[47] are in Locke's view analogous to 'external visible resemblances' of the things and beings that exist outside of the 'closet' and, as he will later argue, so long as the mind can have 'no other immediate object but its own ideas, which it alone does or can contemplate, it is evident that our knowledge is only conversant about them. . . . knowledge then seems . . . to be nothing but *the perception of the connexion of and agreement, or disagreement and repugnancy of any of our ideas*'.[48] Thinking is therefore no more than a process in which the material given in experience is manipulated in a variety of ways. Locke uses the number of words that can be generated from the twenty-six letters of the alphabet to illustrate the multifarious ideas that can be established on the basis of this primary material.[49]

It can therefore be seen that Locke rules out the very possibility of the mental warfare that is the basis of Eternity. Within the closet the other is perceived as 'an external visible resemblance', a simple idea; and reason manipulates these resemblances as if they were fixed coins or tokens. There is certainly no room for dialogue, or for the relationship between call and response that is the ground of Eternity. This is not to say that Locke allows no room for revelation, but that there is no relationship between revelation and the world of the self.

A striking formulation of Blake's objections to Locke can be found in *Jerusalem*. Towards the end of the fourth chapter Los sends his Spectre to the 'Fiends of Righteousness' (of whom one was undoubtedly Locke). Los exhorts him to 'Tell them to obey their Humanities, & not pretend Holiness' (91: 4 and 5, E251). As Los warms to his theme he speaks as if the fiends were themselves present:

> You accumulate Particulars, & murder by analyzing, that you
> May take the aggregate; & you call the aggregate Moral Law:
> And you call that Swelld & bloated Form; a Minute Particular.
> But General Forms have their vitality in Particulars: & every
> Particular is a Man; a Divine Member of the Divine Jesus.
>
> (91: 26-30, E251)

The particulars accumulated by Locke are simple ideas. For Los, however, these ideas are not the primary data of sensation beyond which we cannot go, for 'every | Particular is a Man' who has the capacity to engage us in discourse. Locke turns away from relationship with others and retains as the ground of knowledge only that portion of the world that has been assimilated to the self. In *Jerusalem* the foundation of the fallen world is the relationship between Albion, Christ, and Los. By contrast, Locke turns away from the relationships in which his simple ideas appear. He murders the other by being deaf to his/her call, and then weighing, analysing, counting, and building a world from the 'external visible resemblances' of the other which are retained by the reasoning memory. For the former, our constituted worlds have significance in that they constantly point beyond themselves to a surplus which both exceeds their grasp and engages the self in discourse. For the latter, 'resemblances' have become the property (hence the word 'accumulate') of a 'cavern'd' and withdrawn man.

When Locke wishes to come to an understanding of an idea such as Eternity, he fabricates this idea from the material available within the closed world of the self. His general forms are therefore swelled and bloated forms, whereas for Los there is only one general form and this form is a living being. The only true and general form (within which our identities are comprehended) is Christ. At both ends of Locke's epistemological concerns Blake affirms a universe in which others exist. In *The Four Zoas* Ahania describes the Fall in terms of an overwhelming of Man by his Shadow (40: 2-8, E327). It appears that Locke has also fallen under the sway of his Shadow. In turning away from relationship with others and retaining only that which has appeared within his constituted world, he has become entranced by his own image. Like Narcissus he is mesmerized by 'a watry vision' of himself and a 'watry Shadow' which in turn is used to regulate his life.

An analogous case can also be advanced against Bacon and Newton. Alexander Koyré writes in 'The Significance of the Newtonian Synthesis' that Newton split our world into two. The first world is one 'in which we live, and love, and die . . .'; the second world is centred upon the observations and reasoning of the detached observer (in Blake's parlance, the 'reasoning memory').[50] Yet it is the second world that in Newtonian physics forms the locus of reality. Similarly, the scientific method advanced by Bacon in, for example, the *Novum Organum*, also locates truth firmly within what appears inside the closed world of the (reasoning) self. For Bacon the knowledge generated by this method is closely linked to the desire to gain power over what lies outside of the self. In his own words, he hoped 'to restore and exalt the power and dominion of man himself, of the human race, over the universe'.[51]

It is important to recognize, however, that Blake is *not* suggesting that Locke, Bacon, and Newton are wrong in their descriptions of fallen humanity. In fact they are correct. Fallen existence is a retreat into the closet, a separation of the self from the living world in which others are found. Fallen existence is a world in which one isolated self is pitted against another. Bacon, Newton, and Locke therefore all can be seen to play an important role in the consolidation of Error. In *Europe* it is Newton who blows the 'Trump' of the last doom (13: 5, E65), and in the apocalypse which closes *Jerusalem* 'Bacon & Newton & Locke' are seen alongside 'Milton & Shakspear & Chaucer' (98: 9, E257). Their influence is pernicious, however, because they contend that the world that they (correctly) trace is the only world. Blake, on the other hand, is a prophetic visionary who attempts to reveal the relationships in which this world is grounded, who tries to open the closed world of the self to others, and by these means hopes to open the possibility of transformation and regeneration.

The similarities and dissimilarities between this visionary project and the project undertaken by Derrida in the twentieth century are both instructive and illuminating. Derrida argues that metaphysics has always been based on presence.[52] This foundation, however, is less than secure, for at the heart of what is present to the self an 'irreducible nonpresence can be found to have constituting value, and with it a nonlife, a nonpresence or nonself-belonging of the living present, an ineradicable nonprimordiality'.[53] The sign, for example, is not an autonomous thing in itself, for it is constituted only in relation to other signs. As Saussure observes in the *Course in General Linguistics*, 'in language there are only differences. Even more important: a difference generally implies positive terms between which the difference is set up; but in language there are only differences *without positive terms*'.[54] The meaning of a sign is therefore never fully present, for it finds itself situated in a chain of significations which continually defer the moment in which a fully present meaning could be recouped. The same argument can be applied to the notion of identity, or of a self-same thing, for all 'determinations of identity are broken apart by the necessity of alterity'.[55] Similarly, the apparently autonomous and self-standing things which appear within the world are also caught up in a web of differentiation. They are things only because they stand within a complex series of relationships. Derrida coins the word *différance* to describe this spatial and temporal separation which produces the effect of presence.[56]

*Différance* ensures that no unshakeable foundation for metaphysics can be found. It is impossible to discover a set of axioms which are not themselves caught within the web of differentiation. This means that the world is itself a text in the sense that it does not escape this constitution in differentiation. There is no outside to the text ('Il n'y a pas de hors texte') because there is no certain ground, no absolutely present object, which is not itself constituted by *différance*. We cannot have unmediated access to a first ground or essential substance which will allow us to ground knowledge. As Derrida observes, 'contrary to what phenomenology—which is always phenomenology of perception—has tried to make us believe, contrary to what our desire cannot fail to be tempted into believing, the thing itself always escapes'.[57] It is as if, in terms of the image introduced by Derrida at the end of *Speech and Phenomena*, we are domiciled within a gallery where the paintings achieve definition only in relation to other paintings and other galleries: 'Of the broad daylight of presence, outside the gallery, no perception is given us or assuredly promised us. The gallery is the labyrinth which includes in itself its own exits.'[58] It therefore

> remains... for us to *speak*, to make our voices *resonate* throughout the corridors in order to make up for [*suppléer*] the breakup of presence. The phoneme, the *akoumenon*, is the *phenomenon of the labyrinth*. This is the *case* with the *phone*. Rising toward the sun of presence, it is the way of Icarus.[59]

Our attempts to leave this space and attain pure and unmediated presence must, like the attempts of Icarus to leave his labyrinth, end in failure and, perhaps, in death.

Quite clearly several broad parallels can be drawn between deconstruction and Blake's poetry. In the course of his œuvre Blake develops, for example, a far-reaching critique of all philosophies which rely for their ground on what is present to the corporeal self. It is characters such as Vala and Rahab, or the Deists in *Jerusalem*, who celebrate the world that is present to the closeted self. As I shall argue, this world gains definition only in relationship with what is not present to the corporeal self. It is also possible to argue that Blake is concerned to criticize any philosophy which rests on a set of immutable axioms or rules. The attempts of Urizen, for example, to find a perspective from which he can hold the entire world within his gaze end in failure. The fallen world is indeed a labyrinth and it is also one which includes its exits within itself. However, unlike Derrida, Blake is not concerned simply to show the impossibility, the violence, of all attempts to close this world within a metaphysics based on a limited set of axioms, but to uncover the relationships in which this labyrinth itself appears.[60]

As I shall argue, in Blake's poems—as in Derrida's philosophy—the labyrinth of the fallen world appears as a result of a spatial and temporal distancing (*différance*) which occurs prior to the appearance of the world in which we live. In Derrida's work *différance* is a mysterious, self-motivated, abstract movement whose existence is postulated by inference from what is. For Blake, *différance* is an effect of a particular (let us say, an ontological) comportment of Albion towards the Zoas which make up his identity and towards the other inhabitants of Eden. It is a result of the withdrawal of Albion from relationship. The fallen self and the fallen other which are introduced as a result of *différance* are in Blake's œuvre not the very beginnings of life, but a radical and far reaching reduction of life. As Blake peremptorily states:

Many suppose that before [Adam] <the Creation> All was Solitude & Chaos This is the most pernicious Idea that can enter the Mind as it takes away all sublimity from the Bible & Limits All Existence to Creation & to Chaos To the Time & Space fixed by the Corporeal Vegetative Eye & leaves the Man who entertains such an Idea the habitation of Unbelieving Demons Eternity Exists and All things in Eternity Independent of Creation which was an act of Mercy. (VLJ, E563)

It is this rather different understanding of *différance* which forms one of the major points of divergence between Derrida's sceptical philosophy and Blake's visionary art. It is because, in Blake's understanding, the world is not formed in an anonymous, ahistorical movement of *différance*, but in a particular stance taken by Albion towards others, that this stance and therefore the world can be changed. Blake's work is therefore prophetic in that he attempts to show us the relationships in which this world is formed, and it is visionary in that he is able to figure forth the possibility of transformation.

I am, of course, not denying that it is in Albion's withdrawal from others that the distinctions with which we order our world (such as those between self and other, inside and outside) are formed. It is not this which is fundamentally at issue in Blake's œuvre but, as I shall later argue, the conclusions that are drawn from this particular articulation of existence. On the one hand Albion pits inside against outside in deadly battle. On the other hand Christ follows withdrawal with embrace, and opens the world of the self again and again to others. It is important to underline that when Christ calls Albion to return he does not do away with the movement of *différance*, or with the closed world which is its fruit. Even in the apocalypse of *Jerusalem* the 'Human Forms' return 'wearied | Into the Planetary lives of Years Months Days & Hours' (99: 2-3, E258). Christ does, however, radically displace and so transform this world. In Eternity the world that is formed in withdrawal is a seed: it forms the ground for an expansion in which the world of the self opens to others. The formation of the world of the self opens the possibility of 'Friendship', 'Brotherhood', and the 'Mysterious | Offering of Self for Another' (96: 20-1, E256). At the time of the Fall, however, this outline becomes a horizon which forms the absolute limit of the world of the 'cavern'd man'. Blake is concerned to describe and to induce in his readers a movement which brings us to the perimeter of the labyrinth, and which once more brings contraction into a contrary relationship with expansion.

In what follows I will therefore be arguing against the assumption held by the vast majority of Blake critics that Blake's apocalypse is a matter of perception and not a question of being.[61] The traditional view on this question is put by Northrop Frye as follows:

There is no 'general nature', therefore nothing is real beyond the imaginative patterns men make of reality, and hence there are exactly as many kinds of reality as there are men. 'Every man's wisdom is peculiar to his own individuality', and there is no other kind of wisdom: reality is as much in the eye of the beholder as beauty is said to be. Scattered all through Blake's work are epigrams indicating this relativity of existence to perception.[62]

Yet the epigrams offered by Frye as a sample of those which can be found 'all through Blake's work' subtly contradict these claims:

> Every Eye sees differently. As the Eye, Such the Object.
>
> Every thing possible to be believed is an image of truth.
>
> The Sun's Light when he unfolds it
> Depends on the Organ that beholds it.

The first and second passages certainly do suggest that 'there are exactly as many kinds of reality as there are men', but this does not in itself prove the relativity of existence to perception in Blake's œuvre. The second, for example, counters the multiplication of realities with the implication that there is a single 'truth' and that our beliefs are images of that 'truth'. The first suggests that it is the way in which our Eye/I is constituted, the mode or state of being in which it/the I exists, that determines the appearance of the object. The third quotation offers more substantial support for Frye's view, for it seems to contend that 'the Organ that beholds' the 'Sun's Light' is able to give that 'Light' any form that the self can imagine. Yet even here the simple reduction of existence to perception is qualified, for an equally plausible reading would be to say that the appearance of the 'Sun's Light' is dependent upon the way in which the Organ is constituted or, alternatively, on the *kind* of organ that apprehends it.

Throughout Blake's work one can find epigrams which indicate the relativity of perception to existence. In the 'Mental Traveller', for example, Blake writes:

> The Guests are scatterd thro' the land
> For the Eye altering alters all
> The Senses roll themselves in fear
> And the flat Earth becomes a Ball.   (61-4, E485)

In other words, it is when the Eye/I is altered that the form of 'the land' is changed, and when the 'Senses roll themselves' into a circular shape that the Earth appears to be 'a Ball'. In the letter to Dr Trusler dated 23 August 1799, Blake is even more explicit. He writes that 'As a Man is So he Sees. As the Eye is formed such are its Powers':

Every body does not see alike. To the Eyes of a Miser a Guinea is more beautiful than the Sun & a bag worn with the use of Money has more beautiful proportions than a Vine filled with Grapes. The tree which moves some to tears of joy is in the Eyes of others only a Green thing that stands in the way. Some See Nature all Ridicule & Deformity & by these I shall not regulate my proportions, & Some Scarce see Nature at all But to the Eyes of the Man of Imagination Nature is Imagination itself. (E702)

The Miser feels that a 'Guinea is more beautiful than the Sun' because he has withdrawn into the closet of the self and therefore values things only to the extent to which they are useful within the economy of the self. The 'Man of Imagination', however, takes up a position in the world from which others are able to appear. It is therefore not enough for the Miser to attempt to imagine a new world from his position of withdrawal; he must be induced to change his position in the world;

he must alter his state of being. At the end of *Jerusalem*, for example, it is when Albion changes his comportment in the world, when he throws 'himself into the Furnaces of affliction', that the suffering endured in the Furnaces becomes 'a Vision' and 'a Dream', and the Furnaces themselves are transformed into 'Fountains of Living Waters flowing from the Humanity Divine' (96: 35-7, E256).

It would, however, be unwise to replace Frye's subordination of existence to perception with its mirror opposite. Blake's poetic and prophetic poems attempt to change the way in which we perceive the world in order to induce us to change the relationships that we take up to others. If this were not possible then Blake would not have written prophecies. However, perception in this sense is very different from what Frye calls by the same name and it is constrained within much narrower limits than Frye's formulation would suggest. Blake's prophetic poems attempt to 'instruct' their readers and in this way induce them to change their comportment in the world. In *Visions of the Daughters of Albion*, for example, it is arguably the instruction offered by 'The Golden nymph' that prompts Oothoon to 'turn [her] face to where [her] whole soul seeks' (1: 13, E45), but it is this change of comportment (from withdrawal to embrace) that alters the appearance of her world. The living world that she discovers is closed to both Bromion and Theotormon for so long as they remain within a state of withdrawal. Similarly, in *Milton* it is the Bard's prophetic Song that calls Milton, but this Song does not in itself replace the world in which Milton has been domiciled with a new one. It is when Milton arises and goes 'down to the sepulcher to see if morning breaks!' (14: 21, E108) that his perceptual world changes.

It is precisely movements of self-transformation such as these which Derrida and Locke do not undertake or countenance within their philosophy. Locke does not leave his position of immobility and stasis at the centre of his closet and therefore others do not and cannot appear. Similarly, a Blakean critique of Derrida's description of language and reality (advanced before an appreciation) would begin with the observation that his argument is advanced from the position of the stationary, reasoning self. It is not concerned with what occurs to language in relationship with others, in embrace, or in movement. It is unconcerned with such questions as what happens to the semiotic system in which we are enclosed when it is broken by the force of an other's appeal, or when it is distended by the emotions of fear and hope. For Blake, emotions and engagements such as these can bring us to the very edge of our linguistic world: in the striking epigram from 'For the Sexes: The Gates of Paradise', 'Fear & Hope are—Vision' (E266). This is why the passage quoted above from *Speech and Phenomena* is, within the context of Derrida's work, so uncannily resonant. It figures forth the very shape of Derrida's own polemic, but in doing so it also traces a partner that, within Derrida's discourse, remains silent.

Icarus's flight takes him up and out of the labyrinth and into proximity with the sun of presence. For Derrida this sun of presence is an illusion which is given form by the movement of *différance*. Any attempt to grasp this sun is therefore doomed to failure. Presence emerges only in relation to what is not present and, therefore, as Icarus approaches the sun his ascent turns into a fall and then concludes in death. The labyrinth contains its exits within itself. Nevertheless, Icarus does not return to the same labyrinth, his fall in fact leads him to a labyrinth which is more encompassing and more intricate than the one from which he has escaped: Icarus is lost in the abyss of the sea and the nothingness of death. We can therefore interpret the story of Icarus in a different although still related way. To approach the sun of presence is to lose the movement of *différance* which founds the very distinction between self and other. The blinding illumination of the sun leads to the void of death which is indeed the only outside to the text. The story therefore confronts us with an opposition between withdrawal and deferral on the one hand, and a presence which cannot be attained because it involves the eradication of the self on the other hand. The first opens the spaces of life: the second opens the spaces of death.

There is, however, a third interpretation of the story of Icarus. Our previous interpretations have treated the sun only as the Apollonian, or material sun. A sun such as this is held only in the reasoning memory, and therefore, as Hume, Blake, and Derrida would all affirm, is a mere appearance. In a remark made to Crabb Robinson Blake speaks of a very different kind of sun:

I have conversed with the spiritual Sun—I saw him on Primrose Hill. He said: 'Do you take me for the Greek Apollo?' 'No', I said. 'That' (and Blake pointed to the sky)—'that is the Greek Apollo. He is Satan'.[63]

This Sun that is the Greek Apollo is the Guinea Sun: the Spiritual Sun is that seen in the Hallelujah-Chorus. If Icarus rises towards a Sun that is not a mere appearance held by the reasoning memory, but a person who can call and respond, then this myth suggests the possibility of moving to a position from which the voice of the other can be heard. This does not usher in a world of pure and unmediated presence, nor (as we shall see in our discussion of the apocalypses of *Milton* and *Jerusalem*) does it suggest that we are able to grasp the other or his/her intentions once and for all. Nevertheless, it does open within the world of the self the possibility of engagement and therefore the possibility of transformation and of exodus. This alternate reading of the Icarus story can be seen in the figure of Daedalus, Icarus's companion. Concerning this second portion of the Icarus story Derrida remains silent, yet it is Daedalus who fashioned the wings for Icarus, and who warned Icarus of the dangers of flying too close to the sun. Moreover, it is Daedalus who, without remaining in the labyrinth, flying too close to the sun, or plunging into the sea, flew a middle path between self and other, the present and the non-present, and so was able to re-enter a speaking community. The story of Icarus is in fact a moment within a larger story.

It is this twin narrative, the story of Icarus and of Daedalus, which describes the twin poles of visionary art. Visionary construction, as I shall argue in a later chapter, is not achieved once and for all. This new world which is opened in response to the call of another is, of course, itself a system and must itself be subject to a visionary deconstruction. But this deconstruction is in turn the prelude to another movement towards the other. 'The thing still escapes', the other is beyond our reach, but the *différance* which makes this inevitable is itself the ground for a conversation in 'Visionary forms dramatic' (98: 28, E257).

The question of the relationship between the forms and conventions of what is present to the self and the irruption of the other within that world is, of course, not altogether absent from Derrida's work. In 'Violence and Metaphysics' this question takes the form of a confrontation between, on the one hand, the Apollonian/Greek care for the world of what is present to the self, and, on the other hand, the Hebrew concern for and experience of the other, which is manifested in prophecy.[64] At the end of this essay Derrida writes:

Are we Greeks? Are we Jews? But who, we? Are we (not a chronological, but a pre-logical question) *first* Jews or *first* Greeks? And does the strange dialogue between the Jew and the Greek, peace itself, have the form of the absolute, speculative logic of Hegel, the living logic which *reconciles* formal tautology and empirical heterology after having *thought* prophetic discourse in the preface to the *Phenomenology of the Mind*? Or, on the contrary, does this peace have the form of infinite separation and of the unthinkable, unsayable transcendence of the other? To what horizon of peace does the language which asks this question belong? From whence does it draw the energy of its question? Can it account for the historical *coupling* of Judaism and Hellenism? And what is the legitimacy, what is the meaning of the *copula* in this proposition from perhaps the most Hegelian of modern novelists: 'Jewgreek is greekjew. Extremes meet'?[65]

Although questions such as these are inevitably posed by deconstruction, it is only within a discourse which attempts to suppress neither Icarus nor Daedalus that they can be approached.

What makes Blake's approach to the relationship between time and Eternity, self and other, so peculiarly fascinating is that his affirmation of vision (of the possibility of opening time to Eternity) is not made by a naive or innocent turning away from the realities of existence. In fact, in Blake's poetry the universe of loss (of Los and Enitharmon) is the ground necessary for visionary expansion. An investigation into the nature of Blake's visionary construction and his visionary deconstruction is therefore *ipso facto* an investigation into the character and identity of Los (loss).

Los first appears in the Lambeth prophecies, where he is already a striking and complex figure. He is described as 'the *Eternal Prophet*' (*SL* 3: 1, E67), a Urizenic figure whose children give 'Laws & Religions to the sons of Har' (*SL* 4: 14, E68), a gaoler who attempts to keep knowledge of Urizen's withdrawal apart from the Eternals (*BU* 5: 38-40, E73), a watchman who attempts to remain in relationship with Urizen and awaits his return (*BU* 10: 9-10, E75),[66] a blacksmith who gives form to the chaotic body of Urizen-in-withdrawal (*BU* 10: 8-9, 15-18, 28-30, E76), a demiurge who gives form to the fallen world and creates time and space (*BU* 10: 1-13: 19, E74-6),[67] the father of Orc (*BU* 19: 10-20: 7, E79) and the ground for the fallen world itself. There is also, particularly in *The Book of Urizen*, the suggestion that Los is a printer and an engraver (10: 15-30, E75).[68] The name of Los is similarly polyphonous. It suggests loss and Logos,[69] and it is an anagram for Sol.[70] In addition Los is, of course, a figure for the poet, and many critics see him as a character who can be closely identified with Blake himself.[71]

28  Introduction

These identifications link Los with a wide variety of mythic and literary figures. Northrop Frye has pointed out that as blacksmith and goldsmith Los is similar to the smith who is associated by Isaiah with the building of a New Jerusalem.[72] Los can also be associated with Vulcan and Hephaistos. The latter is 'one of the binders of Prometheus in Aeschylus, who escapes Prometheus' fate because his work in fire has been done for immortal gods rather than mortal men', while the former is the blacksmith of the gods.[73] A similar breadth of association is provoked by the identification of Los as demiurge and watchman. The word Sol, or Sun, is of course, also the alchemical symbol of the *prima materia*, and a word which is often associated with Christ.[74]

Many of these associations are far from unambiguous. As Damrosch notes, 'the text to which Frye points [Isa. 54: 16] is suggestive of a frightening display of energy' and in 'Ezekiel too this symbol has connotations of purgation and anger'. The smith of Ezekiel is 'no fabulous artificer, but an agent of divine retribution'. Damrosch goes on to observe that in Milton the 'sons of Cain are smiths ... in contrast with the pastoral sons of Seth' and 'Mammon, the architect of Hell, is expressly related to the Mulciber or Vulcan whom Jove cast down from heaven'.[75] The demiurge in Gnostic philosophy is a figure who is both good and evil, and although Sol is the *prima materia*, in Los we are dealing with the reverse, or mirror image, of this substance. These various associations and identifications are, however, not incommensurate, but can be shown to be a function of the conflicting tendencies and warring divisions of the fallen prophet. In order to trace a path through these associations and so gain a first glimpse of Los as he emerges in Blake's œuvre, we will begin with his role as 'Eternal Prophet'.

Blake writes in an annotation to Watson's *An Apology for the Bible* that

Prophets in the modern sense of the word have never existed Jonah was no prophet in the modern sense for his prophecy of Nineveh failed Every honest man is a Prophet he utters his opinion both of private & public matters/Thus/If you go on So/the result is So/He never says such a thing shall happen let you do what you will. a Prophet is a Seer not an Arbitrary Dictator. (E617)

In Eternity, where life is grounded in relationship, the prophet performs a crucial role. The prophet gives form and expression to the results of a particular action or style of life. In this way he confronts an individual or a nation with the reality of their actions and so makes a world of relationship possible. The Bard in *Milton*, for example, exhorts his readers to 'Mark well' his words for 'they are of your eternal salvation' (2: 25, E96), and the prophetic Song which follows attempts to reveal the reality which underlies, and the future which is projected by, the fallen world. This same prophetic function can be seen in *The Song of Los*. The 'song', which Los sang '*to four harps at the tables of Eternity* when '*Urizen faded!*' and '*Ariston shudderd!*' (3: 1, 2, 4, E67), is at least initially an attempt to point out to the Eternals, and to Urizen in particular, the result of their actions. It is a prophetic song which attempts to induce the Eternals to leave the closed world of the self and to enter a world of relationship. The 'song' is therefore not a prediction, but an attempt to rouse 'the faculties to act' (E702).

Prophetic art is perhaps the most fundamental precondition for a universe where life is founded on relationship, for the forms fabricated by the prophet give expression to our life and so induce us to change and expand. We can therefore say that the world forged by the prophet in his furnaces is the ground for the leap of eternal life. For this reason the unfallen Los can indeed be called Sol, for the ground which he forges is the site of a radiant movement and expansion. In *The Four Zoas* these characteristics of the unfallen Los are given expression in the figure of Urthona, or 'earth-owner'. As the name suggests, Urthona is the owner of the earth: he fabricates the very ground of eternal life. This ground is, however, not the inert material which forms the ground of the fallen world. Urthona is engaged in the manufacture of intellectual tools: the 'spades & coulters' (E312) of peace and 'the golden armour of science | For intellectual War' (E407). In Eternity the prophetic elaboration of the reality which underlies or is portended by the actions of the Eternals is a tool which is used to make those actions fruitful (the 'spades & coulters' of peace) or to provide a form which will enable the Eternals to engage in 'intellectual War' (the 'armour of science').

Our discussion of the work of the unfallen prophet should not, of course, distinguish too closely between the prophet and his prophetic productions. Frye writes that 'As Blake goes on he becomes more and more impressed by the contrast between a man's imagination, his real life as expressed in the total form of his creative acts, and his ordinary existence.'[76] In the fallen world this separation is accompanied by the division that exists between the poet and his Spectre. However, in Eternity

Los, Enitharmon, and the Spectre, form a single identity. The prophet is embodied in his work. *The Song of Los*, for example, is therefore both a song which is sung by Los, and a song which is made up of the very fibre of Los. We can glimpse this function of the unfallen poet/prophet in the role of the fallen poetic imagination. Paul Ricoeur observes that

> In no way does poetic imagination reduce itself to the power of forming a mental picture of the unreal; the imagery of sensory origin merely serves as a vehicle and as material for the verbal power whose true dimension is given to us by the oneiric and the cosmic. As Bachelard says, the poetic image 'places us at the origin of articulate being'; the poetic image 'becomes a new being in our language, it expresses us by making us what it expresses'.[77]

The poet/prophet is therefore the ontological ground of the unfallen world and, as Los (loss), of the fallen world as well. Los is therefore the smith who builds the form of the fallen world and himself the ontological time of that world.[78] This is why in *Jerusalem* the withdrawal of Albion does not mean simply that Urthona must now confront Albion with the reality of loss, but that Urthona becomes Los:

> In the Fourth region of Humanity, Urthona namd[,]
> Mortality begins to roll the billows of Eternal Death
> Before the Gate of Los. Urthona here is named Los.
> (35[39]: 7–9, E181)

The Los that we meet in the early plates of *The Book of Urizen* is still engaged in a prophetic activity that resembles that undertaken in Eternity. Rather than himself withdrawing from the 'horror' that has appeared in Eternity, Los remains in relationship with Urizen and gives him form. He is, however, in an extraordinary situation. Los is now a prophet whose audience has withdrawn. He is therefore caught between the globe created by Urizen's withdrawal and that created by the Eternals' withdrawal. This means that there is no other to whom Los can relate and therefore that he is himself trapped within a closed world. Los is now used by the Eternals 'to confine | The obscure separation alone' (5: 40, E73). This results in a series of reversals. Rather than being Sol—the ground of an expansion—the Eternal Prophet is now Los; he is enclosed within his constituted world. Rather than being embodied in his work, Enitharmon now forms the horizon of his world. The poet/prophet posits a world without being able to give it any basis in existence apart from that of loss.

The simple fact of enclosure is not in itself a problem. In Eternity the world formed by Los (loss) is a seed. This state can therefore be the prelude to a radiant expansion. While Los remains within the space opened by a double withdrawal, however, there seems to be no possibility of escaping the world of loss. The seed falls on rocky ground and Los is now the demiurge, the creator of the fallen world and, rather than being a blacksmith and a worker who contributes to the fabrication of the 'New Jerusalem', he is now a person who closes life within a fixed form.

In this transformation the positive connotations of the blacksmith are not entirely lost, for Los's creation is still a potentially redemptive activity. In *The Book of Urizen* (and, as I shall argue, *Milton* and *Jerusalem*) Los gives form to the shapeless death of the fallen world and in this way preserves Urizen (and Albion) from complete annihilation. By giving Urizen a fixed form, he opens the possibility that Urizen will return. It is at least possible that the *Song of Los* could function as a prophetic work which, by revealing to us the ground of our existence, calls out to us to 'Turn away no more' (30: 16, E18).

Los is the ontological ground of the fallen world and the creator of the world in which we live. The universe of Los and Enitharmon is therefore the *prima materia*, the base material, with which any attempt at regeneration must work. The difficulty is, however, that as the Lambeth prophecies proceed the possibility of regeneration seems to become more and more remote. Los's plight within the fallen world is so extreme that he also withdraws from relationship. In *Milton* and *Jerusalem* the question therefore becomes, how can Los be inverted so that he becomes the radiant sun once more? How can the fallen world become a womb rather than a cavern which entraps humanity?

Quite clearly there are considerable methodological problems in a study of this kind. When I first began research into the relationship between time and Eternity in Blake's œuvre, I assumed that I would be able to begin by elaborating working definitions of time and Eternity, and sketching a philosophical approach to the problematic with which Los is concerned. With this accomplished I hoped to have in my grasp a series of keys or tools with which to approach the poems. The poems are, however, extraordinarily resistant to this kind of strategy. Moreover, whatever such a study might reveal about the texts, it could not uncover the way in which the poems open to Eternity for the simple reason that both terms of my question (time and Eternity) are, in this approach, from the very beginning the property of the reasoning, critical self. It soon became clear that if I were to escape this impasse I would have to adopt a more vulnerable relationship to the texts. The way in which the poems open the reader's world to Eternity can only be described from within a reading of the poems themselves. This is, with regard to the study of Blake, a course of action which is often avoided. While testifying to a strange beauty that they have glimpsed in *The Four Zoas*, most critics have argued that the poem is chaotic and unfinished.[79] Although much of the criticism which has addressed itself to *Jerusalem* has been concerned with its structure, the 'architecture' of this poem, as Stuart Curran tells us, has 'yet to be satisfactorily explained. For that task must necessarily dissipate the mists of obscurity through which we view this epic, and most attempts have merely cast a light upon them.'[80] Even *Milton* is introduced by a Bard's prophetic Song which, like much of Blake's poetry, continues to raise fundamental questions about the nature of Blake's poems and the way in which we read them. Yet it is only when the reader engages with the poems that they can be allowed to exert a force which acts back on the reader.

The necessity of turning to a reading/encounter with the poems also emerged as a result of my attempt to outline the character of Los. No sooner had I begun than I was struck by a curious correspondence between Los and the form of the poems themselves. Los is the being, or the stance in the world, that allows creation in time. In *Milton*, for example, Los's creative work includes the whole visible world. It can therefore be argued that Blake's poems are themselves part of this wider set and that therefore Los lies thematically and structurally at their centre; in fact the poems are in a sense the body of Los. The nature of Los and the relationship between time and Eternity in Blake's œuvre can therefore be elaborated only within a discussion of the body of Blake's poetry. The poems self-consciously present themselves as a paradigmatic instance of the world which separates time and Eternity, self and other, and yet which at the same time offers the possibility of an opening to Eternity. For this double reason, the following argument proceeds as a reading of Blake's major illuminated poetry. Such a course must inevitably be selective. First, a number of issues which arise from and complicate my readings —most glaringly, the extent to which Blake's 'sexism' qualifies or even undermines his constructive vision and visionary deconstruction—are not explored in the present study. Second, rather than attempting to discuss Blake's entire œuvre, I have concentrated on *Milton* and *Jerusalem*. In my view, however, it is these poems that express most eloquently Eternity's love for 'the productions of time'.

# PART I
# The Moment of Embrace

# 1. Visionary Deconstruction

> In other words, in his nascent state, man is never simply man. He is always, necessarily, and essentially, either Master or Slave.
>
> Alexandre Kojève[1]

PAINTERS, SCULPTORS, AND ARCHITECTS

The first two copies of *Milton* begin with a rousing call to the Painters, Sculptors, Architects, and 'Young Men of the New Age' to 'Rouze up' and set their foreheads against the 'ignorant Hirelings' who are in possession of the 'Camp, the Court, & the University' (E95). The call seems to be clear and unequivocal until we learn towards the end of Book I that while 'in Eternity the Four Arts: Poetry, Painting, Music | And Architecture which is Science: are the Four Faces of Man. . . . in Time & Space . . . Three' of these faces

> are shut out, and only Science remains thro Mercy: & by means of Science, the Three Become apparent in Time & space, in the Three Professions
>
> Poetry in Religion: Music, Law: Painting, in Physic & Surgery.
>
> (27: 55-60, E125)

But Blake does not call on Priests, Lawyers, and Doctors in the preface, he calls on Painters, Sculptors, and Architects, of which only Architects remain as Scientists. The reader is therefore confronted by an extraordinary gap between the task that Blake sets in the preface and the possibility of its accomplishment. The poet's call is directed towards a possibility or potentiality which lies hidden within the world.

The face is both a sign and an event: it finds its existence within a world that is constituted by us, but at the same time it is the centre of a force which irrupts within our world and charges it with a surplus and excess. It is both inextricably part of the person or thing (the face of a cube, for example) and yet it is turned towards others; it includes a relationship with others in its definition. The face therefore evinces a strange duality: it is both sign and epiphany; symbol and allegory; it remains within the constituted world of the self and yet it pierces that world with another's glance. The face is both open to our discourse and yet it must ever elude our attempts to encompass it.

A profession, on the other hand, is both an institution and something that an individual claims as his belief or work. The word implies that it is that which is professed, rather than that which is encountered, which determines the relationship between self and other. It is now the profession, rather than the glance, that structures and defines what is possible within discourse. It is, however, unwise to establish too rigid an opposition between face and profession. The relationship between these two terms is, perhaps, that between face and mask, where a mask is a face that has become stationary and inert. If it were, however, to be reanimated, unfrozen, so that it were once more flexible and expressive, the mask would become a face.

In the eighteenth century Milton was, indeed, a profession and an institution. *Paradise Lost*, for example, was considered a poem worthy of comparison with the epics of Greek and Roman antiquity.[2] However, one can argue that as a result of this institutionalization Milton was no longer a prophetic force; he had become a profession rather than a face, a priest rather than a poet. Milton had become, as Blake's title page for *Milton* implies, a poem in two books, *Paradise Lost* and *Paradise Regained*, which had been rather happily assimilated into the world of eighteenth-century England (see Fig. 1).[3]

Within the poem it is, of course, not simply the professions of others that hem Milton in. When the poem begins Milton has

>                              walk'd about in Eternity
> One hundred years, pondring the intricate mazes of Providence
> Unhappy tho in heav'n, he obey'd, he murmur'd not. he was silent
> Viewing his Sixfold Emanation scatter'd thro' the deep
> In torment!
>                                         (2: 16-20, E96)

In this situation Milton clearly allows a profession (his belief in a transcendent Providence, for example), to determine his relationship to others. Milton is himself closed within his constituted world.[4] However, the title page does not show a person closed within a profession. On the contrary, this enclosure has been ruptured, the name Milton has been broken and at the point of fracture Milton is shown striding forward, right hand extended, in a movement which manifests a prophetic presence. Milton is now seen as a naked body and, for those in

1. Title-page to *Milton*.

the abyss before him, as a face. It is this movement projected outside of the closed world of the self—from sedimented language to speech, from the world held by the Daughters of Memory to that created by the Daughters of Inspiration—that the narrator of *Milton* sets out to describe and to induce in his readers. The immediate provocation for the event depicted on the title page is a Bard's prophetic Song—sung to the Sons of Albion as they sit at eternal tables in heaven—and it is to this that we must now turn.

THE BARD'S SONG

Most readers come to the Bard's Song with expectations of a forceful, immediately persuasive appeal to action. This 'prophetic Song' (2: 22, E96) is, after all, the appeal which 'mov'd Milton' to the 'unexampled deed' (2: 21, E96) of entering 'the deep' and so giving up his life in order to redeem his Emanation. These expectations are quickly dashed, for the Bard's Song appears, in the words of Stuart Curran, as a Covering Cherub: the very mask that, in the frontispiece, Milton is attempting to discard.[5]

The immediate difficulty is that the Bard's Song appears to deal with fallen time and space with extraordinary licence. Events are fragmented, there is a dizzy movement from myth to history and back again, and events from radically disparate times and places are juxtaposed. In this way space seems to be continually turned inside out and time gains a radically disjunctive and episodic character. However, to point only to this aspect of the Bard's Song is radically to simplify one's experience of the poem, for there is, co-existing with this first experience, a definite sense of progression and an almost uncanny force which draws the reader through the Song.

The tension between the narrative and the episodic is repeated in the criticism on *Milton*. John Howard, for example, in his book *Blake's 'Milton'*, recognizes a narrative movement in the poem and yet he describes the plates that Blake interpolated into copies C and D of the poem as 'apparently disorganized material'.[6] In *Fearful Symmetry*, Northrop Frye argues that the poem has no narrative sequence; yet in his 'Notes for a Commentary on *Milton*', he retreats from this position. He now argues 'that a sequence does appear if the editor eliminates plate 5 and re-orders the others to read 2.7.4.6.3.8', an ordering which he assumes (mistakenly) to be that of copy C.[7] The most obvious solution to the conflicting claims of narrative order and episodic disorder is to foreground one at the expense of the other. David E. James argues that in the Bard's Song narrative is so fractured that it is almost non-existent, while Susan Fox, reversing this critical judgement, contends that the Bard carries through the 'seeming disorder' of his song 'a simple and revealing narration'.[8] What are we to make of this oscillation between narrative order and disorder, of a narrative which is and is not there? As James Rieger observes with reference to Frye's views of the poem:

> The Bard's Song is perhaps the most puzzling episode anywhere in the poetry published by Blake himself. Is that because one's normal expectations of narrative do not apply in this case, or because Blake was on the Homeric nod when he wrote it? ... Either the narrative structure is a ruse, then, or Blake garbled it.[9]

We need not reach such an extreme conclusion, however, if we remember that the Bard's Song is a *prophecy* and is therefore (like biblical prophecies such as Revelation) meant to be unsettling. In the pages which follow I will argue that the Bard is not trying to comfort or to amuse us, but to show the set of relationships which ground our world. This cannot be done by using the time and space of our world, for it is precisely that which is in question. It is only in the fracture of the phenomenal appearance of time and space that this structure can appear. The poem's episodic and disjunctive form is therefore closely related to the sense that the poem has a narrative movement. Superimposed upon the poem's episodic and disjunctive form there is therefore a definite sense of progression and an almost uncanny force which slowly draws the reader from a state of confusion to a moment of recognition. It is this movement which generates the strong and sometimes overwhelming sense of a narrative progression. It coexists with and does not supersede a sense of temporal and spatial disorder because it is a narrative which appears in the midst of, and is traced against, the fracture of our time and space.

THE THREE CLASSES

The Bard begins by focusing our attention on what will be one of the central motifs of his Song: the production by Los and Enitharmon of the Classes of the Elect, the Reprobate, and the Redeemed. In doing so he confronts his audience with a rather startling conjuncture of temporal locations:

> Three Classes are Created by the Hammer of Los, & Woven
> By Enitharmons Looms when Albion was slain upon his Mountains
> And in his Tent, thro envy of Living Form, even of the Divine Vision.
>
> (2: 26-3: 4, E96)

On the one hand, the creation of the three Classes is linked with the fall of Albion—an event which occurred in the past—on the other hand, we are told that they are created in the present by Los. For Susan Fox this difference in tense simply 'juxtaposes the continual creation by Los and the fatal abruptness of Albion's fall';[10] however, the syntax of this passage links the creation in the present to the fall of Albion in the past much more closely than the word 'juxtaposes' would suggest. The three Classes are created in the present by Los and Enitharmon *when* Albion was slain in the past.

In speaking of the death of Albion as an event which has already occurred, it is crucial to remember that Albion is not a mortal individual whose death can easily be located at a particular point in time. Albion is, in an important sense, the very shape of history itself. He is not simply the readers of *Milton*, nor is he the poem's potential audience; Albion is all of humanity and for this reason he includes all people who have existed and will exist in fallen time. In Eternity all of humanity can be seen as a single being; however, in the course of the Fall Albion is dismembered and this single identity is fragmented. Eternal annihilation is, in fact, averted only by Los who gives form to Albion as the six thousand year cycle of fallen history. The fall of Albion is therefore not an event which occurs at a certain point in our time; instead, fallen time is the form given by Los to the fallen Albion.[11] History can therefore be seen as a creation (throughout the six thousand year history of the fallen world) which is continually directed towards a being who, in terms of this present, has already withdrawn. It is a creation which is occurring in the very moment (six thousand years long) in which Albion was slain.

For the reader this opening passage has the rather unnerving effect of placing the time of individual existence within the context of a relationship or interaction between two giant forms. Our individual lives find themselves within a history which is formed in the relationship between the event in which Albion is dismembered and the continuing work of Los. Moreover, the substance of this interaction is not the diversity which is often attributed to time, but the simple and elemental production of three Classes. These lines therefore have the effect of making our time and space eerily transparent: under their pressure a fissure or rift has opened within our perceptual worlds. At this point in the Song we can do no more than glimpse what lies beneath, but it is the corrosive force of this vision as it is progressively uncovered by the Bard's words that now forms the centre of the Song. Implicit in this passage are all of the shifts of time and place that characterize the following plates, for if all of time can be read as a production of the three Classes by Los, then the events and moments of time are strangely interchangeable. At the same time the vision glimpsed in this disordering of our perceptual worlds begins, at this point in the poem, to make its claim on us heard.

The lines which follow the Bard's introduction to his Song seem to offer some respite from the temporal dislocations of the opening passage. Plate 3 is for the greatest part taken up with a myth which, although radically condensed, recalls the creation story of *The Book of Urizen*. The narrative begins with Los attempting to give body and form to Urizen, who lies 'in darkness & solitude, in chains of the mind lock'd up' (3: 6, E96). In Eternity the body is the site of an encounter between self and other; by contrast, the body that Los forms for Urizen is a thing which encloses him. It gives form and body to the state of withdrawal that he has entered.

Los's creation of a body for Urizen has unforeseen consequences. With the withdrawal of Urizen (and by implication Albion), Los must work in solitude. This means that Los is also in a state of withdrawal and is himself trapped by the form that he has created. Los therefore becomes the very thing that he has created. Rather than facing others, Los is now caught between his Spectre and his Emanation (3: 28–36, E97). As in earlier poems, the Spectre and Emanation form a world which encloses the active power. In this divided state, Los forms the outline of fallen history (3: 37–40, E97).

With the opening words of the Song still ringing in our ears, what is most striking about this brief narrative is a still not completely articulated sense of the presence of the three Classes (and therefore the creative work of Los in response to the fall of Albion) throughout fallen history. The fabrication of a body for Urizen, for example, divides the world into the world of the self and the world of the other. The body itself (whether it is imagined as a physical body, nature, or the body of social jargon and opinion) represents a third force which now mediates between self and other. With this social formation the world is *ipso facto*—on the levels of the individual, the group, and the collective—divided into three Classes, for the elaboration of any boundary between self and other must inevitably distinguish between those whose interests are served by and actively propagate this division (the Elect); those who are able to work within the space defined and regulated by the Elect (the Redeemed); and that group of people who are excluded by this division (the Reprobate).

This division is repeated in the person of Los, who now becomes what he beholds. Moreover, the history that is constructed within the triangular relationship between Los, his Spectre, and Enitharmon is centred on the three Classes.[12] We are threefold and sexual in our very being and therefore the Starry Mills of Satan are built throughout the twenty seven heavens and six thousand years of the Mundane Shell.

In listening to the Bard's creation story one therefore has an extraordinary sense of the identity of apparently dissimilar things. The events of history are seen as the serial repetition of an original fragmentation. This sense is heightened by a striking similarity between the descriptions of Urizen and Satan: both figures attempt in vain to 'refuse' the form that is forged for them by Los and Enitharmon. This similarity seems to bring the story full circle, for it suggests that the consolidation of Satan is the completion of a process that Los began when he gave form to Urizen. Later in the Bard's Song we will learn that 'Satan is Urizen' (10: 1, E104). Beneath the linear progression of the Bard's creation narrative we can therefore glimpse the three Classes referred to in the opening lines of the poem. In a first reading the exact shape and nature of their interaction remains to a large extent unseen. It is felt, perhaps, as an uneasy, almost uncanny dissolution of what had been perceived as difference into sameness. As the poem proceeds their interaction gradually comes into focus.

To this point in the poem the Bard's narrative has proceeded in the third person, with the dispassionate voice of an observer. In the lines which follow the creation narrative, the distances between the narrator and the events that he is describing, and between the reader and the story that he is following, are closed; the narrator's voice is overtaken by the voice of Los:

> If you account it Wisdom when you are angry to be silent, and
> Not to shew it: I do not account that Wisdom but Folly.
> Every Mans Wisdom is peculiar to his own Individ[u]ality
> O Satan my youngest born, art thou not Prince of the Starry Hosts
> And of the Wheels of Heaven, to turn the Mills day & night?
>
> (4: 6-10, E98)

The effect of this sudden irruption of Satan and Los within the present of the reader is nothing short of startling. First, we see Los and the Class of the Elect not as inert forces but as beings actively engaged in argument. Second, there is a sense of this hitherto unseen (and still only partially glimpsed) quarrel as a force which underlies our world.

If history is grounded in the production of the three Classes by Los, then quite clearly the events of fallen time are, in terms of this ground, interchangeable. In the passage which follows our glimpse of Los and Satan, the Song begins to embody this insight. It now moves rapidly between the past, present, and future, as if it were fascinated by the interchangeability of historical epochs and times. The narrative itself almost disappears and the poem becomes extraordinarily episodic. This section of the poem begins:

> Between South Molton Street & Stratford place: Calvarys foot
> Where the Victims were preparing for Sacrifice their Cherubim
> Around their loins pourd forth their arrows & their bosoms beam
> With all colours of precious stones, & their inmost palaces
> Resounded with preparation of animals wild & tame
> (Mark well my words! Corporeal Friends are Spiritual Enemies)
> Mocking Druidical Mathematical Proportion of Length Bredth Highth
> Displaying Naked Beauty! with Flute & Harp & Song
> Palamabron with the fiery Harrow in morning returning
> From breathing fields. Satan fainted beneath the artillery.
>
> (4: 21-5: 2, E98)

So extreme is the disruption in this passage of our habitual ways of perceiving the world that the first response to these lines is usually one of confusion; yet beneath the apparent disorder of these lines there is a continual evocation of the three Classes and the mediated relationships in which they find their being.

In the very first line Blake mentions 'Calvarys foot'. This allusion to the site of the crucifixion invokes what is, perhaps, the paradigmatic instance of a mediated relationship. Christ was judged a malefactor (and therefore of the Reprobate) because of the threat he represented to the world of the Pharisees and the Romans (the Elect). Calvary is, however, not limited by this passage to a place and time in Israel, for the Bard locates 'Calvarys foot' in the London of his day. The location is, in fact, rather precise: it can be found at the point where South Molton Street, the street in which Blake took up residence when he returned from Felpham, and Stratford Place intersect. This place was, as Damon tells us, where Tyburn brook, a stream which ran past the site of the gallows in London, plunged underground.[13] This superimposition of a Palestinian and an English location suggests that the legal system with which we try and convict our fellow creatures is akin to those which convicted Christ. In both cases a third force is interposed between self and other (whether judge, policeman, or executioner) and this force is used to regulate society. The Reprobate, those who are born to damnation, are damned because they disrupt the system fostered by the Elect.

As we continue reading the Bard's Song there is a temptation to leave Calvin's three Classes intact and merely shift blame from one Class to another. It is the Reprobate who become Calvin's Elect, while Blake's Elect are seen as those who must be judged.[14] The Bard, however, makes this kind of transposition extremely difficult to sustain. This can be seen in the extraordinary ambiguity of the lines which immediately follow the reference to Calvary's foot. As James remarks, these lines 'may mean that the victims were preparing themselves for sacrifice, while the cherubim were attacking them. Or they may mean that the victims were preparing the cherubim for sacrifice.'[15] It is, however, not only impossible but unnecessary, in this context, to decide between these possible readings. In both cases we are dealing with the preparation for sacrifice of one group by another. We sacrifice others only in an attempt to propitiate or meet the demands of a third party, whether a god, an ideology, or a more subtle source of law, such as expedience, order, or the public good. Whether we sacrifice criminals for the public good, prophets in order to preserve the social order, or tyrants in order to bring into being a revolutionary order, we reproduce the triangular and mediated relationship that we have been discussing. One cannot judge judgement without reintroducing judgement into the world. This point is emphasized by the parenthetical comment which divides 4: 21-5 from 4: 27-5: 2: 'Mark well my words! Corporeal friends are Spiritual Enemies'. The preservation of order in our constituted worlds, the confinement or eradication of those forces that threaten our world (even if those forces can be collectively described as Satan), may in effect be to collaborate with our spiritual enemies. Crucifixion, sacrifice, mocking, execution, all stand in stark contrast to the next line of the poem in which the reader gains a glimpse of an action which promises to place the fallen world on a very different footing. The Bard tells us that, in the place of 'judgement', Christ 'took on Sin in the Virgins Womb, and put it off on the Cross' (5: 3, E98).[16]

In the remainder of plate 5 the vision implicit in this temporal and spatial disorder moves into sharper focus. These lines begin with a description of the Daughters of Albion, the passive powers who help to establish the form which separates self and other. In Eternity, male and female are part of a single identity, but here the females merely take 'whom they please ... into their Heavens' (5: 9-10, E98).[17] The body of humanity, rather than being a place of relationship, has become a cave which interposes itself between self and other. The Females sing:

> Ah weak & wide astray! Ah shut in narrow doleful form
> Creeping in reptile flesh upon the bosom of the ground
> The Eye of Man a little narrow orb closd up & dark
> Scarcely beholding the great light conversing with the Void.
>
> (5: 19-22, E99)

It is to the accompaniment of this Song that the Females create 'the Three Classes among Druid Rocks' (5: 38, E99). This insight into the work of the Daughters allows us to see the three Classes in even greater clarity. In the most precise definition to this point, the Bard tells us that they are 'the Two Contraries & the Reasoning Negative' (5: 14, E98). The Reasoning Negative interposes itself between the first two terms and in so doing changes their relationship into one of warfare and negation. It is the reasoning memory that forms the apex of the triangular relationship between self and other that we have been discussing.

With this clarification the poem moves from myth back into the arena of history, where we see the result of the Daughter's work. The notion of the three Classes has now gained such a corrosive power that almost all distinction seems to be on the point of being lost. For the reader this can generate a feeling strikingly akin to vertigo. In what is, perhaps, the most disconcerting passage in the entire Song, the Bard tells his audience that the Females sing in this way as they create

> the Three Classes among Druid Rocks
> Charles calls on Milton for Atonement. Cromwell is ready
> James calls for fires in Golgonooza. for heaps of smoking ruins
> In the night of prosperity and wantonness which he himself Created
> Among the Daughters of Albion among the Rocks of the Druids
> When Satan fainted beneath the arrows of Elynittria
> And Mathematic Proportion was subdued by Living Proportion.
>
> (5: 38-44, E99)

In his notes to *The Complete Poetry and Prose*, Harold Bloom identifies Milton as a member of the Reprobate, Cromwell as the Redeemed and Charles and James as the Elect (E912). This seems to be a common-sense allocation of roles, however, it is in practice hard to sustain.[18] Milton would seem to be not only a candidate for the Class of the Reprobate but for the Redeemed as well. He is the author of *The Reason of Church Government* and *Areopagitica*, for example. It is therefore quite plausible to argue that in line 39 the Reprobate Milton is being asked to atone for his sins. A position such as this immediately raises the question of whether Milton was still in the Class of the Reprobate when Charles I was beheaded, or when he took up his duties as Cromwell's Latin secretary? It would seem to be a much more likely argument that at this point he belonged to the Class of those who take part in the orthodoxy of their day.[19] It would be unwise to discount this last possibility in a poem in which Milton admits that in his own Spectre he is Satan. A contention such as this is also supported by an ambiguity in line 39 which suggests that, in calling on Milton, it is Charles who is seeking to atone for his sins.

As king of England, Charles I was quite clearly a member of the Elect. Just prior to his death, however, Charles seems to have become, just as clearly, a member of the Class of the Reprobate: at that point he had become a figure who represented a threat to the new, democratic and puritan orthodoxy of the day. Similarly, as king, James II was a member of the Elect, however, when overcome by William III and fleeing to France he can hardly be seen as a member of the same Class. A new orthodoxy was in the process of being established and with regard to this it was James who stood outside its bounds. It was now, as William announced, inconsistent for a Protestant country to have a popish king.

Readers encounter the same kind of difficulty as soon as they attempt to determine the Class to which Cromwell belonged. In his struggle against the royalists, and in his demands for democratic reform and for the abolition of the episcopacy, Cromwell was without doubt a member of the Reprobate. However, as Puritan general and then, for a period of five years, the absolute ruler of England—a person who was twice offered the title of king—he seems to have been a member of the Satanic Elect.

The Bard locates the historical events alluded to in this passage by relating them to the quarrel that we have glimpsed in previous plates. These events occur

When Satan fainted beneath the arrows of Elynittria
And Mathematic Proportion was subdued by Living Proportion.
> (5: 43-4, E99)

Susan Fox writes that in these lines it is clear that

> Satan has been felled ... by Palamabron's return ... that act, like the incarnation, is the subduing of mathematic by living proportion. It is achieved on all levels of reality through the appropriate operations of the Three Classes of Men ... and their female concomitant.[20]

It is, of course, not incorrect to see the victory of Cromwell over James as a victory for Living Proportion: the people asserted their authority against that of the king and so the Elect were cast out. Unfortunately, this victory of Living Proportion over the Mathematical led to the loss of Living Proportion and a reassertion of Mathematic Proportion. Under the protectorate we have, superficially, a new doxology, a new public enemy and a new group of people who decide to co-operate with society; however, in a fundamental sense this transformation leaves the three Classes of society intact. For Living Proportion to subdue Mathematic Proportion is for the former to adopt the tactics of, and so become assimilated to, the latter. As the Bard observed on plate 4, 'Corporeal Friends are Spiritual Enemies'.[21] The effect of these lines is, therefore, to demonstrate the absolute ubiquity of the three Classes; the three Classes have become terms which define the structure of life itself.

Plate 6 reiterates the insights of the preceding plates on a higher level of clarity. The three Classes, as we learnt in the opening lines of this Song, are formed by Los from out of the chaos of Albion's withdrawal. In our discussion of the preceding plates we have concentrated on the negative aspects of this creation. The production of the three Classes is, however, also a saving action: it gives form to what would otherwise be nothing but chaos. As the Bard tells us, Los and Enitharmon are weaving the 'Web of Life' from out of the 'ashes of the dead' (6: 28-9, E100). By retaining the body of Albion, Los's creation opens the possibility of regeneration. Los is, therefore, also involved in the production of the spiritual Golgonooza and from this perspective the three Classes help to prepare for the apocalyptic harvest which marks the end of time (6: 8-13, E99). The production by Los of the three Classes therefore stands at the centre of the fallen world, between the cycles of violence which constitute its temporal history and the possibility of regeneration.

At this point in the Song the Bard's visionary deconstruction of our everyday world has reached such a pitch that his audience stands on the edge of vision. In the plates which follow, his listeners are given an account of the quarrel between Satan and Palamabron in which they are able to see in detail a dynamic which they have hitherto only glimpsed.

The quarrel is the moment of recognition: that moment in which a recalcitrant problem unveils itself and one perceives what has been hidden. As a prelude to my discussion of this quarrel, I will, using the additional information it provides, describe the three Classes in a little more detail. I will begin with the attributes that the poem ascribes to these characters. On this level, Rintrah is the Ploughman and is associated with wrath. Palamabron is in charge of the Harrow and his emotion is pity, while Satan, in his role as Miller of Eternity, is concerned with Eternal Death.

### THE ELECT, THE REPROBATE, AND THE REDEEMED

The Ploughman prepares the ground for sowing by opening to the light what has been closed in darkness. He tears the shell of the world to reveal what has been hidden. Rintrah is therefore associated with an iconoclastic wrath that overthrows accepted boundaries. In this activity we can see him beginning a dialogue between darkness and light, earth and sky, self and other. Rather than protecting 'the organic growth from alien actuality', as Bracher contends,[22] Rintrah's Plough in fact tears open the constituted world of the self so that others can appear in our world. It is this activity which prepares the ground so it can receive seed. The Reprobate are 'form'd | To destruction from the mothers womb' (7: 2-3) because they transgress accepted boundaries and are therefore always subject to the judgement of those powers (the Elect) who preserve the status quo. The Bard is identified as a member of the Class of the Reprobate (7: 3, E100) because the act of prophecy is an attempt to plough (and so open) the constituted world of his listeners. It is this activity which prepares Milton's constituted world for the reception of seed. Ploughing is therefore a necessary prelude to the growth and expansion described by *Milton*. Nevertheless, despite the important role played by Rintrah in cultivating the ground, it is important to observe that in isolation Rintrah's role is destructive. It is necessary for Rintrah's work to be coupled with that of his contrary.

## Visionary Deconstruction

Palamabron's Harrow turns the achieved exteriority of the Ploughman back into interiority. The Harrow is used to pulverize the soil, destroy weeds and clods which have been left unchurned by the ploughing process, and cover in the seed. In so doing it closes the fissures which have been opened by the Plough and imposes a new surface (albeit this time of fine, friable soil). The Harrow therefore enables the seed to grow by rendering the re-enclosed surface penetrable by the shoot. Harrowing is, therefore, not the contrary of Satan's milling (as Bracher argues), but of Rintrah's Ploughing. It is only in the contrary relationship between Rintrah and Palamabron that there lies the possibility of growth. Harrowing therefore does not involve merely the 'indirect or mediated preservation of that which is destroyed', as Bracher argues.[23] If this were so it would suggest that the Harrow was in some way involved in the grinding or reduction of others. The action of the Harrow is consequent upon the *opening* of the self to the other. It therefore follows a process which, far from destroying others, opens the self to others, and it is the results of this encounter which are held by the ground as seed. The Harrow therefore does not reduce *others* to fine, friable soil. Instead, it breaks up those elements of the ground (of the self) which would imprison and so assimilate the seed. It turns the outer surface of the *self* into a form which can be penetrated by the shoot. The Harrow circumvents the possibility that the seed will itself be reduced to soil, by ensuring that the ground can be breached by new growth. Nevertheless, it is important to see that without the Plough, the Harrow does become involved in a process which is simply a form of destruction. It can be used as a scarifier, to raze all growth and return the world to the simple and warring oppositions of earth and sky. When the Harrow is used in this way the exterior becomes so dominant that the interior will not show itself. As Los observes: 'pity divides the soul'.

The Miller of Eternity has a different and perhaps more ambiguous role to play. Clearly, the first part of his job is to abstract a part from the whole. The Miller is concerned with the grain, rather than with the whole plant, and even here his Mills translate whatever individual difference is left into indistinguishable units. The Miller of Eternity is also described as a Judge. At the end of *Milton* we see Satan

> Coming in a cloud, with trumpets & flaming fire
> Saying I am God the judge of all, the living & the dead

## 52  *The Moment of Embrace*

> Fall therefore down & worship me. submit thy supreme
> Dictate, to my eternal Will & to my dictate bow.
>
> (38: 50-3, E139)

These two identities are complementary, rather than contradictory, for the Satanic Judge grinds the world every bit as finely as the Eternal Miller. Miller and Judge both attempt to grind the world into submission to their will. One can therefore see a literal truth to Satan's claim that he is 'God alone | There is no other! let all obey my principles of moral individuality' (9: 25-6, E103). Satan's principles of 'moral individuality' are the grinding surfaces of his Mills. As Bracher observes: 'Satan is the principle which destroys the unique identities of individuals, grinding them down (into uniform, elementary forms)'.[24]

What is striking about the Bard's depiction of Satan, however, is that he destroys the individuality of others in order to 'enhance' and extend his own *individuality*. His laws are based on 'principles of moral individuality', he is the 'Sick-one' who 'calls the Individual Law, Holy' (13: 4, 5, E106), and it is Satan who affirms that he is 'God alone | There is no other!' (9: 25-6, E103). In changing grain into flour, Satan is changing the possibility of growth contained in the seed into a form which can be assimilated by other individuals. Flour can be made only into things which are edible and, therefore, can be assimilated to the self. The only other alternative is that it be wasted. We can therefore define Satan's role as the translation of the other into the constituted world of the self.

It is important to mention at this stage that prior to the Fall Satan had a much more positive role to play. In the prelapsarian world Satan, Palamabron, and Rintrah form different aspects of a single identity, what we can call 'living form' because its outline is fluid, open, dynamic; the body is a site of interaction between self and other, a place where, in words taken from *Jerusalem*, there are 'cominglings' from the head even unto the feet. Satan's place of work in this world, the starry heavens, is the surface of the body of Albion. We can therefore see Satan's milling as an ordering of identity, an organization of a living body. In the fallen world what once was open, as a face to others, has become a profession or a mask: a body of rules, laws, and conventions which determines the relationship between self and other. In the fallen world the surface that is established by Satan interposes itself between self and other; he attempts to change the living surface of life into an impenetrable exterior, what Blake would call Mathematical Form.[25]

This can be seen quite clearly in Leutha's account of the usurpation of Palamabron's Harrow. In the unfallen world Satan gives the surface or outer form of existence the measure of stability that is necessary if Palamabron and Rintrah are to perform their work. In attempting to appropriate the Harrow, however, Satan is attempting to interrupt the interaction between this implement and the Plough and, in so doing, enclose life within an opaque, impenetrable form. This attempt meets more resistance than Leutha and Satan had anticipated. The Harrow is living and Satan can only exert his control over such a body by attempting to enclose it in an inert, impenetrable form, but this is to change life into a raging fire, a repressed energy, which encircles Satan's own life:

> Satan astonishd, and with power above his own controll
> Compell'd the Gnomes to curb the horses, & to throw banks of sand
> Around the fiery flaming Harrow in labyrinthine forms.
> And brooks between to intersect the meadows in their course.
> The Harrow cast thick flames: Jehovah thunderd above:
> Chaos & ancient night fled from beneath the fiery Harrow:
> The Harrow cast thick flames & orb'd us round in concave fires
> A Hell of our own making.
>
> (12: 16-23, E106)

The Spectre, Satan, the Reasoning Negative, the Elect, all of these names describe the force that has now interposed itself between self and other. The contrary relationship between Rintrah and Palamabron has been interrupted and the openness of a face has been changed into the opacity of a profession.

In this way we can see that the three Classes describe a condition which is endemic to our world. Perhaps the best description of this condition is given by Locke when he writes that 'the understanding is not much unlike a closet wholly shut from light, with only some little openings left, to let in external visible resemblances, or ideas of things without'.[26] It is here the closet wall, the form or outline of the self, which both separates and determines the relationship between self and other. It is not the other that appears, but the other as it has been graded and assessed by the forms and conventions of our world. We are caverned beings, closed individually and collectively within our constituted worlds, and from this perspective thought is reduced to a process in which we reason upon no more than our 'own Dark Fiction' (EG[k]: 91). In the Bard's terms, Locke's closet is another name for the world that has been outlined by Satan. Its interposition between self and other divides the world into the Redeemed, those that fit into the perspectives of the self, and the Reprobate, those that do not and are therefore 'form'd | To destruction from the mother's womb' (7: 3, E100).

Despite my quotation from Locke it would be unwise to limit the possibilities of Los's world in too precipitate a manner. It is quite clear that the production of this world, although representing a diminishing of the life of Eternity, is itself a saving action and prevents a fall into formlessness. Unfortunately, this same world can also be the site of a further fragmentation and loss of identity. It is with this possibility that the Bard is now concerned as he turns to a quarrel between Satan and Palamabron which threatens to destroy even the outline of the self that we have described.

THE QUARREL

The quarrel begins with a simple, almost homely situation: Satan entreats Los 'to give to him Palamabrons station' (7: 6, E100). Palamabron and Los both refuse this request until, after repeated entreaties, Los gives Satan 'the Harrow of the Almighty' (7: 10, E100). As a result, Satan labours with the Harrow for a day of one thousand years duration (7: 13, E100). The next morning Palamabron wakes to find that 'the horses of the Harrow | Were maddend with tormenting fury' (7: 17–18, E100). The 'servants of the Harrow | The Gnomes' (7: 18–19, E100) accuse Satan, and Palamabron asks Los to judge who is at fault. Los finds, somewhat to the reader's surprise, that he is unable to determine who is the malefactor. As the narrator himself asks:

What could Los do? how could he judge, when Satans self, believ'd
That he had not oppres'd the horses of the Harrow, nor the servants.

(7: 39–40, E101)

He therefore does nothing more than urge everyone to keep to their 'own station | . . . nor in pity false, nor in officious brotherhood, where | None needs, be active' (7: 41-3, E101). Satan now returns to his Mills and finds that his own servants are 'drunken with wine and dancing wild | With shouts and Palamabrons songs' (8: 8–9, E101). Satan therefore returns to Los, 'not fill'd with vengeance but with tears, | Himself convinc'd of Palamabrons turpitude' (8: 6–7, E101). Los responds to this new development by declaring the day to be one of mourning, and claiming that he is himself to blame for these events. The quarrel between Satan and Palamabron, however, now expands and gradually draws all of existence into its orbit.

In our first glimpse of the quarrel we see Los roll 'his loud thunders' and tell Satan in no uncertain terms that he cannot 'drive the Harrow in pitys paths' (4: 16, E98). Eve Teitlebaum articulates a common judgement of Los's outburst when, with evident approval, she describes it as a 'thunderous response to Satan'.[27] It is a 'thunderous response', but in retrospect one wonders why, in the midst of a quarrel which began with the usurpation of the role of one by another, Los is not at his forge giving the three Classes their fixed destinations. As the story progresses we discover that Los is no longer forming Golgonooza, or creating and orienting the three Classes; instead he has become an arbitrator, or a judge, in a dispute. There is therefore a curious similarity between Satan's usurpation of Palamabron's Harrow and Los's assumption of the role of arbitrator. Los does precisely what Satan is accused of: he gives up his own work and identity in order to adopt that belonging to someone else. Moreover, in attempting to judge, and so arrange the world from his perspective, Los can be seen as performing the work of Satan and so being assimilated to the state of Satan.

Much the same kind of criticism can be levelled at Palamabron. Satan's usurpation of Palamabron's Harrow is mirrored by the day spent by Palamabron in charge of Satan's Mills. In rebuking Satan Los says:

> If you account it Wisdom when you are angry to be silent, and
> Not to shew it: I do not account that Wisdom but Folly.
>
> (4: 6-7, E98)

Yet this is what Palamabron is guilty of when he 'fear'd to be angry lest Satan should accuse him of | Ingratitude' (7: 11-12, E100). After Satan has laboured with the Harrow and Palamabron has worked in the Mills, Satan embraces Palamabron with a 'brother's tears' and Palamabron 'also wept'. It is as if in these lines there is a recognition of a secret and repressed collusion between these two brothers. It seems that both Los and Palamabron can be judged to be guilty of the crime that Satan has committed.

I do not, of course, mean to suggest that there are no meaningful differences which can be used to distinguish between these three figures. However, in withdrawing from their identities and either judging or relying on a system of judgement,

Palamabron and Los repeat Satan's usurpation of another's identity and adopt Satan's role of judging and arbitrating. As a result they are assimilated to Satan's world. Satan drives us to suspend creativity and induces us to avoid a relationship of openness with others, in order to judge others by ourselves. It is this which reduces individuals to a homogeneous substance, for in the state of Satan individuals are fundamentally alike: they are closed, inert, and impervious globes, or grains, which in the aggregate form Satan's Polypus. The three Classes should have not a triangular but a spiral relationship. Their interaction should in fact be like a dance step which is initiated by Rintrah and completed by Satan, after which the dancer moves to another part of the floor. Judgement allows Satan to hold all in stasis: one step is, indeed, marred by a 'fall'.[28] One therefore cannot simply say that one side is innocent and the other guilty because they have become assimilated to the very force that Palamabron hopes will be found guilty. They have entered the state of Satan. There is something of a logical paradox here, for so long as Los and Palamabron leave their stations unattended in order to take part in a process of judgement they extend Satan's empire. They cannot pass judgement —or even judge Satan (the Judge)—without themselves being assimilated to what they hope to judge.

Partial recognition that this is the case occurs on plate 8. Los takes off his sandal and declares the day a 'blank in Nature'. In this day, which is one thousand years long, Los takes over the work of Rintrah and so becomes completely identified with wrath. Nothing is produced in nature, the three Classes are no longer sent to their particular destinations and the Plough, driven by Los, works ceaselessly to translate everything into exteriority. Los is attempting to break Satan's grip on the world by forcing the self to be receptive to the other. A new day can begin only when a new seed is able to enter the ground. Unfortunately, until Palamabron and Rintrah enter into relationship with each other the seed cannot grow, and Los's wrathful rending of the surface of the self is ineffective.

At this point in the poem Los is in a double bind similar to that of the student whose teacher says to him: 'If you answer this question correctly I will punish you, if you answer it incorrectly I will punish you and if you don't answer I will punish you'. Los has said 'yes', 'no', and then refused to make any further decision and yet each step has led him further into Satan's world. Palamabron, however, in a move which is probably equivalent to taking a legal matter to a higher court, calls down a 'Great Solemn Assembly'

> That he who will not defend Truth, may be compelled to
> Defend a Lie, that he may be snared & caught & taken.
>
> (8: 47-8, E102)

This course of action, however, merely translates the triangular relationship between Los, Palamabron, and Satan on to a different level and for as long as this triangular structure is maintained we can expect to see a consolidation of Satan's power. In accepting the position that Los has vacated, the Solemn Assembly find themselves in his dilemma. Whatever the precise content of their judgement they have still left their Edenic vocation and identities, they have been defined by the dispute between Palamabron and Satan, and adopted the Satanic role of judge. They are therefore themselves guilty of usurping another's identity. The extent of this change of vocation and identity is suggested by the movement of all Eden into Palamabron's tent: it seems that even Eden has adopted the point of view of Palamabron.

When this new court is called to order it is with some surprise that we learn that the two witnesses are Rintrah and Palamabron, no longer as contraries but on opposite sides of a legal dispute. Rintrah now exerts himself on behalf of Satan because he has been deceived by Satan's mildness. Rintrah has, therefore, also been appropriated by Satan; so complete is this appropriation that it becomes 'a proverb in Eden' that 'Satan is among the Reprobate' (9: 12, E103).

The Assembly judges Rintrah to be the guilty party, but this judgement is one more victory for Satan. The triangular relationship between Los, Palamabron, and Satan has now become one in which the Divine Assembly is at the apex and Rintrah has assumed the position of Palamabron. One can represent the proliferation of the world of Satan, based on the idea of judgement and the translation of the other into the constituted world of the self, as a sequence of triangles in which each triangle extends and engulfs its predecessors (see below).

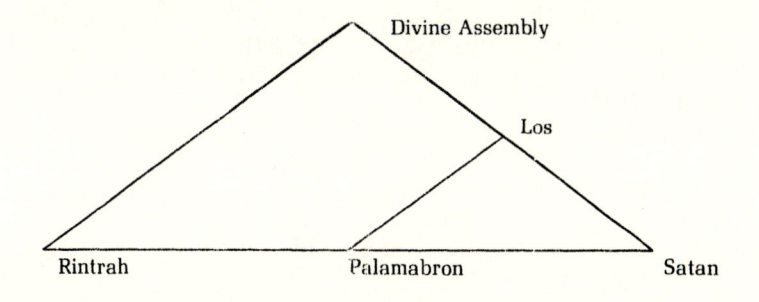

The irony is, of course, that the true apex is Satan and that this triangle represents the mechanism by which Satan hopes to reduce the diversity of the living world to 'One Great Satan', to a world where he is able to assert:

> I alone am God & I alone in Heavn & Earth
> Of all that live dare utter this, others tremble & bow
> Till All Things become One Great Satan, in Holiness
> Oppos'd to Mercy, and the Divine Delusion Jesus be no more.
>
> (38: 56–39: 2, E140)

At this stage of the Bard's Song it appears that no one is able to escape this process. The Divine Assembly, while still secure in their position as judge, notice a world of 'Deeper Ulro' open up within their ranks (9: 34–5, E103). One can sense the despair that envelops them. None of the actors can see their complicity and yet everything that they do widens the empire of Satan. It is as if they have eyes to see Satan, but no sight to see how his power is generated.

The Assembly's judgement and the events which result from it cause a certain amount of consternation on the part of those who have observed the progress of this trial. It is therefore enquired 'Why in a Great Solemn Assembly | The Innocent should be condemn'd for the Guilty?' (11: 15–16, E105). The judgement is defended by an Eternal who tells us that

> If the Guilty should be condemn'd, he must be an Eternal Death
> And one must die for another throughout all Eternity.
>
> (11: 17–18, E105)

This rationalization is, at best, highly ambiguous. It is, on the one hand, possible that the Eternal is referring to the saving action of Christ. A reading such as this is, however, compromised by the observation that Christ gave up his own life in order to redeem humanity, while in this instance the Assembly, like Pilate, has agreed to condemn an innocent party in order to retain law and order. The Eternal is apparently not entirely convinced himself and feels it necessary to confirm his argument with a 'thunderous oath' (11: 27, E105). Within this state of affairs Satan is able triumphantly to divide the nations (10: 21, E104).

Blake encapsulates the process by which Satan has been able to reduce the world to 'one Great Satan' in the illumination which makes up plate 10 (see Fig. 2). Here we see Satan standing on one of the 'paved terraces of his bosom'[29] burning with Rintrah's flames 'hidden beneath his mildness'. In front of

2. *Milton*, plate 10: 'Satan, Palamabron, and Rintrah'.

Satan is Rintrah and at Satan's side is Palamabron.[30] In the arrangement of feet, eyes, bodies, and hands one can see a series of triangular and mediated relationships. Palamabron and Rintrah face each other and show that in reality they should be contraries. However, no real contact occurs between them and instead Palamabron has defined himself by touching Satan's right foot with his left. This is the only direct relationship between the three characters and clearly even this is repressed. Palamabron's eyes and hands express no shadow of an intention to admit his participation in Satan's world. Rintrah seems to be apart from this Satan–Palamabron axis. However, this very separation means that he is no longer in a contrary relationship with Palamabron (their faces no longer meet) and that therefore he is still defined by Satan. It is interesting to note that not one of the three characters catches another's glance. Rintrah looks in the general direction of Satan but is clearly looking at something far to the right. Satan looks in the direction of Palamabron but could catch no more than the faintest glimpse of him from his position. Palamabron is looking between Satan and Rintrah but in the general direction of Rintrah. Rintrah and Palamabron are perhaps both looking at the Solemn Assembly for clarification of their decision. What should be a relationship between two contraries becomes projected into a third term: as the equivalent of Judge or judgement Satan defines Palamabron and Rintrah.

Satan has adopted the facial features and bodily attributes of Palamabron to an extraordinary extent. He has also acquired Rintrah's flames. Rintrah and Palamabron are watching the transformation of their worlds into the world of Satan. Palamabron's hands show an intention to do something resolute. Perhaps he intends to invoke another mediator. Rintrah's hands indicate that he has been mesmerized, defined by the actions of others. He is therefore in a state of supplication and consternation. In the spatial arrangement of feet, bodies, hands, and eyes we see the translation of a face-to-face relationship into the triangular structure of a mediated one. The only real contact is that which inaugurates this reified world and is subsequently repressed. It is now Satan that structures and defines the world, and under his grinding surfaces all difference is on the point of being lost. The world of the three Classes is on the verge of being reduced to a Polypus.

At this point and from this perspective the Bard's Song counsels despair. There seems little hope of inducing Rintrah and Palamabron to form the surface of a 'Living' rather than a

'Mathematical' form. In the course of the poem Los, Palamabron, Rintrah, the Solemn Assembly, even the Eternals all leave their vocations and become immobile, locked into the system of judgement represented by Satan.[31] One after the other they consolidate the world of Satan.

THE BARD'S AUDIENCE

The Bard's Song has two audiences: the Mortal sons and daughters of Albion in fallen time and space—characters such as ourselves—and those Sons who sit with the Bard at eternal tables. For the latter group the Song introduces such a radical doubt into their world that 'the roots & fast foundations of the Earth' (14: 8, E108) are shaken. The Sons therefore respond defensively:

> The Bard ceas'd. All consider'd and a loud resounding murmur
> Continu'd round the Halls; and much they question'd the immortal
> Loud voicd Bard. and many condemn'd the high tone'd Song
> Saying Pity and Love are too venerable for the imputation
> Of Guilt. Others said. If it is true! if the acts have been perform'd
> Let the Bard himself witness. Where hadst thou this terrible Song.
> 
> (13: 45-50, E107)

This response, however, represents yet another expansion of Satan's web of death. The Sons of Albion now become the judges while Pity and Love are the accused.

This resistance to the disturbing power of the Bard's Song is repeated in much of the criticism that is proffered by the temporal Sons and Daughters of Albion. There is, for example, a tendency, in certain critics of the poem, to attempt to confine its thrust to the very world that the Bard is concerned to deconstruct. James, for example, writes that in 'The Bard's Song' 'Blake implies an existential psychology in which fulfilment of self is the foremost moral obligation of each individual.'[32] Howard makes a similar point when he argues that

> Though Blake's ethical valuation may disturb us if we see it as a code for interaction between men, his valuation makes sense to us as a psychological principle working within the mind. Blake's insistence on reliance on freedom, forgiveness, and love means that man must free his impulses, feel no guilt, attempt to restrict no feeling, and respond affectionately to his own true nature. In short, Blake's moral teaching strikes its most profound note when heard as a voice to the psyche. The harmony of mind that Blake would have man hear and feel and sing, is from himself to himself.[33]

Or to take another example, Mark Bracher writes that

> The Bard's Song has articulated a metaphysical problem to which the rest of the poem must find a solution: what fulfillment is possible for individuals in a world in which life lives on death and in which one individual attains completion or fulfillment of its being only through the expropriation of another individual's being?[34]

But the whole thrust of the Bard's Song is not to suggest that the fulfilment of *self* is our 'foremost moral obligation', or to suggest a 'harmony of mind' which, for man, proceeds from 'himself to himself', but to open the constituted world of the self to its ground in relation to the other. The whole question of our 'true nature', the very status of our feelings and impulses (such as love and pity), is therefore made highly problematic. The Bard's visionary deconstruction is an attempt to reveal the foundations of precisely that world in which 'one individual attains completion or fulfillment of his being only through the expropriation of another individual's being.'

The Bard's visionary deconstruction is, however, not concerned simply to establish the existence of a gap between illusion and the abyss which it hides, between the self-assurance of the speaking voice and the rhetorical or fictive ground of that voice, but, in so doing, to open the possibility of a change in relationship between self and other. His visionary deconstruction is, therefore, in the service of a vision which tells us that the triangular relationships which we have been describing will be radically changed (13: 30-4, E107). It is in the figure of Milton and his 'unexampled deed' that this hope is embodied.

## 2. 'To bathe in the Waters of Life; to wash off the Not Human'

> There is a Moment in each Day that Satan cannot find
> Nor can his Watch Fiends find it, but the Industrious find
> This Moment & it multiply. & when it once is found
> It renovates every Moment of the Day if rightly placed...
> (M 35: 42-5, E136)

### THE DESCENT OF MILTON

While the Sons of Albion contend with the Bard, Milton is silent. It is only when the 'foundations of the Earth' are shaken by the 'great murmuring' of the Sons, and the Bard has taken 'refuge in Miltons bosom', that he speaks. In the course of his response, the grave questions of the Sons are displaced by a radical change of comportment. Milton breaches the confines of heaven—the ultimate reference point and transcendental signifier for the fallen world—with a levitation which treats the highest of the high as its ground. He is, therefore, no longer contained by the triangular structure of Satan's world of judgement. Rather than judging Satan, Milton recognizes that in his 'Selfhood' he is Satan. Punishment of the malefactor is replaced by self-annihilation and, what is even more striking, an attempt to loose Satan from his hells and to claim those hells as his own (14: 14-32, E108). Milton is no longer engrossed by the 'intricate mazes of Providence' (2: 17, E96), nor is he content merely to view his 'Sixfold Emanation scatter'd thro' the deep | In torment!'; instead, he begins a movement which will take him 'into the deep her to redeem & himself perish' (2: 19-20, E96). We can gain a first glimpse of the nature of this movement if we return for a moment to Locke's human understanding.

For the self in the state of existence described by Locke, the closet forms the horizon or furthest extreme of his/her world. One wonders, however, why the self in such a predicament remains in the middle of the closet, dependent upon the few rays of light that penetrate its darkness. Even if the door of the closet is locked, why doesn't he/she at least get up and look out of the openings which even now allow a certain amount of light to enter? The reason is probably, as the fairy wryly remarks in the preface to *Europe*, that 'stolen joys are sweet, & bread eaten in secret pleasant' (iii: 6, E60). To remain within the closet of the self is merely to reason upon your 'own Dark Fiction' (EG[k]: 91, E520). Blake does not suggest that there is a way of transforming the fiction into an apodictic truth, or into a set of axioms for establishing a metaphysics; however, we are able to use our fictions to open on to the world in which others exist. As the 'Everlasting Gospel' states in summary fashion:

> This Lifes dim Windows of the Soul
> Distorts the Heavens from Pole to Pole
> And leads you to Believe a Lie
> When you see with not thro the Eye.
>
> (EG[k]: 97-100, E520)

Milton's movement is, therefore, one which attempts to move to the very periphery of his closet, to the horizon of the world in which he is enclosed. In a situation which is the inverse of that pertaining to the natural world, the sun rises because the closeted man moves to the edge of his enclosure and so into proximity with the burning light of relationship. At the very periphery of one's constituted world, Christ is no longer a distant 'disk of blood' from which we are separated by 'heav'ns & earths' which 'roll dark between'; instead Christ will appear as a human form. It is to a consideration of this movement that I will now turn; however, my discussion must be introduced by a brief description of the geography of the land through which Milton will pass.

THE GEOGRAPHY OF ETERNITY

In *Poetic Form in Blake's 'Milton'*, Susan Fox observes that the place in which the Bard sings his Song is ambiguous. The Bard and his audience are placed in 'the old Christian heaven transposed to Blake's cosmology, where it is rather less than heavenly, but Blake assures us that the Bard sings "at eternal tables"'.[1] This kind of ambiguity—in which some of the Sons of Albion seem to be in, and yet in some important way not of, Eternity—is a necessary feature of 'heaven' as it is understood within the postlapsarian world described in Blake's major prophecies. As I have argued in previous chapters, the Fall begins with withdrawal; this does not mean, however, that withdrawal can be adequately described as a movement in spatial or physical terms. To withdraw from the interactions which form the basis of Eternity is not in the first instance to move from one place in Eternity to another, but to replace movement with stasis, openness with closure, and transparence with opacity. The Fall is therefore a phenomenon which in a certain sense occurs within and leaves its mark upon Eternity. On plate 54 of *Jerusalem*, for example, the fallen world is portrayed as an inert globe which is surrounded by the myriads of Eternity. Similarly, in *The Book of Urizen* we are told that 'All the myriads of Eternity: | All the wisdom & joy of life: | Roll like a sea around' Urizen (13: 28-30, E77).

I am not, of course, suggesting that Eternity and the fallen world occupy the same space; *The Book of Urizen* is full of images of separation. However, the separation is not simply a movement in physical terms from one location in Eternity to another, but a change of ontological state. This has the effect of creating a nadir or zero that opens (or more correctly closes) out from the life of Eternity into a bottomless abyss. It is as if a 'black hole'[2] were to be discovered in the life of Eternity, a space which appears to be 'Limited | To those without but Infinite to those within' (10: 8-9, E104). In Blake's œuvre the dimensions of the Fall are measured by the distances between Ulro, Generation, and Beulah.

Beulah is described in *Milton* as a space which exists in order to provide a habitation for the passive powers, who would otherwise be reduced, by the energy and dynamism of Eden, almost to a state of non-existence. It is, however, also described as a realm which surrounds Eden on all sides (30: 8-14, E129). We must therefore argue that Beulah is characterized by the additional role of giving form and shape to Eternity. Without the work of the passive powers the life of Eden would be completely unbounded and such a life is no life at all.

Unfortunately, Beulah not only preserves the life of Eternity, but at the same time opens the possibility of withdrawal. Normally this is no more than a possibility; in *Jerusalem*, for example, Los at first thinks that the events of the Fall are nothing more than visions seen in the shadow of possibility. In the course of the Fall this possibility becomes an actuality and the 'pleasant Rest' (30: 14, E124) of Beulah becomes a deathly sleep. Beulah still ministers to the fallen Man—the daughters of Beulah feed the sleepers on their couch—but the sleepers now wander in the states of Generation and Ulro which open beneath Beulah. Beulah is therefore the highest state possible in the fallen world and at the same time a portion of Eternity. To withdraw is, as I have argued, to enter into a state of non-being. This fate is, however, averted by the work of Los who, as the Bard asserts in the opening plates of his Song, gives form to the fallen Albion as the six thousand year span of fallen time. We can therefore say that beneath or within the form that is held by the daughters of Beulah, in the worlds of Generation and Ulro, non-being is spatialized and temporalized as fallen history.[3]

With this brief and necessarily simplified description of the geography of Eternity and its nether regions we can see that Blake is, in an ironical sense, remaining within a quite traditional conception of the relationship between time and eternity. For Augustine, eternity offers a vantage point from which the full sweep of fallen time can be taken in at a single glance.[4] In *Milton* Blake has given John Milton a similar vantage point; however, this eminence is now itself placed in a wider context. The static heaven which affords a glimpse of the inert and fragmented body of Albion is itself a moment of stasis within an otherwise active Eternity. Its inhabitants are unable to move precisely because their bodies (the world of time and space) lie far beneath them. In other words, eternity in Augustine's sense is merely the furthest extension of the fallen world, the apex of the triangle described in the Bard's Song. It is a repetition on a macro-cosmic scale of a metaphysics of withdrawal. Locke's philosophy is therefore merely a translation into a secular idiom of a theology of withdrawal. There is a relationship of congruence between the plight of the individual caught within the closet of his constituted world and that of the Sons of Albion who gather, after death, in a heaven which is closeted away from the activity of Eternity. Time is not, as in Augustine's scheme of things, merely the transitory or ephemeral, but the very body of Albion and therefore that which must be embraced if Milton is to look forth for the morning of the grave. If Milton is to wake from his heavenly sleep, he must descend to time and gather to himself both his Spectre and his Emanation. In an ironic reversal of the Neo-Platonic descent of the soul to the body, Milton descends to time in order to enter Eternity. This is a movement which offers a profound alternative to Thel's flight from the realities of the fallen world. It is to a consideration of this journey that we must now turn.

THE DESCENT TO THE SEPULCHRE

Beulah is, as I have argued, the point from which the fallen world opens out (or closes in) from the active life of Eternity. It is, therefore, towards Beulah that Milton makes his way. On the verge of this world he discovers 'his own Shadow; | A mournful form double; hermaphroditic: male & female | In one wonderful body' (14: 36-8, E108). The Shadow is the side of his existence that Milton has repressed; it is the night or nether side of the heavens in which the Sons of Albion are domiciled. The Shadow which appears in Beulah is, of course, only a two dimensional phenomenon when it is viewed from the perspective of Eternity. For the person who enters it, however, it can be seen as a form which stretches from Beulah into the depths of the fallen world: the 'dread shadow' is 'twenty-seven-fold' and reaches 'to the depths of direst Hell, & thence to Albions land' (14: 39-40, E108-9).[5] Milton does not avoid this grotesque form; instead, in a movement which is akin to Los's embrace of his Spectre in *The Four Zoas*, he enters into it (14: 38, E108).

For those 'Who dwell in immortality', Milton seems to be 'as One sleeping on a couch | Of gold' (15: 12-13, E109), but for the Seven Angels of the Presence who enter the shadow with Milton, the perception of his sleeping body is supplemented by the sight of his Shadow vegetating 'underneath the Couch | Of death' (15: 9-10, E109). The accounts conflict, but are not incommensurate, for the former, because they remain in Eternity, see only the eternal aspect of Milton's descent, while the latter enter the abyss with Milton and so see his descent into Generation and Ulro. Milton himself offers a third perspective on his descent. As a person who has given up the security of his constituted world and has freely undertaken the Neoplatonic descent of the soul into the sea of time and space, Milton is not aware of his conscious body. As Blake writes: 'But to himself he seemd a wanderer lost in dreary night' (15: 16, E109). In each account it is clear that Milton has left the light of Albion's heaven in order to encounter the night which forms its ground.

It is important to underline at this stage of my argument that Milton's descent does not miraculously render harmless the grotesque body in which he is now embodied; the reader is told, in fact, that the shadow kept 'its course among the Spectres' (15: 17, E109). Milton has simply embraced the body which forms the horizon or limit of his world. However, within the trajectory of this body there is now opened a quite different movement:

> Onwards his Shadow kept its course among the Spectres; call'd
> Satan, but swift as lightning passing them, startled the shades
> Of Hell beheld him in a trail of light as of a comet
> That travels into Chaos: so Milton went guarded within.
>
> (15: 17-20, E109)

Milton has begun the journey towards the periphery of his constituted world.

## TURNING ONE'S SELF INSIDE OUT

Milton's descent to the sepulchre in which Albion is enclosed is quite clearly not completed with his entry into his Shadow. The opposition between up and down, heaven and hell, form and shadow, day and night, is rehearsed, in the first instance, within the figure of the individual Milton. Milton has, one could say, as a first step, embraced his *own* shadow. This embrace, however, takes place within the collective ground of Albion. Milton, like Jonah in the belly of the whale, is himself enclosed in a larger form. To emerge from his own tomb is therefore to become aware of the cavern in which humanity is enclosed. Milton's Shadow finds its individual existence within this larger form. This is why it is described as 'twenty-seven-fold' and as an entity which reaches to Hell and to 'Albions land'. If Milton is to 'look forth for the morning of the grave', his embrace of his *own* shadow must therefore exceed itself, pass beyond its own perimeters, and move to the body which encloses humanity. It is at the limits of the world constituted by Albion-in-withdrawal that morning will break.

The poem begins this second stage of Milton's journey with a marvellous discourse on the nature of infinity. The reader is assured that

> The nature of infinity is this: That every thing has its
> Own Vortex; and when once a traveller thro Eternity.
> Has passd that Vortex, he perceives it roll backward behind
> His path, into a globe itself infolding; like a sun:
> Or like a moon, or like a universe of starry majesty,
> While he keeps onwards in his wondrous journey on the earth
> Or like a human form, a friend with whom he livd benevolent.
>
> (15: 21-7, E109)

Vortexes, as W. J. T. Mitchell observes,

occur in nature as the focus of the encounter between conflicting forces; whirlpools arise from the interaction of conflicting currents. ... But ... the vortex is not simply the product of two equal and opposite forces. ... [It] depends upon a third element to give progression to the cycle of contraries, to bring it to a critical point with a conical apex like the point of the Gothic arch.[6]

If we trace this account of a natural vortex onto Blake's descriptions of prelapsarian existence we can say that the conflicting (or contrary) forces within an individual are the male and female powers which make up his/her identity. The form established in the relationship between these powers is drawn to a point, and therefore fashioned into a cone, by the movement of the whole person to relationship. We are able to call this form a vortex, however, only if we remember that in Eternity our fallen world is inverted. In the prelapsarian world a vortex is perhaps what we would call a fountain: the apex is a point of openness and the psyche looks towards others rather than assimilating others to itself. In withdrawal, the movement of the active self towards others ceases and in its place the Spectre merely retains the shape of the world that has appeared to the self. The fountain has now become 'a whirlpool fierce to draw creations in'.

In the fallen world, particularly in the light of deconstruction and Freudian psychotherapy, it takes no great leap of faith to believe that the self is a vortex which assimilates others. The lines which follow the passage quoted above, however, make a distinction between the weak traveller who is 'confin'd beneath the moony shade' of his/her own constituted world and the strong traveller who is able to pass from his/her own vortex to that of others (15: 32-5, E109).[7] As extraordinary as this capacity to 'travel' appears to be, it is important to recognize that it does not in some way miraculously renovate the world. The travel described in *Milton* 15 occurs within the fallen world.[8] Nevertheless, it does produce a change of perception. The world is no longer conceived solely on the basis of that which has been assimilated to the constituted world of the self; instead, it can be seen to be composed of many vortexes and therefore many persons. As Blake writes in *Jerusalem*:

> For all are Men in Eternity. Rivers Mountains Cities Villages
> All are Human & when you enter into their Bosoms you walk
> In Heavens & Earths; as in your own Bosom you bear your Heaven
> And Earth, & all you behold.
>
> (71: 15-19, E225)

It is this perception which enables us to understand the nature of infinity.

Locke describes infinity as a form of mental exhaustion. He writes that

Every one that has any idea of any stated lengths of space, as a foot, finds that he can repeat that idea; and joining it to the former, make the idea of two feet; and by the addition of a third, three feet; and so on, without ever coming to an end of his additions, whether of the same

## 70  The Moment of Embrace

idea of a foot, or, if he pleases, of doubling it, or any other idea he has of any length, as a mile, or diameter of the earth, or of the *orbis magnus*: for whichever of these he takes, and how often soever he doubles, or any otherwise multiplies it, he finds, that, after he has continued his doubling in his thoughts, and enlarged his idea as much as he pleases, he has no more reason to stop, nor is one jot nearer the end of such addition, than he was at first setting out: the power of enlarging his idea of space by further additions remaining still the same, he hence takes the idea of infinite space.[9]

By this kind of reasoning infinity can be imagined as a more intense version of the weariness that some readers might experience at the end of the lengthy sentence quoted above. If, however, we begin a definition of infinity with the characterization of it as that which (unlike a point of limit or exhaustion) cannot be reduced to our representation, or perception of it, then we can say that the clearest and most eloquent symbol of infinity is the person.[10]

In the Bard's Song the fallen world appeared as a Polypus, a conglomerate of identical particles. By contrast, Milton's descent into the world and embrace of his Shadow reveals a world that is peopled with others and in which the natural world is 'one infinite plane', 'the heaven a vortex passd already, and the earth | A vortex not yet pass'd by the traveller thro' Eternity' (15: 34-5, E109). In other words, it reveals a world of many vortexes, and therefore a world of numerous persons and many infinities.

This brief description of infinity and the vortex enables a further visualization of Milton's journey. In entering the deep, Milton is attempting to invert the vortex of assimilation (the triangle) which was the subject of the Bard's Song. As I have argued, this cannot be done simply by turning to the active life of Eternity, for Milton's body lies in the deep far beneath him. Milton's journey therefore involves moving from the static position of Satan at the apex of the vortex of the fallen world, where he is 'confin'd beneath the moony shade' of his own constituted world, to his body beneath him. The cone or vortex that stretches from Beulah down to the six thousand year *cycle* of fallen history is therefore inverted by this movement, and the 'endless circle' of the fallen world changed into the kind of eternal vortex that we have characterized as a fountain.

ON THE EDGE OF THE PRESENT

Milton's embrace of his shadow therefore brings him, first of all, to the edge of his constituted world and therefore the edge of his own vortex. At this point of the poem Milton is able to 'travel' from his own vortex to that of another. His movement into the abyss takes him from the vortex of an individual to that of all humanity, from the vortex of heaven to that of time. The resulting change of perspective is described in a striking passage:

> First Milton saw Albion upon the Rock of Ages,
> Deadly pale outstretchd and snowy cold, storm coverd;
> A Giant form of perfect beauty outstretchd on the rock
> In solemn death: the Sea of Time & Space thunderd aloud
> Against the rock, which was inwrapped with the weeds of death
> Hovering over the cold bosom, in its vortex Milton bent down
> To the bosom of death, what was underneath soon seemd above.
> A cloudy heaven mingled with stormy seas in loudest ruin;
> But as a wintry globe descends precipitant thro' Beulah bursting,
> With thunders loud and terrible: so Miltons shadow fell
> Precipitant loud thundring into the Sea of Time & Space.
>
> (15: 36-46, E109-10)

The *raison d'être* of Milton's journey is, as I have argued, to reach a point from which it is possible to look forth for 'the morning of the grave'. Such a point must be one in which others can be encountered, and it must also represent the furthest extent of Albion's fallen body. Quite clearly the furthest extreme of Albion's temporal body is the present. Moreover, the present is, as Bultmann observes, a point of encounter.[11] The present is, however, also the furthest point in Milton's body, for it is in the present that Milton's own works are subject to re-reading and re-interpretation and, therefore, in the present that Milton is open and subject to encounters with others. We can therefore say (with certain qualifications which I will discuss later in this chapter) that the present is the point at which morning will break. It is only at this point in his journey, as Milton's prophetic presence erupts within the time and space of early nineteenth-century England, that Blake is able to see him:

> Then first I saw him in the Zenith as a falling star,
> Descending perpendicular, swift as the swallow or swift;
> And on my left foot falling on the tarsus, enterd there;
> But from my left foot a black cloud redounding spread over Europe.
>
> (15: 47-50, E110)

Milton's descent is experienced by Blake as a presence within his very flesh and blood. Milton falls on Blake's tarsus and, moreover, enters there. This is, of course, a rather extraordinary idea as long as we picture the self as an autonomous self-enclosed identity and the body as a physical, corporeal substance. Locke's closeted man need not fear such an event for he can have direct contact only with those 'external visible resemblances' that manage to filter into his cavern. By contrast, in Blake's œuvre the self is not isolated and autonomous, but emerges in relationship; the body is not simply a physical form, but includes our spiritual body. In this latter sense our body is the sum of all of our experiences, relationships, commitments and so on; it is the mental and emotional, as well as physical, shape of our lives.

It is in terms of this wider body that Christ asserts that he resides within our bosoms, and that we reside within his (J 4: 19, E146), or Merleau-Ponty contends that 'Whether speaking or listening, I project myself into the other person, I introduce him into my own self.'[12] Similarly, Milton's descent is experienced by Blake within this wider sense of the word 'body'. We can begin to understand this phenomenon by drawing an analogy from the reading process. Merleau-Ponty writes that

With the aid of signs agreed upon by the author and myself because we speak the same language, the book makes me believe that we had already shared a common stock of well-worn and readily available significations. The author has come to dwell in my world. Then, imperceptibly, he varies the ordinary meaning of the signs, and like a whirlwind they sweep me along toward the other meaning with which I am going to connect.[13]

As a result of this process Merleau-Ponty can say: 'I create Stendahl; I am Stendhal while reading him. But that is because first he knew how to bring me to dwell within him.'[14] We can observe an analogous mutuality and exchange in the relationship between Milton and Blake.

Milton's descent from heaven to time animates the hitherto static edifice of his poetic works with a prophetic presence. It is, however, the author of *Milton* who gives body to Milton within time and is therefore the immediate vehicle for this presence. As the author and printer of *Milton: a poem in [1]2 books*,[15] Blake has created Milton; Milton has come to dwell within Blake. This creation was possible only because Milton knew how to bring Blake to dwell within him.

This relationship is suggested in the illumination to plate 32 where we see Milton, as a falling star, about to fall on Blake's tarsus. At first sight Blake's body is falling backwards and away from the illumination represented by Milton. In fact the falling body is balanced and precariously held by a movement upwards which has stretched Blake's chest almost to breaking point. Milton's journey to the edge of his constituted world has called forth a response in Blake, for now Blake's physical body, the body of his constituted world, is pressed almost to breaking point by an answering desire to look forth for the morning of the grave. Milton must come to dwell in Blake's world if he is to complete his journey. Yet, as the illumination makes clear, it is Milton that draws Blake into his world and hence calls forth an answering movement within his very being. Blake and Milton depend upon one another in the same way that readers and writers, in Merleau-Ponty's analogy, gather each other to themselves. For a writer in the prophetic tradition this interaction is particularly important for, as Wittreich writes, paraphrasing Richard Brothers: 'every prophet communicates through a precursor prophet, the precursor providing the key that unlocks the vision of his successor, holding up the lamp without which the new prophecy receives no illumination.'[16]

This kind of interdependence is not confined to Blake and Milton. A similar relationship exists between Blake and the Bard, the Bard and Milton, and Blake and Los. At the close of his Song, as the Sons of Albion 'shook the heavens in doubtfulness', the Bard took refuge in Milton's bosom. However, the Bard was able to dwell within Milton only because the Bard, through the force and power of his 'prophetic Song', was able to bring Milton to dwell within him. Similarly, it is in the orbit of Blake's poem that we hear the Bard's voice: the Bard dwells within Blake's world. Yet, it is the Bard's prophetic Song that begins the poem; it is in the orbit of the Bard's Song that Blake finds his own poetic voice. Similarly, later in the poem Blake becomes 'One Man' with Los and so arises in his 'strength' (22: 12, E117). The syntax of the lines which follow this announcement suggest that it is Blake who now claims to be 'that Shadowy Prophet who Six Thousand Years ago | Fell from my station in the Eternal bosom' (22: 15-16, E117). Yet this passage finishes with the clear assignment of these lines to Los (22: 26, E117). It is, indeed, Los who speaks. He has brought Blake to dwell within his giant form. But Los is himself able to speak only to the extent that Blake, through the vehicle of his poem, brings Los to dwell within his world. The voices of Los and Blake, like those of Blake and the Bard (in the opening plates of the poem), and Blake and Milton (throughout the course of the poem), are distinct, and yet curiously intertwined with each other. However, to describe the interaction between Blake and Milton in this way is to raise the question of the subject matter of their encounter.

The poem offers the reader a clue as to the significance of the encounter between Blake and Milton by nominating the tarsus as the point at which the latter entered the body of the former (15: 49, E110). The tarsus is 'the flat of the foot between the toes and the heel' (*OED*), and for most people it represents a singularly uninteresting part of our anatomy. Nevertheless, this place in our body has the virtue of an association with the birthplace of St Paul, a figure whose singular experience on the road to Damascus offers several close parallels with Blake's experience of the falling Milton. There is of course no suggestion in *Milton* that Blake was waging a physical war against the Christians prior to the descent of Milton; however, the point is perhaps that this kind of activity is characteristic of any world in which the self is closeted away from others. Saul's encounter with Christ, and Blake with Milton, can therefore be seen as a conversion in which the closed world of the self is opened. The subject matter of Blake's encounter with Milton (and of the poem which bears his name) is, ultimately, Christ: the network of relationships in which the fallen world finds its existence.

The relationship between Milton and Blake, at this point in the poem, is not yet one in which Blake encounters Jesus although, as I shall argue, this is its issue. Moreover, even this opening is not unequivocal, for Milton's entry into Blake's body results in the appearance of 'a black cloud' which 'redounding spread over Europe' (15: 50, E110). This could be taken to imply that Blake, like Paul, will spread only a black cloud as the result of his conversion. In fact, the foot of an upright person *must be* the place where his shadow begins and this beginning place is located directly under the tarsus. The brighter the light from above, the darker the shadow; the more sharply focused the revelation, the clearer the shadow's outline. As a result of Paul's work and influence, the shadow of the law became extremely clear and dark. Similarly, one consequence of Milton's descent is that Error is consolidated and the Covering Cherub is revealed. In presenting the beneficial effect (clarification of Error) of revelation by the spreading of a cloud, Blake shows us something of the pain of receiving a revelation and of being a prophet.[17]

At this stage of my argument, it is clear that my analogy with the reading process, although remaining instructive, needs to become more inclusive. The descent of Milton to time and the experience of this phenomenon by Blake exceeds any possible encounter between these two figures which could occur in a reading of Milton's poetry. Milton's descent, for example, spans a long period of time, it occurs in the 'nether regions of the Imagination' and is seen by 'all men on Earth, | And all in Heaven' (21: 5-6, E115). Moreover, Blake tells us that Milton's descent was taking place within his members for quite some time before he was able to recognize it consciously:

> But Milton entering my Foot; I saw in the nether
> Regions of the Imagination; also all men on Earth,
> And all in Heaven, saw in the nether regions of the Imagination
> In Ulro beneath Beulah, the vast breach of Miltons descent.
> But I knew not that it was Milton, for man cannot know
> What passes in his members till periods of Space & Time
> Reveal the secrets of Eternity: for more extensive
> Than any other earthly things, are Mans earthly lineaments.
>
> (21: 4-11, E115)

Quite clearly, Milton's influence is not limited to that experienced when we read his poetry. The works of a great poet become part of our cultural heritage and in so doing bequeath to language certain possibilities of thought and expression. It is in this sense that Milton appears to all men on earth and in heaven. Milton is a presence and a prophetic force within the tradition that addresses us and in which we stand. All men on earth see Milton's descent, albeit in the 'nether regions' of our imaginations, because from within our linguistic and cultural heritage, and as part of the linguistic world in which we stand, Milton addresses us.

BLAKE, MILTON, AND LOS

The Shadowy Female, Urizen, Rahab, and Tirzah all gain their power within the enclosure of the fallen world. Bloom defines the Shadowy Female as 'the material environment of natural man', Rahab as 'the image of the visible church', and Tirzah as 'the necessity of natural limitation' (E916). They are the passive powers which have become separated from man and now define his being. Urizen is identified in *Milton* as Satan and as the Spectre. He is the masculine reasoning memory that retains the shape of the fallen world. For each of these characters, Milton's descent is a threatening and ominous event because, by attempting to breach the confines of their world and so render transparent the cavern in which Albion is enclosed, Milton threatens the very foundation of their power. It is for this reason that they respond to Milton's descent by attempting to assimilate him to their world. With Urizen this takes the form of open conflict. He attempts to baptize Milton into this world, to enclose him within the material world. Milton, on the other hand, attempts to give Urizen a Human Form which will enable him to enter into relationship with others (19: 6-14, E112).[18]

Rahab, Tirzah, and the Shadowy Female respond to Milton's descent by attempting to entice Milton away from his struggle to humanize Urizen and into a material Canaan (20: 3-6, E113-14). If Milton were to accept their invitation he would necessarily forgo any attempt to look forth for the morning of the grave. It would now be the cavern of the fallen world, with its incipient warfare between the contraries, that would remain the horizon of his world.

It is, in fact, only Enitharmon who explicitly welcomes Milton when he first appears within the fallen world. This response is predicated upon Enitharmon's perception of Milton as a 'wintry globe'—as Satan—rather than as the 'awakener'. Enitharmon is the Emanation of Los and, therefore, she is the shape or body of the fallen history that is forged by Los. Within this world Enitharmon's power exists only in concert with the Spectre, who holds the outline of fallen history and is limited by the shape originally given to the fallen Albion by Los. The descent of Milton suggests to Enitharmon a cataclysm in which the bounds of the fallen world will be broken. The fallen world will sever its relationship with Albion, and Satan will be free to assimilate even the sleeping body of Albion into his kingdom:

> Los the Vehicular terror beheld him, & divine Enitharmon
> Call'd all her daughters, Saying. Surely to unloose my bond
> Is this Man come! Satan shall be unloosd upon Albion.
>
> (17: 31-3, E111)

Los responds to Enitharmon's words with terror, for although the world that he has forged is that in which Satan gains his power, it is also all that stops Albion from sinking into the abyss. He therefore pits his strength against Milton (17: 34-6, E111).

Los's initial inability to understand the significance of Milton's descent is owing to his position outside of Golgonooza, in the position of stasis and inactivity which characterizes the various actors of the Bard's Song. When many of the Eternals rise 'up from eternal tables' and—in a striking parallel to the various judgements of the Bard's Song—respond with wrath to

Milton's descent (20: 43-7, E114), Los can only retreat further into inactivity: 'He sat down on his anvil-stock; and leand upon the trough. | Looking into the black water, mingling it with tears' (20: 54-5, E115). In the act of rage (and implicitly of judgement) in which the Eternals 'rend the heavens round the Watchers' in a 'fiery circle', and in Los's response to this act, we can see a further consolidation of Satan's empire.

It is at this nadir that Los remembers

> an old Prophecy in Eden recorded,
> And often sung to the loud harp at the immortal feasts
> That Milton of the Land of Albion should up ascend
> Forwards from Ulro from the Vale of Felpham; and set free
> Orc from his Chain of Jealousy, he started at the thought.
> (20: 57-61, E115)

For W. J. T. Mitchell 'there is an unmistakable element of the ridiculous in the convenient timing of Los's memory here'.[19] However, this judgement is based on a misunderstanding of the nature of Milton's descent. Milton is attempting to open a relationship with Albion-in-withdrawal. One can therefore say that Milton repeats the original openness of Los to Albion-in-withdrawal in which the fallen world was forged. I will return to this point later in this chapter; however, for the moment it is important to observe that the openness of Milton to Albion (and of Blake and Los to Albion) is, paradoxically, both the first and the last event of the fallen world. It is, therefore, quite in order that the descent of Milton, which to Los in the time of memory occurs at the end of fallen time, should provoke a memory from the very beginnings of the fallen world, in which the possibility of transformation inherent in Milton's descent is celebrated. With the recollection of this prophecy, Los begins a movement which will take Milton (in Blake in Los) to the edge of the tomb in which Albion is enclosed.

When Milton entered Blake's body, the 'Vegetable World' appeared on his 'left Foot, | As a bright sandal formd immortal of precious stones & gold'. Blake therefore 'stooped down & bound it on to walk forward thro' Eternity' (21: 12-14, E115). Blake's encounter with Milton therefore involved an extraordinary transformation, for it changed the world from a cavern into a sandal: from a form which hinders movement to one which assists it. This transformation is, nevertheless, not complete. Blake is at this point unable to 'walk forward thro' Eternity' because his encounter with Milton takes place within the body of the fallen Albion. Blake and Milton are at this point like Oothoon in *Visions of the Daughters of Albion*. Although Oothoon's closed world has been opened and she is able to enter a universe which is living, she is unable to enter a fully human world, for she is herself closed within a collective body of withdrawal. Milton's journey can be completed only within the giant form of Los:

> While Los heard indistinct in fear, what time I bound my sandals
> On; to walk forward thro' Eternity, Los descended to me:
> And Los behind me stood; a terrible flaming Sun: just close
> Behind my back; I turned round in terror, and behold.
> Los stood in that fierce glowing fire; & he also stoop'd down
> And bound my sandals on in Udan-Adan . . .
>
> (22: 4-9, E116-17)

It is this embrace which takes Milton, Blake, and Los to a position where they are present to the six thousand year extent of the fallen Albion's body:

> I am that Shadowy Prophet who Six Thousand Years ago
> Fell from my station in the Eternal bosom. Six Thousand Years
> Are finishd. I return! both Time & Space obey my will.
> I in Six Thousand Years walk up and down: for not one Moment
> Of Time is lost, nor one Event of Space unpermanent
> But all remain: every fabric of Six Thousand Years
> Remains permanent: tho' on the Earth where Satan
> Fell, and was cut off all things vanish & are seen no more
> They vanish not from me & mine, we guard them first & last
> The generations of men run on in the tide of Time
> But leave their destind lineaments permanent for ever & ever.
>
> (22: 15-25, E117)

Milton's descent has provoked, and itself become part of, an answering movement within the very texture of the fallen world. We can understand this if we observe that, as prophets, Blake and Milton are members of the Eternal Prophet, Los. Milton's descent can therefore be compared to the Nightingale who, in the second book of *Milton*, begins the 'Song of Spring'. Milton and the Nightingale both call forth and themselves become part of a larger movement. The reader therefore has the sense of a gradual awakening of powers. The whole world now wakes with Milton to look forth for the 'morning of the grave'.

Quite clearly Milton's perpendicular descent to time still presents the reader with a set of conceptual difficulties and paradoxes. Not least of these is the question of how we are to conceive of a movement to the very peripheries of our linguistic/

mental worlds, a movement which appears to enter the world at right angles to the movement of fallen time. The answer that is usually given to this question depends upon the assertion that the poem's events are simultaneous, that they occur in the instant of vision, and that the whole thrust of the poem's apocalypse is to abolish time. Damon writes, for example, that 'Practically all the action of the epic passes in one moment',[20] and a similar case is urged by critics as diverse as Fisch, Frye, James, Mitchell, and Rose.[21] Perhaps the clearest statement of this point of view is provided by Susan Fox, who writes that 'All the actions of the poem occur in the last measurable segment of the moment, the last fragment of time itself, the instant before apocalypse puts an end to time.'[22]

From the linear perspective of the fallen world it is true that Milton descends at the very end of time. However, if time itself is the six thousand year body of Albion, then we can see that Milton's intention to 'look forth for the morning of the grave' is fulfilled, not simply with the embrace of the closet in which he is enclosed, but with an embrace of the body of fallen time. It is, in fact, an extraordinary image. The empire of Satan, with the Elect at the apex of a mediated relationship, has been replaced with a presence to the very body of the world, an expectant looking forth for the morning of the grave, and an attempt to make fluid the body in which Albion is enclosed. To adopt this kind of comportment to others is to enter the city of Golgonooza and it is to this location that the reader, with Los, Blake, Milton, and the Bard, now proceeds.

GOLGONOOZA

The sight of the city of Bowlahoola, which lies on the outskirts of Golgonooza, generates an extraordinary sense of déjà vu. The journey that we have traced, 'outward to Satans seat' and 'inward to Golgonooza' (17: 29-30, E111), suggests that we should now find ourselves at a point far removed from the time and space described in the Bard's Song. Instead, there is a curious penetration of Golgonooza and its environs by the world in which Satan has gained dominion; it is almost as if the Polypus were in some way superimposed on Bowlahoola. In this place stands Los's Anvils and Hammers, but it is a place of 'horrid labours' and its labourers dance 'the dance of death, rejoicing in carnage' (24: 57, 62, E120-1). Bowlahoola is called 'Law. by Mortals' and we are told that it is 'the Stomach in every individual man' (24: 48, 67, E121). How is Bowlahoola, one may well ask, different from the process of assimilation with which Satan translates difference into sameness?

If we measure the movement of Milton in terms of chronological or clock-time, then a considerable period separates Milton's decision to descend to Ulro and the arrival of Blake, Los, and company in Golgonooza. The movement that has been described by the poem is, however, not one that can be measured in chronological terms, for it proceeds at right angles to the passage of fallen time. Milton's journey involves a progression from a stationary position in which Nature is the bound of the self to one in which the world has been embraced. At this point history is no longer a Polypus without form, but a six thousand year period to each moment of which Los (and Milton and Blake in Los) is present. The journey traced by the poem is therefore, to this point at least, not an account of a passage to a different world, but of a radical change of comportment *within the same world*. Golgonooza does not exist in some ideal realm apart from the world of time and space; it is the spiritual form or ground of that world, and for this reason we can see the realities of temporal history, or at least the possibility of those realities, woven into its fabric. The perspective that we adopt to these realities is, however, now very different, for we no longer see the world solely as it is retained by our reasoning memory; instead, we see it in terms of the relationships which give it being. Within Blake's myth these relationships constitute 'the Universe of Los and Enitharmon' (19: 25, E113).

As a result of this change of comportment what had appeared to be a purely natural phenomenon, an appearance within the closet of the self, is now seen in relationship to its ontological foundation. The narrator writes:

> Thou seest the gorgeous clothed Flies that dance & sport in summer
> Upon the sunny brooks & meadows: every one the dance
> Knows in its intricate mazes of delight artful to weave:
> Each one to sound his instruments of music in the dance,
> To touch each other & recede; to cross & change & return
> These are the Children of Los; thou seest the Trees on mountains
> The wind blows heavy, loud they thunder thro' the darksom sky
> Uttering prophecies & speaking instructive words to the sons
> Of men: These are the Sons of Los! These are the Visions of Eternity
> But we see only as it were the hem of their garments
> When with our vegetable eyes we view these wond'rous Visions
> (26: 2-12, E123)

To see the 'Trees on mountains' as Sons of Los, and hear the prophecies that they utter, involves a decentring of the corporeal self which is every bit as radical as that demanded by Freud or Marx. The whole thrust of the third and final section of Book I is therefore not to deny all truth value to the statement that Bowlahoola is called 'Law. by Mortals' but, through the eyes of Milton/Blake/Los within the time of embodiment, to return the Satanic Law to the ground from which it has become separated. For example, in the Bard's Song Law is Satan's Law; it is the source of 'Moral laws and cruel punishments'. As Los approaches Golgonooza, however, Law is seen as a city, a forge, and a stomach. Moreover, we are told that Bowlahoola was established by Tharmas 'Because of Satan' (24: 49, E120). Bowlahoola is, in other words, a direct response to the chaos and fragmentation resulting from the withdrawal of Albion. Bowlahoola is the place within the workshops of Los where the 'piteous Passions & Desires' are clothed and fed and 'the various Classes of Men' are 'all markd out determinate' (26: 37, E123). It is the stomach and the forge; the point at which the sleepers are ingested, made pliable and malleable in the heat of Los's furnaces, and then given a shape.

The transformation of perception described above raises the question of the precise relationship between the world seen through the vegetable memory and that seen in the time of embodiment. Blake's description of natural causes as a 'Delusion | Of Ulro: & a ratio of the perishing Vegetable Memory' certainly does not mean that the world in which they appear is not real for those who exist within it, or that the sufferings which are experienced by those in Ulro are illusory.

The world of Ulro is not simply Golgonooza as it appears to mortal humanity, it is that appearance severed from its ground. Ulro is the world of semblance that Urizen, in the frontispiece to *Europe*, scatters on the void. The ultimate ambition of this world is to sever the fallen world entirely from its ground, 'To bring the shadow of Enitharmon beneath our wondrous tree | That Los may Evaporate like smoke & be no more' (FZ 80: 5-6, E355), and in this way reduce the world to its surfaces. We can imagine the movement of Los to embodiment as an attempt to re-member the scattered body of Albion; to return the semblances of himself, which Urizen has scattered upon the void, back into relationship with himself. In the passage describing the Sons of Los which was quoted above, it is still *possible* to focus our attention on the dance of the

## 82  The Moment of Embrace

flies and be mesmerized by their beauty. Similarly we may fix our gaze on the hem of the garments worn by the Sons of Los. With this kind of narrowing of perception it would perhaps appear as Newton's linear time. The gap at the front of the garment, where the two ends of the hem are brought together, would from this perspective appear to be the beginning and end of time, creation, and the apocalypse. In the time of embodiment, however, the possibility of this kind of perception is seen only in the 'Outward Spheres of Visionary Space and Time' (J 92: 17, E252). It represents a falling away from appearance into a world based on semblance.

The point of this visionary return to the relationships which ground the fallen world is not to provide a foundation for human understanding, as in, for example, Husserl's philosophy. In Blake's œuvre the vision of the relationships which ground our world becomes a prophetic call. Where Husserl grounds philosophy in a phenomenology, Blake (like Los) attempts to open that world to Eternity. The fallen world is held by Los in order to confront Albion with the shape of his own withdrawal and so open the possibility of regeneration. This can be seen in Blake's description of the 'Wine-press' of Los.

As Los descends to Golgonooza we are told that

> The Wine-press on the Rhine groans loud, but all its central beams
> Act more terrific in the central Cities of the Nations
> Where Human Thought is crushd beneath the iron hand of Power.
> There Los puts all into the Press, the Opressor & the Opressed
> Together, ripe for the Harvest & Vintage & ready for the Loom.
>
> (25: 3-7, E121)

The wine press is 'eastward of Golgonooza, before the Seat | Of Satan'; its foundations were laid by Luvah '& Urizen finish'd it in howling woe' (27: 1-2, E124). It is a place of great torment:

> But in the Wine-presses the Human grapes sing not, nor dance
> They howl & writhe in shoals of torment; in fierce flames consuming,
> In chains of iron & in dungeons circled with ceaseless fires.
> In pits & dens & shades of death: in shapes of torment & woe.
> The plates & screws & wracks & saws & cords & fires & cisterns
> The cruel joys of Luvahs Daughters lacerating with knives
> And whips their Victims & the deadly sport of Luvahs Sons.
>
> (27: 30-6, E124-5)

Not surprisingly the wine press is called 'War on Earth' (27: 8, E124); it is nothing less than the reality that is formed in withdrawal, an apt symbol of a world where 'the Contraries of Beulah War beneath Negations Banner' (34: 23, E134). The wine press is, however, not simply associated with the work of Luvah and Urizen, for the poem identifies it as belonging to Los. For the Eternal Prophet to have anything to do with an instrument such as this is nothing short of scandalous. Unfortunately, in the time of embodiment, the link between Los and the wine press is made even closer, for the wine press is described as 'the Printing-Press | Of Los; and here he lays his words in order above the mortal brain | As cogs are formd in a wheel to turn the cogs of the adverse wheel' (27: 8-10, E124).

When confronted by the withdrawal of Albion, Los has only two choices: to do nothing and so withdraw from his friend's dilemma, or attempt to give form to Albion-in-withdrawal. The latter course of action, however, means giving form to loss, providing a body and form for the warring Spectres. The wine press of 'War on Earth' belongs to Los in the sense that it prepares the materials for the Loom of Enitharmon and, therefore, for the fabric of the fallen world.

A printing press, like a wine press, performs the same set of operations no matter what is placed within it. For the printing press it is of no consequence whether it prints the works of Burke or Paine. In this respect it is similar to the mortal brain of the cavern'd man which (in Locke's description) is forced to perform the same set of mental operations on whatever simple ideas enter its enclosure. Los's prophetic words are placed above the mortal brain in order to confront the self with the reality of its actions: loss is the ground to the figure of the self. Similarly, the world that is forged by Los (which is the form of Albion in withdrawal) is a cog which is inserted into the printing press (the withdrawn, anonymous body of Albion), not as one which works happily within the machine, but as a cog which attempts to turn or convert the printing press itself. Los's prophetic production of the fallen world is an attempt to renovate the press itself, to awaken Albion and so turn the manufacture of books by the press into the production of 'Visionary forms dramatic'. Los is, like all prophets, attempting to give form to the lack that is represented by the withdrawal of Albion, and to use this lack as a means of changing people. War becomes a call which attempts to move the 'cogs of the adverse wheel'. The adverse (opposing anyone's interest, the injurious or calamitous) is confronted and potentially moved to act by its own reality.

## 'NATURE IS A VISION OF THE SCIENCE OF THE ELOHIM'

To this point in my discussion I have largely been concerned to distinguish between the world described in the Bard's Song and that seen in the time of embodiment. As I have already argued, however, any attempt to rigidly separate these terms encounters a number of difficulties. If the closeted man is to leave his closet he must recognize that the form in which he is enclosed is not the limits of the world, but the horizon of *his* world, the outer limits of *his* body. This final portion of the first Book of *Milton*, therefore, underlines again and again the curious phenomenon that we first observed with regard to Bowlahoola. The passage that describes Los as 'the Spirit of Prophecy' and 'the ever apparent Elias', for example, continues with the observation that 'All the Gods of the Kingdoms of Earth labour in Los's Halls. | Every one is a fallen Son of the Spirit of Prophecy' (24: 74-5, E121). Similarly, Los's printing press is 'before the Seat | Of Satan' (27: 1-2, E124) and Cathedron's Looms (a crucial part of the process of giving form to the Spectres) weave 'only Death | A Web of Death' (24: 35-6, E120). Although Allamanda is 'the Cultivated land | Around the City of Golgonooza' and is the place where the 'Sons of Los labour against Death Eternal' (27: 43-4, E125), it also provides a location for the labours of the Sons of Urizen and for the 'Seat of Satan' (27: 45, 49, E125). The most striking example of this interpenetration is with regard to both Milton and Los.

When Rintrah and Palamabron see Milton it is not as someone who has escaped the enclosure of the self, but as one who has

> enterd into the Covering Cherub, becoming one with
> Albions dread Sons, Hand, Hyle & Coban surround him as
> A girdle; Gwendolen & Conwenna as a garment woven
> Of War & Religion.
>
> (23: 14-17, E118)

Milton is, of course, embracing this body in order to look forth for the morning of the grave; however, it is important to see that this embrace does not immediately or in itself renovate the body. At the end of the poem Ololon is still able to see Milton striving 'upon the Brooks of Arnon' with 'a dread | And awful Man ... oercoverd with the mantle of years' (40: 4-5, E141). The descent of Milton in fact seems to herald an intensification of Satan's world. Rintrah and Palamabron want to bring this figure 'chained | To Bowlahoola' (23: 17-18, E118), a judgement which would extend once more the kingdom of Satan, and even at the gates of Golgonooza Los warns of the danger that Rintrah and Palamabron will be vegetated.

Los's response to Milton's descent is now very different from that seen on plate 20 or the kind of reaction he displays in the Bard's song. He exhorts his Sons to 'come, come away . . . give all your strength against Eternal Death | Lest we are vegetated' (24: 33-5, E120). However, even here Los's reaction is not unequivocal. Rintrah and Palamabron, for example, observe a very different response that coexists with the first and suggests the Los who exists within the time of memory: 'They saw that wrath now swayd and now pity absorbd him | As it was, so it remaind & no hope of an end' (24: 46-7, E120).

The intermingling of closure and openness, the world of memory and that of embodiment, does not ease as Los enters Golgonooza. This moment occurs (from within the perspective of the fallen world) within the last moment of chronological time. It is the Last Vintage and here the Sons of Luvah sing:

> This is the Last Vintage! & Seed
> Shall no more be sown upon Earth, till all the Vintage is over
> And all gatherd in, till the Plow has passd over the Nations
> And the Harrow & heavy thundering Roller upon the mountains.
> (25: 8-11, E121)

In preparation for this Vintage Los demands that they 'Throw all the Vegetated Mortals into Bowlahoola' (24: 40, E120), and he recommends to his Sons that they

> bind the Sheaves not by Nations or Families
> You shall bind them in Three Classes; according to their Classes
> So shall you bind them. Separating What has been Mixed
> Since Men began to be Wove into Nations by Rahab & Tirzah
> Since Albions Death & Satans Cutting-off from our awful Fields;
> When under pretence to benevolence the Elect Subdud All
> From the Foundation of the World.
> (25: 26-32, E122)

Los's basic strategy is quite straightforward. Albion is the six thousand year history of fallen time and therefore, if he is to awake, he must resist assimilation to Satan's Polypus. Rather than responding with wrath to the approach of Milton, Los uses his forge in Bowlahoola to mark 'out determinate' the three Classes and so separate what Satan's world has mixed. What is striking about this advice is that it takes the reader back to the very beginning of the poem: to separate what has been mixed 'Since Albions Death & Satans Cutting-off from our awful Fields' is to reaffirm and reiterate the world (based on the three Classes) that was 'Created by the Hammer of Los, & Woven | By Enitharmons Looms when Albion was slain' (2: 26–3:1, E96). The end of time is therefore, in this sense, its beginning, for Los will bind the Elect, in order to save them from the 'fires of Eternal Death', into the 'Churches of Beulah' (25: 38–9, E122), the six thousand year history of the fallen world. This is why harvest is conducted with the instruments of seedtime—the plough and harrow and roller—rather than those of a natural harvest. The spiritual harvest of the fallen world is, at least initially, always its beginning.

This primal repetition or reaffirmation of the world is a necessary (but not sufficient) condition of Albion's awakening. It is necessitated by the understanding that the body of Albion in withdrawal encompasses all things (human and non-human) that make up the six thousand year history given form by Los and Enitharmon. For Albion to awake is for him to embrace this world and history as his body. An apocalypse that was limited to the 'furthest moment of calibrated time' would fail to awaken the whole Man. Apocalypse is therefore, in the first instance, a moment in which the entire extent of the fallen world is reiterated and reaffirmed by Los in order to preserve the body of Albion. It is this affirmation which enables the body of withdrawal to become the ground for a leap into regeneration and eternal life.

Los is quite clearly in an extraordinary position. The world that he creates and recreates gives form to the chaos of Albion's withdrawal and so preserves humanity from annihilation; it is also the ground of Albion's return to relationship. Yet this same creation gives form to Satan's world; it creates the three Classes of men and so establishes the preconditions for Satan's assimilation of difference into sameness. In the first Book of *Milton*, however, we do not see a movement from openness to closure (which is the subject of *The Book of Urizen*, for example); instead, the contrary to this regression is traced. The first Book of this poem (and therefore the fallen world as a whole) is a pulsation, a heartbeat, in the life of Los and Albion. In the Bard's Song we see the shell of enclosure and understand the mechanism by which being is assimilated to Satan's Polypus. We are all, like Milton, enclosed within the shells of our constituted worlds. However, from within this enclosure, beginning with the descent of Milton, we gradually see the emergence of a pulse which embraces and so opens this enclosure to others.

It is a movement which fills the Mundane Egg to bursting and places humanity in a posture of hope and expectation. It is important to note that we are, in an important sense, still in the same world, but we have adopted a different relationship to it. It is no longer a nature, a doxa, or a creed which we use to judge others; instead it has become something in which we are embodied. Our perceptions are still semblances, still temporal forms, but now they have become 'Visionary forms dramatic', or in the words of *The Four Zoas*, 'embodied semblances in which the dead | May live before us' (90: 9-10, E370). The horizon of our world has become something which we can both look out from and potentially cast off. As Los says, indicating in his choice of words this intertwining of closure and openness: 'The *Awakener* is come. *outstretched* over Europe' (25: 22, E122, emphasis added).

The movement of the first Book of *Milton* is, therefore, only in a superficial sense from the beginning to the end. The central plates of this book take Milton and the reader from a position in heaven—above the poem and outside of time—to an embrace of the poem/world that lies beneath us. The poem takes us, in effect, back to the world described in the Bard's Song, but in such a way that we see it in the time of embodiment. This return and the openness to Albion that results from it is the occasion for the separation of what Satan has mixed and, therefore, a reaffirmation of the fallen world. This implies, however, that openness is followed by a further enclosure, and that the poem returns to its beginning in a second sense. This regression, or falling away is itself the site for a second reading and therefore another pulsation and expansion. The fallen world is a state where, as Blake tells us in *Jerusalem*, 'Man is born a Spectre or Satan & is altogether an Evil, & requires a New Selfhood continually & must continually be changed into his direct Contrary' (E200). This is why, as the Bard informs us, Golgonooza, 'the spiritual Four-fold London eternal' is 'ever building, ever falling' (6: 1-2, E99). This is the subject matter of the great visions of time and space which form the penultimate movement of the first Book of *Milton*.

The vision of time begins by describing time as a defensive structure, replete with Walls, Terraces, 'invulnerable Barriers with high Towers', Moats, 'Flaming Fire', and Guards (28: 44-61, E126-7). It is an edifice built to protect those who have withdrawn (the sleepers) and to offer a bulwark against annihilation. This defence is, of course, also an enclosure. The repetition of words such as 'and', 'every', and 'is' has a

## 88  The Moment of Embrace

cumulative effect that suggests, from within the body of time as a building, a second time which is no more than a sequence of 'abstract instants'. At the very moment that this sequence seems on the verge of moving into the foreground, when we have moved from Minutes to periods of 'Two Hundred Years' duration, and the cumulative effect of the passage has become quite imposing, the entire structure is collapsed:

> Every Time less than a pulsation of the artery
> Is equal in its period & value to Six Thousand Years.
> For in this Period the Poets Work is Done: & all the Great
> Events of Time start forth & are concievd in such a Period
> Within a Moment: a Pulsation of the Artery.
>
> (28: 62–29: 3, E127)

Blake is careful to describe this Period in such a way that it cannot be confused with a particular interval in calibrated or clock-time. It is a time which is 'less than a pulsation of the artery', it is 'Within a Moment', and therefore escapes the grasp of the reasoning memory. This is the time in which Los/Milton/Blake become present to each moment of the fallen world. All of the events of fallen time start forth in such a Period because it is here that Los is open to, and therefore able to give form to, Albion-in-withdrawal. Time can therefore be seen as an alternation between openness and closure, between time as a monumental institution and time as a continual bringing to stand of Albion-in-withdrawal. The vision of space which follows transforms our notions of time and space in a similar way.

The narrator begins his vision of space by affirming that the world is a tent and not a cavern, a dwelling and not an enclosure that hems us in (29: 4–7, E127). The fixed natural world is a phenomenon that depends upon the reasoning memory (29: 15–16, E127); however, in the time of embodiment the spatial world can be seen to be extraordinarily transparent:

> For every Space larger than a red Globule of Mans blood.
> Is visionary: and is created by the Hammer of Los
> And every Space smaller than a Globule of Mans blood. opens
> Into Eternity of which this vegetable Earth is but a shadow.
>
> (29: 19–22, E127)

The 'Globule of Mans blood' to which Blake is referring in this passage is nothing less than the Sun:

> The red Globule is the unwearied Sun by Los created
> To measure Time and Space to mortal Men. every morning.

> Bowlahoola & Allamanda are placed on each side
> Of that Pulsation & that Globule, terrible their power.
>
> (29: 23–6, E127)

In these lines the entire physical world is seen as a heartbeat in the body of Albion, but it now has a rhythm of contraction and expansion which occurs in every day. The Sun (the Logos or word in which we dwell) is on the one hand a 'red Globule', a form which measures the outline of the natural (and therefore the enclosed) world. On the other hand, it is also a 'Globule of ... blood' and it is kept in motion by the continual movement of Los and his Sons to the perimeter of the fallen world in order to 'see if morning breaks'. It is in the gap opened between systole and dystole that Los is open to Albion and hence able to give form to Albion-in-withdrawal (to create the 'Globule of ... blood') and at the same time preserve that Globule from becoming inanimate matter. Bowlahoola and Allamanda 'are placed on each side | Of that Pulsation & that Globule' because the world that they construct depends upon (and itself supports) the continual openness of the fallen world to Albion. The fallen world is therefore the still breathing body of Albion-in-withdrawal.

These passages force the reader to think on two radically contradictory, but not incommensurate, levels. On the one hand the fallen world, as the Bard has told us, can be seen as a form which is forged in the embrace of the giant Albion by the giant Los. Whenever we enter the time of embodiment we participate in this moment. This moment of embrace is, thanks to the work of Los, spatialized as the six thousand year history of fallen time and space. Coterminous with this movement of Los (within creation) to Albion is a second which sweeps us 'in the tide of Time' (22: 24, E117) from beginning to end. Within the fallen world Los and Albion, Milton and Blake, all participate in both of these times. We are bodies of flesh and of spirit. It is the oscillation between these two times and movements that forms the pulse of the sleeping Albion.

The poem does not allow this vision of time and space to become a dogma, for no sooner has it been established than *Milton* begins again the cycle of openness and closure which it has traced. The openness of vision is immediately followed by a series of qualifications:

> But Rintrah & Palamabron govern over Day & Night
> In Allamanda & Entuthon Benython where Souls wail:
> Where Orc incessant howls burning in fires of Eternal Youth,

## The Moment of Embrace

> Within the vegetated mortal Nerves; for every Man born is joined
> Within into One mighty Polypus, and this Polypus is Orc.
>
> But in the Optic vegetative Nerves Sleep was transformed
> To Death in old time by Satan the father of Sin & Death
> And Satan is the Spectre of Orc & Orc is the generate Luvah
>
> But in the Nerves of the Nostrils, Accident being formed
> Into Substance & Principle, by the cruelties of Demonstration
> It became Opake & Indefinite; but the Divine Saviour,
> Formed it into a Solid by Los's Mathematic power.
> He named the Opake Satan: he named the Solid Adam.
> (29: 27-39, E127-8)

Through the 'cruelties of Demonstration' the fallen Albion 'became Opake & Indefinite'. Death was, however, averted by the 'Mathematic power' of Los who gave form to Albion as the six thousand years of fallen history. In the fallen world Los 'conducts the Spirits to be Vegetated, into | Great Golgonooza, free from the four iron pillars of Satans Throne' (29: 47-8, E128). However, this world is, as we have seen, itself intertwined with the world of Satan and so once more Blake begins a series of qualifications:

> But Enitharmon and her Daughters take the pleasant charge.
> To give them to their lovely heavens till the Great Judgment Day
> Such is their lovely charge. But Rahab & Tirzah pervert
> Their mild influences, therefore the Seven Eyes of God walk round
> The Three Heavens of Ulro, where Tirzah & her Sisters
> Weave the black Woof of Death upon Entuthon Benython
> In the Vale of Surrey where Horeb terminates in Rephaim
> The stamping feet of Zelophehads Daughters are coverd with
>   Human gore
> Upon the treddles of the Loom, they sing to the winged shuttle:
> The River rises above his banks to wash the Woof:
> He takes it in his arms: he passes it in strength thro his current
> The veil of human miseries is woven over the Ocean
> From the Atlantic to the Great South Sea, the Erythrean.
> (29: 51-63, E128)

These lines give the reader a quite haunting sense of a beating heart. It is this extraordinary world, with its oscillation between enclosure and openness, contraction and expansion, that 'is the World of Los the labour of six thousand years'. The first Book of *Milton* does not, therefore, close 'with a moment of illumination in which the whole of reality is absorbed within the perceiving mind of the poet',[23] but with that moment in which 'the perceiving mind of the poet' is opened to others. It is in this period that Ololon descends.

## THE DESCENT OF OLOLON

In *Visions of the Daughters of Albion* Oothoon's passage to the very periphery of her constituted world is not answered by a corresponding movement on the part of Theotormon. Oothoon is, therefore, able to enter a living but still not fully human world. If *Milton* were to end with the close of Book I, we would be in an analogous situation. Los's world would remain on the brink of relationship, but would be unable to proceed beyond this point. In *Milton*, however, the descent of Milton calls forth an answering movement on the part of Ololon, the other to Milton's masculine self. It is this descent which is the subject of the second Book of the poem, and it is the occasion for some of the most moving poetry in Blake's œuvre. As male and female (active and passive) powers approach each other, the world is given a vision of Christ: 'All Beulah . . . saw the Lord coming in the Clouds' (31: 10, E130) and on earth 'all Nations . . . saw the Lord coming | In the Clouds of Ololon with Power & Great Glory!' (31: 12, 15-16, E130).

The descent of Ololon is described as an expansive awakening, a movement to spring and morning:

> Thou hearest the Nightingale begin the Song of Spring;
> The Lark sitting upon his earthy bed: just as the morn
> Appears; listens silent; then springing from the waving
>   Corn-field! loud
> He leads the Choir of Day! trill, trill, trill, trill,
> Mounting upon the wings of light into the Great Expanse:
> Reechoing against the lovely blue & shining heavenly Shell.
>
>             (31: 28-33, E130)

In the first Book of the poem, the reader and Milton have heard Milton 'begin the Song of Spring'; now this call is answered by Ololon. Lark, Thrush, Linnet, 'the Goldfinch, Robin & the Wren' all rise to 'Awake the Sun from his sweet reverie upon the Mountain' (31: 40, 41, E131) and so bring in the morning. In doing so they expand to fill the world in which they are enclosed and, therefore, their voices re-echo 'against the lovely blue & shining heavenly Shell' of the fallen world. This song is, however, 'a Vision of the lamentation of Beulah over Ololon' (31: 45, E131). This is because, as Michael J. Tolley suggests, 'the best lamentations, the best elegies—like *Lycidas* or *Adonais*—are most profoundly paeans of joy'.[24]

The image of the Nightingale and his company filling the world and so calling and waking the sun is not a complete description of the descent of Ololon. Blake juxtaposes this strophe with a second in which he describes the descent of Ololon as an awakening in which 'every Flower: The Pink, the Jessamine, the Wall-flower, the Carnation | The Jonquil, the mild Lilly opes her heavens!' (31: 58-60, E131). The descent of Ololon is also an opening to relationship, and it is within this opening that Christ appears; or to adopt the metaphor used in this passage, as a result of her descent the perfume of Eternity enters into the closed world of the self. The presence of a thing like perfume is, of course, totally inexplicable to those who live within a cavern'd world. Locke perceives the mind as an eye that looks at the inscriptions on a *tabula rasa*. Within his frame of reference, perfume can only be a disruptive force which emerges from the spaces that lie between the simple ideas retained by the reasoning memory; from a centre that is so small that 'none can tell how from so small a center comes such sweets'. In *Milton* this opening is begun by the 'Wild Thyme', a herb which suggests the wild (in the sense of unprecedented and unexpected) movement of Los and Milton that was the provocation for Ololon's descent.

THE MOMENT OF EMBRACE

Milton's descent, as I have argued, is completed only in the presence of Los to each moment of fallen history. The Milton who appears at the end of *Milton* is therefore a being within whom can be seen 'the Covering Cherub & within him Satan | And Raha[b]' (37: 8-9, E137). Blake writes that he saw him

> Descending down into my Garden, a Human Wonder of God
> Reaching from heaven to earth a Cloud & Human Form
> I beheld Milton with astonishment & in him beheld
> The Monstrous Churches of Beulah, the Gods of Ulro dark
> Twelve monstrous dishumanizd terrors Synagogues of Satan.
>
> (37: 13-18, E137)

He then goes on to detail these Churches of Beulah and Gods of Ulro, giving us 'their Names & their Places within the Mundane Shell' (37: 19, E137). All these are seen in Milton's Shadow who is the Covering Cherub. This should not be taken to suggest that Milton has lost all personal identity, for this extraordinary description moves immediately into an account of Milton the individual:

> And Milton collecting all his fibres into impregnable strength
> Descended down a Paved work of all kinds of precious stones

*"To bathe in the Waters of Life'*

> Out from the eastern sky; descending down into my Cottage
> Garden: clothed in black, severe & silent he descended.
>
> (38: 5-8, E138)

Within the figure of Milton can be seen all of humanity, for it is against or within the ground of the whole that he has his individual existence. The inverse of this proposition is, however, also true: Milton is contained within Satan's universe. We can see a similar interpenetration of the individual and the whole in the case of Ololon.

The descent of Ololon at first seems to be very precisely located in terms of fallen time and space. She stands 'In Chasms of the Mundane Shell which open on all sides round | Southward & by the East within the Breach of Miltons descent' (34: 41-2, E134), and when she steps into the Polypus (36: 13, E136) she appears in the garden of Blake's cottage at Felpham:

> And as One Female, Ololon and all its mighty Hosts
> Appear'd: a Virgin of twelve years no time nor space was
> To the perception of the Virgin Ololon but as the
> Flash of lightning but more quick the Virgin in my Garden
> Before my Cottage stood for the Satanic Space is delusion.
>
> (36: 16-20, E137)

Like Milton, Ololon appears to Blake at a particular point in fallen space and time, but the passage in which this is affirmed also admits the inadequacy of this location, for such space 'is delusion'. Moreover, Ololon's descent, like Milton's, calls forth and provokes an answering movement within the body of the world. As a result her descent is carried throughout the six thousand years of creation. The metaphors that Blake uses to describe this are quite startling.

In the moment in which Ololon descends,

> stands a Fountain in a rock
> Of crystal flowing into two Streams, one flows thro Golgonooza
> And thro Beulah to Eden beneath Los's western Wall
> The other flows thro the Aerial Void & all the Churches
> Meeting again in Golgonooza beyond Satans Seat.
>
> (35: 49-53, E136)

The first stream flows thro Golgonooza and Beulah to Eden, while the second passes through the twenty-seven churches of fallen history until it reaches Golgonooza once more. In other words, in the moment of Ololon's descent a fountain rises up to connect, like a gigantic circulatory system, all of Albion's heavens and earths and hells. An analogous movement is carried out by the Larks, who carry the news of her appearance throughout 'all the Twenty-seven Heavens' of the fallen world until they return to the 'East Gate of Golgonooza' (35: 65, 36: 9, E136). These metaphors suggest that, like Milton's, Ololon's descent occurs (in terms of sequential time) in the space between the beginning and end of the fallen world. Secondly, just as Los's continually repeated movement to the time of embodiment can be seen as the pulsating heart of Albion, so Ololon's descent calls forth a movement which suggests both a process of unification and a giant circulatory system.

The world that encloses Milton is of course also that in which Ololon is enclosed. As a result of their respective descents, this world has been embraced and now all that separates them is a thin screen or veil: Milton the Puritan faces Ololon the Virgin. In this encounter time and Eternity, male and female, the individual and the collective, self and other, are on the brink of relationship. Milton stands within his 'sleeping Humanity' (38: 10, E139). Satan responds to this situation by attempting to re-assert his rule:

> Satan heard! Coming in a cloud, with trumpets & flaming fire
> Saying I am God the judge of all, the living & the dead
> Fall therefore down & worship me.
> 
>     (38: 50-2, E139)

In the Bard's Song a claim such as this would have drawn forth a judgement of Satan, which would in turn have assimilated the self to Satan's world. Milton specifically eschews this course of action. He says:

> Satan! my Spectre! I know my power thee to annihilate
> And be a greater in thy place, & be thy Tabernacle
> A covering for thee to do thy will, till one greater comes
> And smites me as I smote thee & becomes my covering.
> 
>     (38: 29-32, E139)

Rather than judging Satan, Milton has embraced the world in which he is enclosed and from this position he is now able to cast off Satan in a movement of self-annihilation. He therefore continues:

> Such are the Laws of thy false Heavns! but Laws of Eternity
> Are not such: know thou: I come to Self Annihilation
> Such are the Laws of Eternity that each shall mutually
> Annihilate himself for others good, as I for thee[.]
> 
>     (38: 33-6, E139)

*'To bathe in the Waters of Life'* 95

In the first Book of *Milton*, Ololon descends as a direct result of Milton's descent. She has, therefore, not heard the Bard's Song and, as a result, when she sees the world beneath her she responds with amazement (34: 49-35: 18, E134-5). It is only at the close of *Milton* that she recognizes the part that she plays in this world, and this recognition of Error allows her to move forward into embrace (41: 34-42: 6, E143). Milton and Ololon now stand face to face, and in this encounter the entire world is seen as Christ (42: 7-15, E143).

The meeting of Ololon and Milton is, as I have argued, not simply a meeting of two individuals. Their separate descents provoke and themselves become part of a corresponding movement within creation itself. Creation, the six thousand year history of fallen time, is now seen no longer as an enclosure, but as a form in which Milton/Blake/Los look out or 'thro'. It is therefore a form that is animated by hope and expectation, by an eager looking forth 'to see if morning breaks!' This animated form is described by Blake as Christ. Jesus still wears 'a Garment dipped in blood', a 'Garment of War' (42: 12, 15, E143), but this will be cast off when Albion arises. It is now that we glimpse the 'morning of the grave':

And I beheld the Twenty-four Cities of Albion
Arise upon their Thrones to Judge the Nations of the Earth
And the Immortal Four in whom the Twenty-four appear Four-fold
Arose around Albions body: Jesus wept & walked forth
From Felphams Vale clothed in Clouds of blood, to enter into
Albions Bosom, the bosom of death & the Four surrounded him
In the Column of Fire in Felphams Vale; then to their mouths the Four
Applied their Four Trumpets & them sounded to the Four winds.

(42: 16-23, E143)

But at this point there is a surprising reversal. Albion does not wake, our vision of 'the morning of the grave' slips from our grasp, and Blake falls back into his corporeal body (42: 24-7, E143). In order to understand this fall, we must distinguish Milton's movement towards relationship from the particular kind of transparence associated with symbolism, with which it is often confused.[25]

RHETORIC AND TRUTH

In 'The Rhetoric of Temporality' Paul de Man writes that towards the 'latter half of the eighteenth century' the symbol came to be ranked above other rhetorical figures such as allegory.[26] In this historical change allegory came to appear as dryly rational and dogmatic in its reference to a meaning that it does not itself constitute, whereas the symbol is founded on an intimate unity between the image that rises up before the senses and the supersensory totality that the image suggests.[27]

Coleridge, for example, writes that

the symbol is characterized by the translucence of the special in the individual, or of the general in the special, or of the universal in the general; above all by the translucence of the eternal through and in the temporal.[28]

The symbol therefore suggests the possibility of identification or union with the world outside of us and, therefore, an abolition of time. However, as de Man argues, if the symbol's identification can itself be shown to be based on a rhetorical figure, then the symbol can no longer be privileged over other figures. Instead its claims can be seen as a suppression of temporality itself and therefore tantamount to a seduction by illusion.[29] In this context what is immediately striking about Blake's poetry is that it is *not* symbolic in Coleridge's sense of the term. Blake does not, in fact, use the word symbol at any point in his œuvre. Symbol has been replaced by the term, vision.

Where the symbol describes a movement and a transparence of the eternal in the temporal, vision relies upon an openness of the temporal to the eternal. Where symbol suggests a relationship of synecdoche between time and eternity, vision relies on a separation and contrary relationship between the two. Where symbol is a rhetorical figure, vision is a relationship which is taken up to a linguistic or perceptual form. The subject of the symbol is static, while that of vision is moving and fluid. The symbolist is stationary and passive, while the visionary in Blake's sense is active, passionate, and engaged in movement. Vision does not deny its temporal base and, therefore, always must place truth at one remove from the self, always outside of our grasp. Vision is, one could almost say, the opposite of symbolism.

Vision is, first of all, a vision of others. In *Milton*, as we have seen, one of the first results of Milton's change of perspective, or change of relationship to the world, is that the natural world is seen as a creation of Los and his Sons. This sudden animation of what had been a closed and silent world is seen most eloquently in the approach of Ololon. What he had seen as 'his Sixfold Emanation scatter'd thro' the deep | In torment!' (2: 19-20, E96) becomes a presence that can be encountered and embraced.

If the intention of the poem were to 'arrive at the far goal of time, full knowledge',[30] or if, as James suggests, 'The achieved clarity of [Blake's] vision is the achievement of form in images that order reality; most specifically it is the establishment of a definite line between the imagination and its enemies,'[31] then quite clearly Blake's fall at the end of *Milton* is a self-conscious admission of the gap which separates rhetoric and truth. The attempt to order reality (without a parallel attempt to open it), the ambition to gain 'full knowledge', and the desire to draw 'a definite line between the imagination and its enemies' are, however, all characteristics of Satan. It is in Satan's inert world, where the being of that which is is located in human representation, that this gap opens a destructive chasm between self and other. But if the other is alive—if the most fitting metaphor for truth was not the adequation of intellect and thing, but the openness of the self to another that was living— then this same gap becomes the moment in which the autonomy of the other is preserved; it is one pole of the oscillation between openness and closure in which the voice of another can be heard. The 'bounding line' of identity is not one that draws a 'line between the imagination and its enemies'. This is the Satanic project that was deconstructed in the Bard's Song. The 'bounding line' of identity is formed when the self casts off the static forms in which it is enclosed.

*Milton* is a poem which urges us to see Imagination not only as a forming power, but as a power of openness, a power of responding to a non-violent appeal.[32] In order to Imagine, our constituted worlds must be open to the Reprobate, to those figures who will always remain outside our world. The Vision that is the result of such an Imagination is, therefore, not the reduction of others to the world of the self, but a power of opening that world. It is, therefore, not simply a matter of grasping vision, but of being open to its appeal. It is the power to hear and respond to this appeal that enables the visionary deconstruction of the Bard to be followed by the visionary construction of Jerusalem.

# PART II
## Visionary Construction

# 3. Los and *Jerusalem*

> But the question at once arises: how does this conversation which we are, begin? Who accomplishes this naming of the gods? Who lays hold of something permanent in ravenous time and fixes it in the word?
>
> Martin Heidegger[1]

## ENTERING TIME

*Jerusalem* consists of four chapters—one hundred plates and two thousand lines—which are linked in an (almost) invariable chain: each chapter is preceded by a full page engraving; the poem begins and ends with a full page illumination; each chapter is framed by half-page designs, and the written text opens and closes with the word 'Jerusalem'. *Jerusalem* is without doubt an extremely 'ORDERD RACE' (26, E171). This regular, measured form suggests that the subject matter of *Jerusalem* will be organized according to an absolute time such as that proposed by Newton in the *Principia*.[2] On this level, *Jerusalem* appears to be a remarkable product of the horological revolution; it is a timepiece capable of measuring out the linear succession of 'nows' which characterize chronological and everyday time. In *Jerusalem*, one could argue, the transparence of *Milton's* apocalypse has been supplanted by opacity. *Jerusalem* has failed to materialize the promise extended by its prelude.

Before we too hastily endorse this conclusion it is as well to observe that up to this point in our argument we have adopted a relationship to the text which is analogous to that taken up by Milton to time, or by the Sons of Albion to the Bard's Song. The frontispiece, however, suggests the possibility of a very different relationship to the poem (see Fig. 3). On this plate we see Los/Blake/the reader—in a movement which is reminiscent of the movement 'thro' the text that we traced in *Milton*—stepping across the threshold of a door which appears to give us access to the interior of the poem. Los seems to be poised on the brink of a movement 'thro' the text.

Unfortunately, the plate does not offer an unequivocal means of achieving this goal. Los does not enter the text, for Los, like the reader, is poised between an imminent entry into *Jerusalem* and a sequential unfolding of the poem which opens out to the right. Erdman writes that a 'wind from the opening ... blows his hair and garments back'.[3] In fact, the wind is coming from the direction in which Los is looking. The passage of sequential time blows each present irrevocably into the past and therefore continually defers the moment of embrace. Entry into the city of *Jerusalem*, like the vision of Christ at the end of *Milton*, is both now and not yet.

Our first step into the poem (in which our foot is placed across the threshold of *Jerusalem*'s gate) places us in the same position as Los. As we read, we stand with Los/Blake outside the door of the heavenly city (we are quite literally, at each point in the poem, facing *Jerusalem*); yet the poem itself sweeps us along a sequential path which continually defers our entry into this city. It should therefore be no surprise that our first experience of the poem gives expression to the tension between what is now and what is not yet, what is present and what is absent, by inducing in the reader an overwhelming sense of vertigo. It is as if one were lost, or as if there were an imminent danger of being swept from a high point. Stuart Curran describes this emotion well. He writes that 'though the reader is generally sure of the immediate ground he treads, the path before and after may be swept with mists.'[4] Damon describes a more extreme variety of the same experience:

But though the plot is so simple, *Jerusalem* is the obscurest of the three epics. ... Time and again the depths are stirred and a gush of half-forgotten names emerges for the moment, to be lost immediately in the impenetrable black.[5]

Interestingly, Damon goes on to say that 'Obscure as Blake's plot may be, his teachings are never in doubt.'[6] We find the same phenomenon in Wicksteed's book on the poem. He writes that it is only after reading *Jerusalem* 'month after month and year after year' that one begins

to find treasures of terse wisdom, epic grandeur, and occasional gleams of lyrical beauty so widely dispersed throughout its hundred pages as to make the fertile oases spread out more and more into the desert sands and rocks that still intervene.[7]

Like Curran and Damon, Wicksteed attempts to give expression in these lines to an experience of clarity which is nevertheless intertwined with a feeling of confusion. Like Los in the frontispiece, these critics seem to be looking in one direction while being irrevocably drawn in another.

3. Frontispiece to *Jerusalem*.

This kind of experience has led Blake criticism to make two closely related critical judgements which have had far reaching consequences for our understanding of *Jerusalem*. It is agreed, first of all, that the poem—despite its periodic form—in some way disrupts or does away with our everyday ideas of time and narrative.[8] Second, given that *Jerusalem* disrupts our normal ideas of time and narrative sequence, critics have looked for a non-temporal ordering principle for the poem. Damon writes, for example, that 'The tale proceeds not by action but by the sequence of ideas.'[9] The exact nature of these ideas is, of course, a matter of contention. Erdman writes that 'the motif of *Jerusalem* is *peace without vengeance*.'[10] Marks tells us that 'the process by which various figures in the poem overcome selfhood to become fully creative is a central ordering element of *Jerusalem*',[11] while Karl Kiralis associates each chapter of the poem with a specific stage in human development.[12]

Other critics attempt to find an external structure which, like the shell of a crustacean, will give the poem a form. The 'outline of the human body', the Four Gospels, the four Zoas, the book of Ezekiel, *Paradise Regained* and the book of Revelation have all been proposed.[13] Paley adds to this list 'a seventeenth-century tradition of the structural analysis of Revelation, Handel's *Messiah*, and possibly Smart's *Jubilate Agno*'.[14]

Other critics delineate atemporal structural patterns within the poem itself. Mitchell sees the poem as a single, static form. He calls it 'an encyclopedic anatomy of the world in which the exemplary actions, descriptions, and personae are drawn from the realms of myth, epic, & romance'.[15] The poem's 'apparent formlessness' is, he says, a characteristic of the genre of anatomy. Stuart Curran sees in the poem a variety of structures. If we look closely at *Jerusalem*, he argues, we find a system of seven interlocking structures.[16] Morton Paley suggests that

Blake develops *Jerusalem* in what may best be called, following Mede, a series of synchronisms. Just as Revelation is in Mede's view not a diachronic structure but a synchronous one, so *Jerusalem* is primarily to be read not for its relatively subordinated story line but for the way in which its inter-related parts explain one another.[17]

And Minna Doskow contends that

the poem's parts fall into place as pieces of a kaleidoscopic whole complementing and reinforcing one another. Each chapter then turns the kaleidoscope to view the theme in a new way. The pieces recompose themselves in new patterns and seem to reveal new appearances of the whole but are only actualizing those patterns potentially present all along. After the first glimpse, no new element is added to the picture. Further turns and glimpses simply rearrange existing pieces to examine the theme from all sides, going, in turn, through all the possible combinations.[18]

There are two striking features of these accounts of *Jerusalem*. First, the sheer number of structures that have been proposed for the poem is nothing short of astonishing. Second, and even more surprisingly, these attempts to delineate a basically atemporal structure for the poem are often divided against themselves and contain the surreptitious and perhaps half unconscious admission that a temporal progression *can* in fact be discerned in *Jerusalem*. Mitchell, for example, has no sooner completed his description of *Jerusalem* as an anatomy than he writes that there are signs that the two middle chapters reflect 'a vision of the historical development of consciousness as a movement from masculine to feminine dominance', and that Jerusalem is a woman with patterns of growth.[19] Similarly, Bloom, Harper, Kiralis, and Marks are unwilling to do away completely with temporal progression, even though they argue that the poem is ordered according to a non-progressive and atemporal structure. This leads them into the difficult position where they must describe a movement in stasis, or a progression in a poem which does not move.[20] Lesnick sharpens this paradox when he writes that 'Although *Jerusalem* continually reiterates and offers variations on a few elements of action and imagery, the narrative may be seen to be somewhat progressive.'[21] The same equivocation can be seen in *The Continuing City*. Despite his contention that 'If we are to understand the form of [*Jerusalem*], we must discover the interrelationships of its parallel acts, its synchrony',[22] Paley admits that the poem has a plot that 'moves as a submarine current producing episodic surface movements'.[23]

An anatomy with patterns of growth; a 'somewhat progressive' narrative in a poem which 'offers variations on a few elements of action and imagery'; a plot which moves as a 'submarine current': it is with paradoxes such as these that critics have attempted to deal with a poem which seems to be constructed of atemporal moments (chapters which seem to be organized around some kind of atemporal organizing principle or theme), but which are themselves embedded in a mysterious progression. The reader is confronted with solid, spatially organized chapters and a relatively hard-to-grasp and ephemeral temporal flow. *Jerusalem* is a physical structure, a city which Los, in the frontispiece, is on the verge of entering. Yet the city is also a woman who grows in time.

What is striking about these accounts of *Jerusalem* is that the experience of the poem that they imply, far from doing away with our everyday experience and conception of time, closely parallels it. Kant, preceded by writers such as Augustine and followed by philosophers such as Bergson and Heidegger, observes the curious paradox that we measure time by something which seems to have no immediate relationship to it, namely space. Temporal progression is for most of us extremely evanescent; we know that things have a duration, that our lives spread themselves out in time, but if we attempt to think about the nature of time our thoughts, like those of Augustine on this subject, quickly reach an impasse.[24] Time is all pervasive and yet we measure it by the non-temporal: the position of the sun in the sky, or the location of a rotating wand on a flat surface. This phenomenon can be clearly seen in Locke's *Essay*:

It is evident to any one who will but observe what passes in his own mind, that there is a train of ideas which constantly succeed one another in his understanding, as long as he is awake. Reflection on these appearances of several ideas one after another in our minds, is that which furnishes us with the idea of *succession*: and the distance between any parts of that succession, or between the appearance of any two ideas in our minds, is that we call *duration*.[25]

Our measures of time such as minutes, days, hours, and years derive from our observation of regular and recurrent appearances. It can therefore be said that the measures do not refer directly to time, but to the length of void between separate appearances of ideas in our minds. Repeating these 'measures of time' gives us, according to Locke, the idea of a past and future. These terms, however, denote no more than the presence of what from this perspective will always remain absent, for, as Locke writes, by this process 'we can come to imagine *duration, where nothing does really endure or exist*; and thus we imagine to-morrow, next year, or seven years hence'. Eternity is the repetition to exhaustion of these measures of absence; and finally, 'by considering any part' of this expansive nothing, 'we come by the idea of what we call *time* in general'.[26] Even Berkeley, although he scoffs at Locke's derivation of the abstract idea of time, agrees that our idea of duration is gained from our experience of the voids between successive appearances.[27]

Our experience of *Jerusalem* and our experience of time are therefore strangely isomorphic. The ordered chapters and lines of *Jerusalem* and the 'succession of ideas' in Locke's mind are both embedded in and give one the sense of a temporal progression, but this temporality is extra-ordinarily elusive. The ideas which appear to the self give us a sense of clarity, but time itself is a void, a space between appearances, an 'impenetrable blackness'.

This eclipse of time by space (by a series of appearances to the corporeal self) is itself a phenomenon which seems to depend upon a withdrawal from relationship. Locke's understanding of time is, for example, developed from the perspective of the closeted man. Succession is evident, as he tells us, to anyone who has stepped outside of himself and in this way observed 'what passes in his own mind'.[28] If time is, in the words of Auden, 'Our choice of how to love and Why',[29] then quite clearly this standpoint reduces the subject of our love (and therefore the substance of temporality) to vanishing point. From this position we are left with a series of appearances to the self rather than with the set of relationships which ground and open time.

I am, of course, not saying that the critics I have discussed are somehow wrong about the poem. Far from it; they are correct and their experiences of the poem are paradigmatic. *Jerusalem* is a poem which is structured, like Lockean time, as a series of appearances to the self. From a position outside of the poem these appearances can be arranged and rearranged in many different ways. Just as the physical universe can be organized to form a Ptolemaic, Copernican, Newtonian, and even an Einsteinian universe, so too *Jerusalem* can be 'ordered' in a startling variety of ways. However, this manipulation of what appears to the self is the work of the Daughters of Albion, rather than of the Imagination. As Los explains in the final chapter of *Jerusalem*:

> And sometimes the Earth shall roll in the Abyss & sometimes
> Stand in the Center & sometimes stretch flat in the Expanse,
> According to the will of the lovely Daughters of Albion.
> Sometimes it shall assimilate with mighty Golgonooza:
> Touching its summits: & sometimes divided roll apart.
> As a beautiful Veil so these Females shall fold & unfold
> According to their will the outside surface of the Earth
> An outside shadowy Surface superadded to the real Surface;
> Which is unchangeable for ever & ever Amen: so be it!
>
> (83: 40-8, E242)

## 108  Visionary Construction

It is this work of the Daughters which is often confused with the work of the Imagination. Hume, for example, writes that

> Nothing is more free than the imagination of man, and though it cannot exceed that original stock of ideas furnished by the internal and external senses, it has unlimited power of mixing, compounding, separating, and dividing these ideas in all the varieties of fiction and vision.[30]

The number of possible arrangements of these appearances is, like those of the alphabet, almost infinite. However, despite this freedom, in Hume's understanding the labour of the Imagination is confined to a single world. No visionary construction occurs with an imagination of this kind; the imagination is not a power of opening or responding, but a power of manipulation.

It is one of the extraordinary achievements of Blake in *Jerusalem* to have created a poem which follows so closely some of our most fundamental experiences of time. Having said this, however, the question remains as to whether this is all that can be said of the poem and of its time. Is there not some way of entering *Jerusalem* and so glimpsing the temporality which from outside the poem is so evanescent? This question is of more than casual importance, for the hero of the poem is, after all, characterized in *Milton* as time itself. To say that Los can appear only as space, as Enitharmon, is to resign oneself to the radical impossibility of reading *Jerusalem*. The concern of the frontispiece with the question of entry into the poem also suggests that there is a perspective which will in some way collapse the distance imposed by the reasoning memory. This possibility is moreover the subject matter of *Milton*, *Jerusalem's* prelude. A reading of the latter poem should quite clearly begin from the embrace and vision of Christ described by the former. Most tantalizing, however, is the narrator's claim in the preface to the fourth chapter that he has given us the end of a golden string. All we need to do is to

> wind it into a ball:
> It will lead you in at Heavens gate,
> Built in Jerusalems wall.                (77, E231)

The most immediate referent for this passage is the line of text which leads us to the fourth chapter. If we are to see 'thro' the window of *Jerusalem* then quite clearly we must follow the temporal unfolding of the poem. We must focus on our participation in the text. The lines quoted from the preface to the fourth chapter suggest that this path will lead, from within the body of Lockean time, to the perimeter of the world, to the gate that in the frontispiece opens to *Jerusalem*.

AN EXPANDING VISION

The opening lines of *Jerusalem* seem, at first glance, to offer the reader an elegant and obvious ordering principle for the poem.[31] Blake writes:

> Of the Sleep of Ulro! and of the passage through
> Eternal Death! and of the awaking to Eternal Life.
>
> This theme calls me in sleep night after night, & ev'ry morn
> Awakes me at sun-rise, then I see the Saviour over me
> Spreading his beams of love, & dictating the words of this mild song.
>
> (4: 1-5, E146)

Blake's theme is, however, a rather unruly affair. It is not an organizing principle which the author or the reader could possess and then use to order a mass of otherwise inert material. The theme, rather than being possessed by Blake, presents *itself* to him every night. What is more, rather than Blake developing the theme (into the work of *Jerusalem*, for example) it is, at least in the first instance, the theme that develops him. The sources of cognition and motivation for the poet are therefore as much outside the self as inside: the theme not only speaks of the passage from sleep to waking, but seems to be able to inspire a parallel movement in its audience.

Blake must, of course, listen to, and himself embrace, the words that he hears, and he must do this in a way which makes them his own; nevertheless, it is the manner in which the theme poses Blake as a question which draws him from sleep to waking and into the presence of Christ. The call that the poet records in these opening lines is therefore a call in the sense of a *vocation*. It must be listened to and embraced by the individual, but to the extent that this is done the individual is led out of him/herself and into his/her calling.

Even with these qualifications it is important to affirm that this theme is *not* the organizing principle of the poem. The entire process described in the first five lines is, strictly speaking, *antecedent* to *Jerusalem*. It tells us of the conditions under which the Saviour's voice, who dictates the poem itself, is heard. The theme calls Blake only in sleep; during the day it is the Saviour who is heard and it is the Saviour who dictates the mild song called *Jerusalem*.

## 110  Visionary Construction

The point at which the vision of *Jerusalem* appears is, therefore, the moment in which one has listened to the theme and under its influence woken from sleep to the voice of the Saviour. *Jerusalem* appears in a moment of vision. We can therefore say that, rather than beginning with the outline of a principle which will organize the material at the disposal of the poet, *Jerusalem* opens with a description of the particular engagement with and comportment towards others in which the poem can be heard.[32] It is at the apex of *Milton*, in a vision of Christ's call to us, that *Jerusalem* begins:

> Awake! awake O sleeper of the land of shadows, wake! expand!
> I am in you and you in me, mutual in love divine:
> Fibres of love from man to man thro Albions pleasant land.
> In all the dark Atlantic vale down from the hills of Surrey
> A black water accumulates, return Albion! return!
>
> (4: 6-10, E146)

Blake writes in *A Vision of the Last Judgment* that 'All Things are comprehended in their Eternal Forms in the Divine body of the Saviour the True Vine of Eternity' (E555). A vision of Christ is therefore a vision of the relationships which underlie and make possible life itself. It is a vision of ontological time.

In the fallen world, however, reality is constituted in a relationship of withdrawal. To withdraw from relationship is not an act which can be completed once and for all; it must be continually repeated, for in order to escape others one must withdraw even from the very fact of withdrawal. One way of picturing this is to say that, for a person in the state of withdrawal, Christ is always solicitous, always calling, and that withdrawal is a constant turning away from his presence. The vision of Christ in *Jerusalem*, therefore, modulates into a vision of this relationship between a call and the refusal to hear. The constitutive relationship which founds the fallen world, and from which fallen time opens out, is that between the caring call of Christ and the continual withdrawal of Albion:

> I am not a God afar off, I am a brother and friend;
> Within your bosoms I reside, and you reside in me:
> Lo! we are One; forgiving all Evil; Not seeking recompense!
> Ye are my members O ye sleepers of Beulah, land of Shades!
>
> But the perturbed man away turns down the valleys dark;
> [Saying. We are not One: we are Many, thou most simulative]
> Phantom of the over heated brain! shadow of immortality!
>
> (4: 18-24, E146-7)

In the first lines of the poem we discovered the particular relationship and moment in which the vision of *Jerusalem* appeared to the narrator. These lines have now opened into a vision of humanity's comportment in the world. There is an interesting relationship between these two foundations, for while the narrator's particular perspective in the world opens, and in a certain sense constitutes, the time and space in which Christ can appear, it is evident that the relationships which are revealed in this way ground and make possible the narrator's position in the world. It is the relationships of call and withdrawal, enacted, respectively, in the persons of Jesus and Albion, which underlie the world of day and night in which Blake is situated.

In the time of embodiment, one perceives the relationships which found and open the ontic world. The fall is, therefore, not something that occurs in the distant past, but a phenomenon which is ever-present. The movement of withdrawal on the part of Albion therefore has a startlingly present reality:

> The banks of the Thames are clouded! the ancient porches of Albion are
> Darken'd! they are drawn thro' unbounded space, scatter'd upon
> The Void in incoherent despair! Cambridge & Oxford & London,
> Are driven among the starry Wheels, rent away and dissipated,
> In Chasms & Abysses of sorrow, enlarg'd without dimension, terrible . . .
>
> (5: 1-5, E147)

In the everyday world in which we live, the founding structures of the world cannot be seen. Locke's closeted man, for example, sees the outline of the closet and not the relationships which bring the world of the closet into being. It is only in the vision achieved in embodiment, or awakening, that we hear the call of the Saviour and see the withdrawal of Albion. It is important to see that this vision does not do away with the caverned world; in fact, it is the basis of it. The narrator must live in the everyday world, but from within this space he is able to see the withdrawal of Albion from the call of Christ, which is its foundation. This is why Blake's friends are astonished at him. They live, with Blake, in the fallen world, but are unable to see the ontological ground of that world. For Blake, however, the theme has become a call that wakes him, and so allows him to hear the voice of Christ, in response to which he must act:

> Trembling I sit day and night, my friends are astonish'd at me.
> Yet they forgive my wanderings, I rest not from my great task!

## 112  Visionary Construction

> To open the Eternal Worlds, to open the immortal Eyes
> Of Man inwards into the Worlds of Thought: into Eternity
> Ever expanding in the Bosom of God. the Human Imagination.
>
> (5: 16-20, E147)

The vision of ontological or foundational time does not stop at this point; instead, it expands in what is at first an extremely disconcerting fashion. The narrator's description of the task that now lies ahead of him makes mention of a number of names and places—Golgonooza, Entuthon, Scofield, Kox, Kotope, and so on—which resist any easy assimilation to what has preceded them. The vision itself follows a similar course and in the second half of the fifth plate this list is expanded to include Tirzah and Her Sisters, the Twelve Sons of Albion, Vala, Jerusalem, Beulah's lovely Daughters and a war by 'Abstract Philosophy . . . against Imagination'.

The basic import of the passage from which these names are drawn is fairly clear. It can be seen as an extremely condensed map of the world that is opened in the time of Albion's withdrawal from Christ. For Albion to withdraw is for him to be fragmented and divide into male and female powers: the whole man becomes his warring sons and daughters. Nevertheless, much of the fifth plate of *Jerusalem* requires a detailed knowledge of earlier poems, or of later parts of *Jerusalem*, in order to make sense. The reader is presented with the brute fact of the attempts by Kox and his brothers to destroy the 'Furnace of Los' and 'desolate Golgonooza' and 'devour the Sleeping Humanity of Albion'. Similarly, the plight of Jerusalem and Vala is described without any real orienting context. Doubtless it is the effect of passages such as these which leads a critic like Northrop Frye to write that 'the initial impression' of the poem is 'of a harsh, crabbed and strident poem', a 'dehydrated epic' in which Blake's symbols 'had become a kind of ideographic alphabet and had thereby lost much of their immediacy'.[33] However, for this reader at least, these opening pages of *Jerusalem* certainly do not lack immediacy. The struggles which are described are all too present. They seem to contain a fury which threatens the reader him/herself. The lack of orienting context only heightens this emotion. The kernel of truth in Frye's comments can, however, be seen if we define the immediate as that which can be readily assimilated to the constituted world of the self. Rather than this kind of immediacy, the opening pages of *Jerusalem* confront readers, (in a way which is entirely appropriate for a vision of Christ and Albion) with a force that bumps up against us, moves us with the force of powerful emotions, and yet remains outside of our grasp.

It is, in fact, extremely difficult to capture this experience within the confines of discursive prose. The world in which we write orderly prose, the comfortable everyday world in which we live, has been torn open by a movement which brings us into the presence of Christ and his call. The world in which we once walked so confidently is now animated, and we are displaced from its centre. What is more, the ground which once seemed so solid and secure can now be seen to be founded on the withdrawal of Albion from the call of Christ. To 'enter into these Images' is to experience an extreme dizziness and vertigo. The ground beneath our feet is itself without foundation. The world is 'drawn thro' unbounded space, scatter'd upon | The Void in incoherent despair! . . . rent away and dissipated, | In Chasms & Abysses of sorrow' (5: 2–5, E147). Our everyday world is a world of loss.

Before we proceed any further into *Jerusalem* it is, quite clearly, important to understand in more detail part of what Blake means by vision, and it is to this discussion that we must now turn.

VISION

In the twentieth century it is without doubt easier to accept Blake's observation that vision is 'infected' (E563) by the weak visions of time and space than it is to feel comfortable with his companion belief that in vision we see more clearly than we do with our mortal eyes:

The Prophets describe what they saw in Vision as real and existing men whom they saw with their imaginative and immortal organs; the Apostles the same; the clearer the organ the more distinct the object. A Spirit and a Vision are not, as the modern philosophy supposes, a cloudy vapour or a nothing: they are organized and minutely articulated beyond all that the mortal and perishing nature can produce. (*DC*, E541)

In attempting to understand what Blake means in passages such as this we must be careful not to confuse a clarity which is gained through the assimilation of one's subject matter to the perspectives of the self with the clarity that is a result of vision. In the above passage Blake's metaphor for what is seen in vision is that of 'real and existing men'. Vision, therefore, has the uncomfortable ability to speak back, to refuse one's outline, to simply walk away and refuse dialogue, and most importantly,

114  *Visionary Construction*

it can even be wrong. The person who experiences such a vision may well feel that it is a corrosive and unsettling force.

A particularly clear depiction of the difference between these two kinds of clarity is shown in the drawing known as 'A Vision'.[34] If the page is a paradigmatic instance of the forms with which we attempt to order the world around us, a two dimensional surface in which we attempt to box and so represent reality, then quite clearly this vision is inaccessible to the series of pages/boxes with which we attempt to encompass it. The figure writing at the table, the light of vision, and the figure seen in vision, all are, from the perspective of the viewer, almost lost. There is something both frustrating and disconcerting about our inability to reach their conference. As we continue to look at the picture this feeling can develop into one of giddiness and vertigo, for the frames and receding corridor which lie in front of us are always about to become a cavity which opens beneath us. In these moments we perhaps gain a glimpse of what it is to see 'thro' the window of our eyes and not with them; in this moment we fall into the unsettling presence of vision.[35] Vision is therefore, for Blake, as much given to, as structured by, the individual. As he writes in a poem which he sent to Thomas Butts on 22 November 1802, 'Now I a fourfold vision see | And a fourfold vision is given to me' (E722).

Something of this sense of a vision which is 'given' is continually demanded of the reader by the first chapter of *Jerusalem*. As I have argued, the poem begins in a moment of awakening in which the closure of sleep is punctured. At this precise point, we hear the voice of Christ and observe the withdrawal of Albion; moreover, we feel the presence of their interaction in our world and our solitude. Nevertheless, in the opening lines of the poem we are able to grasp this interaction only in an intuitive or pre-reflective way. If we focus on this moment, however, what was at first only intuitively grasped becomes more minutely articulated. The vision of Christ's call is supplemented by a vision of Albion's response. This vision itself expands to show the presence of this relationship beneath the entire fallen world. Then the circle of vision itself expands and becomes a map of the world of withdrawal; instead of the relationship between Albion and Jesus we now see the results of it, the world in which it is embodied.

It is difficult to find an adequate metaphor for this expansion. It is in some ways as if a stone has been thrown into a pool of water. After the initial commotion a ripple appears which gradually expands until it reaches the edge of the pool. At the point of impact the shape of the ripple is quite clear; however, in the moments immediately following this event the ripple gradually grows larger and larger. As a result the form that was first only glimpsed is, after some time, seen in great detail. The movement of the ripple and its centre are, nevertheless, always defined by the point of impact between stone and water; and the circle that reaches the river banks is an elaboration, an expansion, of the original circle, not something that supersedes or surpasses it. Similarly, in the moment of vision in which the calm of sleep is broken and Christ's call to Albion-in-withdrawal is heard, we gain, in an unarticulated state, the shape and form of the entire first chapter and, indeed, of the whole poem. The chapter develops as if it were an expanding circle which, while always being defined by the original vision, expands and so articulates and clarifies that vision. Paul Ricoeur writes in *The Symbolism of Evil* that 'The beginning is not what one finds first; the point of departure must be reached, it must be won.'[36] Similarly, as I shall argue, it is only at the end of the first chapter of *Jerusalem*, and then again at the end of the poem, that we grasp its opening lines in full clarity.

Albion's withdrawal from the Saviour immediately places him in the time of loss. This is now the ground of the fallen world. To have a vision of the Saviour is to see Albion withdrawing from his call; to see Albion is to see in a preliminary way the shape of the fallen world; to focus our attention on this world is to see Los, for as we have seen in *Milton*, the fallen world is retained only as a result of the relationship which Los sustains with Albion-in-withdrawal. For this reason the vision now turns to Los.

THE VISION OF LOS, HIS SPECTRE, AND HIS EMANATION

In *Jerusalem*, as in previous poems, Los is a prophetic blacksmith who sustains a relationship with Albion-in-withdrawal; he is called 'the friend of Albion who most lov'd him' (35: 12, E181). Los describes the task of maintaining a relationship to Albion-in-withdrawal in extraordinary terms:

> I saw terrified; I took the sighs & tears, & bitter groans:
> I lifted them into my Furnaces; to form the spiritual sword.
> That lays open the hidden heart: I drew forth the pang

> Of sorrow red hot: I workd it on my resolute anvil:
> I heated it in the flames of Hand, & Hyle, & Coban.
>
> (9: 17–21, E152)

Los's prophetic work involves an attempt to retain the reality—the sighs, groans, and pangs—of withdrawal. If he were not to fulfil this task, the fallen world would dissolve and Albion would vanish. Moreover, in retaining this reality he forms a spiritual sword, a prophetic weapon, which is able to confront Albion with the reality of withdrawal and so call him to return. It is for this reason that Los must establish a world of loss.

Los's relationship with Albion-in-withdrawal is not without personal cost. Our first glimpse of him reveals a figure who is under extraordinary external pressure: 'Scofield! Kox, Kotope and Bowen' bend 'their fury' (5: 27, 28, E147) against him. Their activity is, of course, an attempt—parallel to that conducted by Urizen in *The Four Zoas*—to assimilate Los (loss) and in this way to become blind to the foundation of their world. This external pressure is accompanied by an excruciating internal division:

> Los heard her lamentations in the deeps afar! his tears fall
> Incessant before the Furnaces, and his Emanation divided in pain,
> Eastward toward the Starry Wheels. But Westward, a black Horror,
> His spectre driv'n by the Starry Wheels of Albions sons, black and
> Opake divided from his back; he labours and he mourns!
>
> (5: 66–6: 2, E148)

Los's division in this chapter differs from apparently similar divisions in *The Book of Urizen* and *The Four Zoas* in a number of ways. Most important of these differences is that the fragmentation of Los is portrayed as an event that occurs in every day (each morning Blake awakens to his vision of Christ-Albion-Los). The fragmentation of Los is, within the framework of ontological time, an ongoing event which takes place beneath each moment of the fallen world.

The Spectre appears at the point of withdrawal from others. It is, for example, precisely when Albion turns his 'back to the Divine Vision' that 'his Spectrous Chaos before his face appeard: an Unformed Memory' (29[33]: 1–2, E174). In withdrawal Albion, like Locke's human understanding, can see no more than what his memory is able to retain of past encounters. Withdrawal therefore results in the domination of the active power by the Spectre.

Los, of course, does not himself withdraw from Albion. Nevertheless, he finds himself in a position which is analogous to that of Albion-in-withdrawal: the other has withdrawn and

Los is therefore left in solitude. In this situation, each moment of attentiveness to the plight of Albion must result in the elaboration of a closed world because there is no other to meet Los's embrace. It is this duality in the work of Los which produces the hiatus in his being. Los is, by default, continually torn back from relationship and thrown into a world held by his Spectre. On the one hand he awaits the return of Albion; on the other hand this very process divides the Spectre from him, for in order to do this Los is always engaged in building a closed world. This situation and division is, of course, described in *The Four Zoas*. In *Jerusalem* it is given added cogency and clarity by the elaboration of the Spectre into a complex and striking figure.

Many of the characteristics of the Spectre and of his relationship to Los can be seen in the illumination to plate 6, where this figure appears with large bat-like wings which roof Los in. The Spectre appears because Los has stopped working at his forge and, instead, looks over his shoulder. The implication is that by looking backwards he has stopped facing Albion. This is perhaps why Blake writes that the 'Spectrous Dead' dwell in 'the back & loins' (29[33]: 4, E174): it is only by turning away from relationship that the Spectre divides from the active power and can be seen as a separate part of the personality. In this same illumination, Los's hammer has become an erect phallus. The transformation is quite revealing. In working at his furnaces the hammer is a tool which forges relationship with others. When he ceases work, however, Los adopts a position which suggests masturbation rather than intercourse. In this second position others are present only within the economy of the self. Los is, in this moment, enclosed within the 'Ratio | Of the Things of Memory' which is formed by the Reasoning Power.

The Spectre, as he himself recognizes, is always outside of life. In the terms of Locke's analogy, he exists within a closet where the light of encounter reaches him only as a pale reflection. The Spectre is 'all reversed & for ever dead', and his recognition of this fact is expressed in an intensely moving speech:

> Life lives on my
> Consuming: & the Almighty hath made me his Contrary
> To be all evil, all reversed & for ever dead: knowing
> And seeing life, yet living not; how can I then behold
> And not tremble; how can I be beheld & not abhorrd.
>
> (10: 55-9, E154)

The Spectre identifies himself as despair (10: 51, E153), because his being never reaches the present of life.[37] At the moment in which Los opens the closed world of the self he is transformed, but, in the fallen world at least, only into another memory of life that must be consumed.

The Spectre is a highly ambiguous character. In Eternity, the Spectre is necessary in order to retain the ground against which the leap of the active power towards others is defined. In the fallen world this figure has a role to play which is just as crucial, for, given the absence of Albion, the Spectre must retain the world in which Los stands. If the reasoning memory did not retain the shape of Los's relationship with Albion then the entire world would dissolve. This interdependence means that Los must continually subdue the Spectre to his will. In a sequential narrative this event would occur at a particular place and time (10: 29-36, E153). In the vision of ontological time which composes the first chapter of *Jerusalem*, it is seen as an ongoing struggle and tension because it forms the very foundation of the world in which we live.

The struggle between Los and the Spectre creates an oscillation between enclosure and openness, opacity and transparence. This means that life itself, as I have argued in my discussion of the vision of nature which ends the first Book of *Milton*, is formed in the tension between openness and closure; but now, in the vision of ontological time which composes the first chapter of *Jerusalem*, this oscillation can be clearly seen to be a result of the struggle between Los and his Spectre.

Los is, of course, also subject to a second division in which Enitharmon divides away from him. This is described in terms which are reminiscent of *The Book of Urizen*:

>                              yet still she divided away
> In gnawing pain from Los's bosom in the deadly Night;
> First as a red Globe of blood trembling beneath his bosom[.]
> Suspended over her he hung: he infolded her in his garments
> Of wool: he hid her from the Spectre, in shame & confusion of
> Face; in terrors & pains of Hell & Eternal Death, the
> Trembling Globe shot forth Self-living & Los howld over it:
> Feeding it with his groans & tears day & night without ceasing:
> And the Spectrous Darkness from his back divided in temptations,
> And in grinding agonies in threats! stiflings! & direful strugglings.
>
>                              (17: 49-58, E162)

In this passage the shape of Los's world, which once was the site for a movement towards others, is now projected into the void. The Spectre and Los now struggle with each other for possession of the body of the fallen world. Los's attempt to bend the Spectre to his will is implicitly an attempt to ensure that the passive power gives body to Albion-in-withdrawal. On the other hand, the Spectre struggles with Los in the hope that he will be able to make the world formed by Enitharmon into a closet.

Perhaps the most striking part of Blake's vision of Los, Enitharmon, and the Spectre is the recognition that in retaining the world of withdrawal he is giving form to Albion's withdrawal. When his Sons and Daughters appear from out of his furnaces they are all astonished that Los should give a body to Vala rather than Jerusalem:

> Why wilt thou give to her a Body whose life is but a Shade?
> Her joy and love, a shade: a shade of sweet repose:
> But animated and vegetated, she is a devouring worm.
>
> (12: 1–3, E155)

We will discuss Vala later in this chapter; however, at this stage it can be said that Vala is the outer form or surface of Albion-in-withdrawal. Los gives form to Vala because he is giving form to the world of withdrawal. This is why the Spectre asserts that Los's friendship to Albion assists Albion's Daughters and Sons:

> Wilt thou still go on to destruction?
> Till thy life is all taken away by this deceitful Friendship?
> He drinks thee up like water! like wine he pours thee
> Into his tuns: thy Daughters are trodden in his vintage
> He makes thy Sons the trampling of his bulls, they are plow'd
> And harrowd for his profit, lo! thy stolen Emanation
> Is his garden of pleasure!
>
> (7: 9–15, E149)

Enitharmon is Albion's garden of pleasure because the outline of the world of Los (loss) gives form and body to Albion's withdrawal. The body of Los is in the fallen world the body of Albion. This is also why Enitharmon divides 'Eastward toward the Starry Wheels' of Albion's sons (5: 68, E148).

Los recognizes the danger and ambivalence of what he is doing. He describes himself as a 'horror and an astonishment' (8: 18, E151) and as he works at his furnace he sees the 'soft affections | Condense beneath [his] hammer into forms of cruelty' (9: 26–7, E152). Despite this ambivalence he retains the form of the world of withdrawal in the hope that Albion will

## 120  Visionary Construction

recognize his error and so cast it off. Perhaps the most striking description of Los's strategy is contained on plate 12:

> I saw the finger of God go forth
> Upon my Furnaces, from within the Wheels of Albions Sons:
> Fixing their Systems, permanent: by mathematic power
> Giving a body to Falshood that it may be cast off for ever.
> With Demonstrative Science piercing Apollyon with his own bow!
>
> (12: 10–14, E155)

The world that is created in this way also contains the possibility of openness. One of the major effects of Los's work and of his struggle with his Spectre is the production of the spaces of Erin:

> Then Erin came forth from the Furnaces, & all the Daughters of Beulah
> Came from the Furnaces, by Los's mighty power for Jerusalems
> Sake: walking up and down among the Spaces of Erin:
> And the Sons and Daughters of Los came forth in perfection lovely!
> And the Spaces of Erin reach'd from the starry heighth, to the starry
>    depth.
>
> (11: 8–12, E154)

Erin arises as a result of Los's attempt to remain in relationship with Albion, subdue his Spectre, and so claim his body as his own. In other words, Erin appears in the time of embodiment. As Damon helpfully suggests, Erin is the body;[38] or, perhaps more accurately, Erin is the body that has been embraced. As we found in *Milton*, it is in the time of embodiment that others—the Sons and Daughters of Los and the Daughters of Beulah—are able to appear. Los's work has opened within the sequential time of Ulro a time of 'meeting' and 'loving embrace'. The shape of this world, with its extraordinary oscillations between the Spectre and Los, openness and closure, opacity and transparence, is the city of Golgonooza. It is to this city that the vision now extends.

AN URN OF BEULAH

The first chapter of *Jerusalem* gives us two major sites on which Golgonooza is built. The first is mentioned on plate 10, where we learn that Los builds Golgonooza while he is standing in London (line 17, E153). London is, quite obviously, a city in time and space; and, more particularly, it is a city in which Blake lived and worked for much of his life. However, to say no more than this is to deal only with surfaces. The streets of

London are built upon, perhaps even embody, a wide-ranging dissolution. As I have observed, beneath the everyday world the narrator discovers a drama in which 'Cambridge & Oxford & London . . . Are . . . rent away & dissipated' (5: 3-4, E147). In the second chapter London is given a more specific role in this global dissolution; London is a willing victim of Albion's withdrawal. The very shape and spatial organization of London embodies and expresses a person who has entered the furnaces of privation and separated himself from his human form in order to attempt to recall Albion (34[38]: 29-39, E180). Golgonooza is therefore built on the site of the victim, or martyr. The second location amplifies this reading:

> What are those golden builders doing? where was the burying-place
> Of soft Ethinthus? near Tyburns fatal Tree? is that
> Mild Zions hills most ancient promontory; near mournful
> Ever weeping Paddington? is that Calvary and Golgotha?
> Becoming a building of pity and compassion?
>
> (12: 25-9, E155)

In this extraordinary passage, with an apparent lack of regard for geography, Blake locates Golgonooza in both Israel and England. As Frye notes, in *Jerusalem* Blake draws a series of historical and geographical parallels between English and Biblical geography and history. On the one hand the geography of the Holy Land is simply 'superimposed on England', and on the other Blake is drawing a series of parallels between English and biblical history.[39] This parallelism is a powerful tool for it allows Blake to read English history in biblical terms (and *vice versa*), and at the same time it assists in the construction of a space where events and places are located according to their spiritual significance rather than their spatio-temporal location.

In this instance it allows Blake to add depth to the original location of Golgonooza in London by drawing together a series of places which have associations with the victims of oppression. Ethinthus was one of the daughters of Los and Enitharmon and, as Damon tells us, she represents the 'mortal flesh'.[40] Tyburn was the site of London's gallows, Paddington was a slum district of London (until 1811 when new houses were built),[41] and Calvary and Golgotha are names for the place where Christ was crucified. At the point where the flesh is buried, the victim is sacrificed and where the innocent suffer, the narrator of this passage witnesses an extraordinary transformation. The change is so great that he must ask in a tone of astonishment and bewilderment where Ethinthus is buried?

Can it possibly have been 'near Tyburns fatal Tree?' 'Zion was originally the rocky scarp on the southern end of the ridge between the Kidron and Tyropoeon valleys in Jerusalem ... and in Christian times was taken as a type of heaven';[42] and yet this promontory is now seen near Paddington. Even Calvary and Golgotha are in the process of being transformed. The presence of a 'building of pity and compassion' in such a place would indeed be astonishing, however, rather than simply building on this soil, Golgonooza's 'golden builders' seem to be transforming the event and reality of Calvary and Golgotha into a work of love. Golgonooza is a structure that is built in an attempt to turn the fact of suffering and the triumph of the forces of state and church oppression into a building of compassion.

Golgonooza therefore embodies Los's efforts, as poet and prophet, to forge 'the sighs & tears, & bitter groans' of suffering into 'the spiritual sword. | That lays open the hidden heart' (9: 17, 18-19, E152). If he is to achieve this end, it is the very substance of withdrawal that must be transformed. It is important to note, however, that this activity does not precede or even follow the construction of the fallen world, but is coterminous with it. If Los did not stand in London, and if his builders were not at Golgotha to give privation a form and to 'bring the sons & Daughters of Jerusalem to be | The Sons & Daughters of Los', then all life would cease, for it is Los's care for Albion that grounds the fallen world. Golgonooza is the *locale* that Los's relationship to Albion-in-withdrawal opens and the form that it takes. Golgonooza is, therefore, more than a city of art built within the fallen world, or inside the scaffolding of nature, for its streets, houses, and inhabitants, express and embody the shape and result of Los's relationship with Albion in his absence. The extended account of the city which is given on plates 12 to 14 is therefore one more clarification and expansion of the vision that we have been tracing. In order to follow the movement of this vision, we must learn how to orient ourselves within the spaces of this city.

### INSIDE GOLGONOOZA

We map our position in the fallen world on a two-dimensional grid which extends along axes running north–south and east–west. In Golgonooza place is determined according to a very different system. The four points of the compass which orient the visitor to this city are described as the circumference, zenith, nadir, and centre. These coordinates map out the comportment of a three-dimensional, sentient body, for each direction is a sense or a faculty of a man:

> And the Eyes are the South, and the Nostrils are the East.
> And the Tongue is the West, and the Ear is the North.
>
> (12: 59-60, E156)

Blake describes each point of the compass, and therefore each sense of the man, as a face which looks towards, and opens, one of the 'Four Worlds of Humanity | In every Man'. In the fallen world we perhaps tend to think of our senses as organs for assimilating or registering what exists outside ourselves. The senses of the whole man, however, are described as faces: Noses, Eyes, Tongue, and Ear are the organs through which we face, and are able to form relationships with, others. To orient oneself in Golgonooza, therefore, one must see its spaces as a human body. This being should not be imagined as a corporeal self, for each point of the compass and each faculty of Man is fourfold and forms an animated being. Golgonooza is, therefore, a world of relationship, of care and compassion, where we reside within each other.

Los's city is fourfold, gates open to all levels of existence, and it forms a body which is potentially able to engage in relationship; however, one of the dimensions of this city and this body is closed:

> Fourfold the Sons of Los in their divisions: and fourfold,
> The great City of Golgonooza: fourfold toward the north
> And toward the south fourfold, & fourfold toward the east & west
> Each within other toward the four points: that toward
> Eden, and that toward the World of Generation,
> And that toward Beulah, and that toward Ulro:
> Ulro is the space of the terrible starry wheels of Albions sons:
> But that toward Eden is walled up, till time of renovation:
> Yet it is perfect in its building, ornaments & perfection.
>
> (12: 45-53, E156)

Eden is beyond the western gate and is associated with the circumference. This is closed in the fallen world because Albion has withdrawn and therefore there is no other to meet Los's embrace. The self cannot leave its closet, nor can it make the 'spring of eternal life'. The circumference cannot be escaped: rather than being the ground for a leap it has become the outer bound of our world.

Golgonooza is the city of the prophet; it embodies the comportment that Los adopts towards Albion-in-withdrawal. It is a relationship (four faces which look toward the world of humanity) and yet, in the absence of Albion, it is an enclosure. As the spiritual London, and as the shape of ontological time, Golgonooza is always, in a certain sense, complete. Even the gate towards Eden which is walled up is described as 'perfect in its building, ornaments & perfection' (12: 53, E156). Golgonooza is described as rising and falling (rather than progressing towards Eternity) because it is the very shape of Los's attentiveness to Albion-in-withdrawal and this attentiveness must be assayed again and again. Golgonooza falls in the moment in which Los is enclosed by his constituted world; it rises in the return of Los to his forge.

If the fourth gate of Golgonooza could be opened, then Golgonooza would give way to the movement and dynamism of Eden, and this interaction would be spatialized as the city of liberty, which Blake calls Jerusalem. The apocalypse in which Eden will appear occurs when the fourth gate is opened and the circumference becomes the ground for a leap into Eternity. Even at this point regeneration will occur only on the condition that there is an other to meet the self. In fallen history the fourth gate remains closed because it is surrounded on all sides by 'the land of death eternal; a Land | Of pain and misery and despair and ever brooding melancholy' (13: 30-1, E157). Golgonooza is a bastion and defence against these forces of dissolution. It is constructed by Los in order to prevent the collapse of the world, and its gates are each protected by 'sixty-four thousand' Genii, Gnomes, Nymphs, and Fairies (13: 26-9, E157).

At the same time, as I have argued in previous chapters, the world of Los and Enitharmon has the effect of giving form to these same forces. Without this outline they, and Albion, would fall into non-entity. Blake writes, for example, that 'the abstract Voids between the Stars are the Satanic Wheels' (13: 37, E157), but these voids have a form and are therefore visible because they are negatively defined by Los's universe. Golgonooza forms the figure to the ground of 'death eternal', which surrounds it on all sides. In fact, Blake goes so far as to suggest not merely that the figure of the Stars forms the Voids, but that the reverse is true and that in a certain sense the Voids 'form' the 'Mundane Shell' of the visible universe:

A Concave Earth wondrous, Chasmal, Abyssal, Incoherent!
Forming the Mundane Shell: above; beneath: on all sides surrounding Golgonooza.

(13: 53-5, E157)

Golgonooza is therefore, like Los and the work that he undertakes, itself made ambivalent by the support it unavoidably lends (in the process of giving form to Albion-in-withdrawal) to the world of withdrawal. Some of the smaller cities of Golgonooza are 'The Looms & Mills & Prisons & Work-houses of Og & Anak: | The Amalekite: the Canaanite: the Moabite: the Egyptian' (13: 57–8, E157). The form of the Eastern gate is taken from 'the Wheels of Albions sons; as cogs | Are formd in a wheel, to fit the cogs of the adverse wheel' (13: 13–14, E156), and here we find many of the things which characterized the 'land of death eternal': 'eternal ice, frozen in seven folds | Of forms of death', 'The seven diseases of the earth', 'forms of war' and 'seven generative forms'. (13: 15–16, 17, 18, 19, E156–7).

In the culmination of the vision of Golgonooza we are given an account of the world which Los surveys as he 'walks round the walls' of his city. As a result the interconnection between Golgonooza and the land which surrounds it is made even more self evident. First, Los views within the city of Golgonooza the entire extent of fallen history. He sees:

> all that has existed in the space of six thousand years:
> Permanent, & not lost not lost nor vanishd, & every little act,
> Word, work, & wish, that has existed.
>
> (13: 59–61, E157–8)

This passage, however, goes on to affirm that these events are

> all remaining still
> In those Churches ever consuming & ever building by the Spectres
> Of all the inhabitants of Earth wailing to be Created.
>
> (13: 61–3, E158)

Los then turns his attention to 'the Cherub at the Tree of Life ... the Serpent | Orc' and the condition of all the Zoas and their Emanations. This panoramic view of the fallen world is concluded with the at first surprising statement that 'Such are the Buildings of Los! & such are the Woofs of Enitharmon' (14: 15, E158). The present condition of the Zoas, Orc, the Cherub and the Serpent are all a result of the disintegration of Albion. As in *The Four Zoas* the fall of Albion (and the Zoas) is a fall into the universe of Los and Enitharmon. It is their saving activity which gives a form to the fallen world and, paradoxically, gives substance to their withdrawal. It is in this sense that these characters are 'Buildings of Los'. Los finally turns to Jerusalem. The construction of the fallen world has created a bastion against further fragmentation; however, because the western gate remains closed, Jerusalem is no more than 'a pale cloud arising from the arms of Beulahs Daughters: | In Entuthon Benythons deep Vales beneath Golgonooza' (14: 33–4, E158).

Golgonooza is like the 'Urns of Beulah' (11: 2, E154). It is a funeral Urn which houses beings who have withdrawn from relationship. Although it must be described as a space of loss and privation, it is also a building of compassion: it embodies Los's struggles with his Spectre and Los's solicitude for Albion. It is an Urn which gives form to the relationships which ground life in the fallen world. It is this last characteristic of the city which ensures that it also provides an outline for what would otherwise lack definition. Golgonooza is a city which gives a form to both Albion-in-withdrawal and to Vala and at the same time holds open the possibility of regeneration.

To call Golgonooza a city of 'Art & Manufacture'—the name it is given by 'mortal men' (M 24: 50, E120)—is correct only if these terms are taken in a sense which far surpasses their normal signification. Golgonooza is not an aesthetic object, but a structure which embodies an engagement and relationship with Albion. It is prophetic art which preserves the very possibility of life by establishing the outline of identity in the midst of dissolution. The art that it represents is the work of the titan Los, and it underlies all of existence. It is a city of manufacturing in the sense that this work is done only by assimilating the raw material represented by Albion-in-withdrawal to the world of Los and Enitharmon, and because, at the same time, it establishes the real centre of manufacturing: the wheels and cogs of Satan.

## 'SUCH VISIONS HAVE APPEARD TO ME AS I MY ORDERED RACE HAVE RUN': LOS AND BLAKE, GOLGONOOZA AND LONDON

Los's panoramic view of Golgonooza ends with a striking change of focus. In previous plates we have seen what 'He views' and beholds (13: 56; 14: 2, 16, 31, E157 and 158). Now the text seems to turn itself inside out; the reader discovers that Los's vision is also Blake's 'awful Vision' (cf. 14: 30–15: 5, E158–9). Throughout this plate it is repeated again and again that it is now Blake who sees (15: 6, 8, 21, 30) and Blake who turns his eyes towards the objects of vision (15: 14). This change of perspective places a not inconsiderable stress on the poem's sequential movement, for it brings the expanding vision that we have been tracing back to its ground in the moment of awakening in which Christ dictates the 'mild song' of Jerusalem to Blake. In so doing it makes us aware of the extraordinary tension that exists in this song between vision and the narrative account of that vision, between what is dictated by Christ and what is given form by Blake.

In the opening lines of Jerusalem Blake awoke from sleep and, as a result, was given a vision of the relationships which formed the ground of his identity and of the world in which he lived. However, the call of Christ and the withdrawal of Albion are not, properly speaking, events which can be confined to a moment of ontic time. As I have argued, vision is predicated upon an opening of the world of the self. Moreover, Albion and Jesus are giant figures whose bulk extends across all of fallen history. Yet the vision in which they appear is 'given' to a person who is swept along 'in the tide of time'. The vision of what structures time must be given form and elaborated within time and in a sequential narrative. In Jerusalem the gradual elaboration of Blake's vision can be traced in the gradually expanding circle which moves from Jesus to Albion, to Los and his Spectre, and then to Golgonooza. It can also be seen by comparing plate 15 with plate 4. On the later plate the opening vision has become more detailed and more complex. Blake is now able to see Albion's withdrawal as a sleep, and to perceive the division into Emanation and Spectre which is a result of this withdrawal. Moreover, after the elaboration of the initial vision which is contained in the intervening plates, Blake is able to see all of time 'existing' before him:

> I see the Four-fold Man. The Humanity in deadly sleep
> And its fallen Emanation. The Spectre & its cruel Shadow.
> I see the Past, Present & Future, existing all at once
> Before me.
>
> (15: 6-9, E159)

In the opening plates Blake saw the division and fragmentation that Albion's withdrawal caused in England. Now, he sees the same process at work beneath all of Europe. Where he first was able to do no more than glimpse Los in his world (5: 27-33, E147-8), he is now able to see Los 'raging round his Anvil | Of death: forming an Ax of gold' (15: 21-2, E159) and his sons 'cutting the Fibres from Albions hills' (15: 23, E159). The initial glimpse of the time which structures his world allowed Blake to grasp clearly his own situation (5: 1-15, E147), but now we hear of figures such as Reuben, Noah, Satan, and Adam who take part in a much wider drama.

One way of interpreting this elaboration of vision would be to describe it in terms of a gradual appropriation of vision to the perspectives of the self. On one level this clearly does occur, for, as I have argued, the reader of *Jerusalem* passes along a linear path which strikingly resembles Lockean time. From this point of view, the moment of awakening with which the poem began has been left far behind. Yet such an account would do small justice to the poem. The expansion of vision which I have described is not something which is captured by ontic time. While sustaining a complex and intricate relationship with that time, Blake's vision seems to expand behind or between its intervals. The vision described on plate 15, for example, far from being confined to the ontic moment between plates 14 and 16, takes us back to the very same moment of awakening in which the poem began. It forces us to take seriously Blake's contention that in the moment of awakening with which the poem begins Christ dictates the 'mild song' called *Jerusalem*, or in other words, that the poem itself can be seen and heard in this visionary moment. It is not simply, as Morton Paley suggests, that 'Blake's "I" is ... presented synchronously as the narrator of synchronous events',[43] but that the constant return of the poem to the perspective of the visionary moment with which the poem begins underlines that *Jerusalem* is a visionary construction or elaboration of that vision. The visionary narrator of *Jerusalem* can see 'Past, Present & Future, existing all at once' because he can see Albion/Jesus, not because he is able to hold the entire poem within the purview of his gaze.

A reading of *Jerusalem* must therefore progress on two levels. On the one hand it is possible to read it as a simple narrative which is held in the reasoning memory. In this reading vision is merely that which began the sequence and is now lost in primordial and inaccessible time. From this perspective an interpretation of this poem involves an attempt to order what the reasoning memory has retained of *Jerusalem*. It is, however, also possible to read it in a radically different way. *Jerusalem* attempts to wake us from the slumber of ontic time by returning this time to its ground. To take up the relationship to the text described in the opening plates is to discern, between the intervals of the poem's onward movement, an expansive vision. In this second reading *Jerusalem* takes the form of a visionary construction.

For the reader it is therefore quite literally true that 'SUCH VISIONS HAVE APPEARD TO ME AS I MY ORDERED RACE HAVE RUN'. The vision of Christ/Albion underlies the whole poem and all of time. The sudden shift of focus in plate 15, from Los to Blake, underlines that the poem is vision; it calls us to 'see thro' the text rather than with it. The poem, like time itself according to Blake, is therefore a divine analogy or an 'Allegory addressed to the Intellectual Powers'. It creates a figure of the relationships which hold between ontic, sequential, and ontological time, between the world of the corporeal, closeted self, and the world of vision.

Before proceeding with our argument it is important to affirm that the relationship between vision and its temporal elaboration is not at all a hierarchical one. It is true that the necessity for Blake to elaborate sequentially the moment in which *Jerusalem* appears introduces a gap between that elaboration and vision; however, this gap does not imply that there is a relationship of heteronomy between the two, that the latter is necessarily no more than a second-hand version of the first, or that we can describe one as a 'phantom' generated by the other. In the poem itself the linear narration and the series of expanding circles contradict each other's frame of reference, and yet they are in a relationship of mutual dependence.

The relationship between vision and temporal elaboration can be seen in the lines which follow on from Blake's claim to be able to see 'Past, Present & Future, existing all at once'. Blake writes:

> O Divine Spirit sustain me on thy wings!
> That I may awake Albion from his long & cold repose.
> For Bacon & Newton sheathd in dismal steel, their terrors hang
> Like iron scourges over Albion, Reasonings like vast Serpents
> Infold around my limbs, bruising my minute articulations.
>
> (15: 9-13, E159)

Blake's elaboration of his vision in a temporal form is quite clearly a 'minute articulation': it is an attempt to articulate in physical and temporal form a vision which cannot be contained in this form. His articulations are 'minute' in two ways: first, they are composed of a series of minute physical forms (words, lines, illuminations, paragraphs, pages); and second, these forms are ordered by a temporal spacing. The word 'articulate' means to express, and so give an appropriate form to something which would otherwise remain mute and inchoate. Articulation thus implies both that something is given to the person who articulates, and that the he/she does not articulate what is given in a neutral fashion, but is him/herself involved in giving it body and form. The person who articulates, therefore, shapes what is to be articulated. To 'articulate' therefore also means to link together (without merging or identifying) two separate things. In this understanding the narration of the poem has a crucially important role to play in relationship to vision. It is only in Blake's 'minute articulations' (which yoke time and Eternity) that this vision achieves expression and, therefore, it is only as a result of 'the productions of time' that Albion can be confronted with the reality of his withdrawal.

This kind of interdependence can be seen in the relationships which exist between Blake and Los, and Golgonooza and London. Although Los forges the ground on which London stands, it is also true to say that Los stands in London forging this ground (10: 17, E153). Similarly, although all temporal things can be seen in Los's halls (13: 59, E157), we must also affirm that Los's halls are filled with things that are formed on earth: Los preserves 'every little act, | Word, work, & wish, that has existed' (13: 60-1, E157-8). Perhaps the clearest statement of the influence of Golgonooza on time, and one which has provoked the suggestion that Golgonooza is a realm of ideal Platonic forms, is that contained on plate 16. Blake writes:

> All things acted on Earth are seen in the bright Sculptures of
> Los's Halls & every Age renews its powers from these Works
> With every pathetic story possible to happen from Hate or
> Wayward Love & every sorrow & distress is carved here
> Every Affinity of Parents Marriages & Friendships are here
> In all their various combinations wrought with wondrous Art
> All that can happen to Man in his pilgrimage of seventy years.
>
> (16: 61-7, E161)

Even this passage, however, reveals a curious dependence of Golgonooza on time. 'All things acted on Earth' are not determined by, but 'seen' in, the 'Sculptures of Los's Halls'. This verb leaves the question of where they originate quite open. The sculptures contain 'every ... story possible to happen' because they embody the ontological time of the fallen world. As such they open the site and context of our human freedom. The ground of our life is formed by the relationships between Los, Albion, and Christ; however, the figure we cut in this ground is established by the relationships that we take up to others.

We can therefore say that it is only at this point of the vision that we clearly see the outline of identity of the world formed in the withdrawal of Albion from Christ. This outline is formed in the relationship which exists between Blake and Los, London and Golgonooza. This vision is, of course, not static. Los must return again and again into relationship with Albion, and Blake must awake to Christ each morning. The account of Blake's role in the elaboration of what is given is, therefore, followed by a return to Los's divisions and his contentions with his Spectre. The spaces of Golgonooza exist in the relationship between these two figures.

In the previous section we spoke of a centre of vision which passed from Albion to Los and then to Golgonooza. The modulation in plate 15 from Los to Blake underlines the fact that there is a second centre to this vision. The circles that we have been tracing have a centre in the people who are watching them: the narrator, the poet, and the reader. It is in the contrary relationship between the vision that is given and the vision of Blake (and the reader), between Albion, Los, and Christ on the one hand, and the beings who exist in linear time on the other hand, that *Jerusalem* is forged.

NEGATIVE SPACE: THE WORLD OF VALA

Our vision of Golgonooza and the outline of identity allows a very different clarification and expansion to occur. When a ripple expands to a certain point, the observer's focus often changes and he/she is able to see the negative space that has co-determined that form. Similarly, the completion of the vision of Golgonooza and of the outline of identity allows the ground to this figure (the negative space out of which it emerges) to be seen. This is the 'orbed Void' described on plate 18:

> From every-one of the Four Regions of Human Majesty,
> There is an Outside spread Without, & an Outside spread Within
> Beyond the Outline of Identity both ways, which meet in One:
> An orbed Void of doubt, despair, hunger, & thirst & sorrow.
> Here the Twelve Sons of Albion, join'd in dark Assembly.
>
> (18: 1-5, E162)

We have, of course, seen the land of death eternal from within Golgonooza, but now we are actually surrounded by the voices and conflicts of this world. In this space the contention between Los and his Spectre is replaced by that between Vala, Jerusalem, and Albion. Early in the first chapter we saw Los walking 'round the walls' of Golgonooza 'night and day'. From this new perspective we see him 'roofd in from Eternity in Albions Cliffs' (19: 33, E164).

Prior to this, Blake's vision has progressed from the withdrawal of Albion to Los's struggle with his Spectre, and then to Golgonooza. For the reader this expansion of vision produces the feeling that a form is being elaborated out of chaos. The climax of this expansion is, of course, the delineation of the outline of identity which we have discussed above. In the vision of negative space which follows on from this point there seems to be, by contrast, a slow contraction or regression. We move from the Sons of Albion and the world that they hope to build (18: 1-43, E162-3) to a description of Albion's external condition (18: 44-19: 16, E163-4), to an account of Albion's internal or psychological state and his flight 'inward among the currents of his rivers' (19: 17-39, E164), and then to the contentions between Albion, Vala, and Jerusalem (which are the substance —both cause and result—of this withdrawal). Finally we see Albion utter his 'last words' (23: 26, E168) and 'die' in the arms of Christ (24: 60, E170). We move from what is nearest to the outline of identity and Golgonooza (the Sons who war mightily against the world of Los) to what is evanescent and out of Los's grasp (Jerusalem and Albion). In previous plates we watched the poem slowly elaborate the shape of the relationship between Albion and Christ. Now the poem progressively dismantles the world of the Sons of Albion until we are able to see the relationships which underlie and support it.

For the reader these plates are extraordinarily moving; for the critic they pose certain problems, not least of which is the difficulty of describing, without becoming prolix, a phenomenon before one perceives its ground. For this reason we will, in the course of our discussion of the kingdom formed by the Sons of Albion, digress from the narrative order of the poem and introduce material which properly should appear later in our exposition.

The negative space which lies outside the outline of identity is where the Sons of Albion attempt 'To murder their own Souls, to build a Kingdom among the Dead' (18: 9, E163). They hope to create Babylon—a world where the self attempts to devour and absorb others. Perhaps the most significant features of this world are the appearances in its spaces of Vala as 'Nature' and as the founder of Babylon and of Jerusalem as 'The Shadow of delusions!' and the 'Harlot-Sister' (18: 11, 29, 30, E163). Vala achieves her power over Jerusalem because Albion is close to death. Already,

His Children exil'd from his breast pass to and fro before him
His birds are silent on his hills, flocks die beneath his branches
His tents are fall'n! his trumpets, and the sweet sound of his harp
Are silent on his clouded hills, that belch forth storms & fire.

(19: 1-4, E163-4)

However, this state of being (and the wars fostered by Hand and Hyle) represents the surface effect of a very complex phenomenon. As the vision contracts, our gaze moves from the surface of the 'land of death eternal' to its interior.

The Sons rage against Albion and declare their loyalty to Vala because Albion is 'self-exiled from the face of light & shine of morning' (19: 13, E164). To withdraw is to deny relationship and, as I have argued, to enter a world constituted by the Spectre. Albion's Sons are collectively his Spectres and therefore it is this withdrawal that gives them power to 'gormandize | The Human majesty and beauty of the Twentyfour' (19: 23-4, E164). As the vision continues to contract we therefore find Albion fleeing 'inward':

Albions Circumference was clos'd: his Center began darkning
Into the Night of Beulah, and the Moon of Beulah rose
Clouded with storms: Los his strong Guard walkd round
    beneath the Moon
And Albion fled inward among the currents of his rivers.

(19: 36-9, E164)

This withdrawal is caused by (and results in) the separation of the male and female powers.[44] As Albion flees inward he, therefore, comes across Jerusalem and Vala (19: 40-2, E164), who attempt 'to melt his giant beauty' (19: 47, E165).[45] As the vision contracts once more, we hear in detail the contentions between Vala, Jerusalem, and Albion.

The relationship between these three figures is rather complex. In Eternity Vala and Jerusalem are part of Brittannia, the wife of Albion, but Jerusalem is also the Emanation of Albion and the bride of Christ, while Vala is given to Albion as a bride. Vala is also the wife, Emanation, and daughter of Luvah. Luvah is love in general and sexual love in particular. He is a figure of eros, or sexual desire, rather than *agape* (which in Blake's œuvre is represented by Christ). Frosch writes, for example, that 'The activity of Luvah is a search for sheer pleasure, his energy comprehending desire, affection, beauty, and love'; when he operates apart from the other Zoas 'his quest becomes one of a pure & almost frantic self-gratification'.[46] In the fallen world Vala and Jerusalem fall apart from Albion and from each other.

Desire proceeds because of a lack; it is an attempt to fill in something that is missing and in this way complete the self. The result of desire is paradoxically a completed self, a sense of the self's unity. It should therefore be no surprise that Luvah's Emanation, wife, and daughter is Vala. Desire results in a veil interposing itself between lover and beloved. This is why a person possessed by love is often described as blind: the lover is the veiler. In Eternity Luvah is therefore characterized as a weaver who fabricates the veil or outline of the constituted world of the self (95: 17, E255). In the fallen world Vala is herself described as a being who is formed by the Spectres of Albion. In other words she is the veil of simple ideas (the outline of the closet) which Locke interposes between self and other.

Eternity is clearly a place of plenitude and for this reason Luvah is described as 'the gentlest mildest Zoa' (24: 52, E170).[47] However, life in the fallen world is founded on privation and Luvah therefore becomes a force and energy which continually drives towards a now unreachable completeness. Here Luvah is Orc (see, for example, FZ 78: 30-9, E354). In Eternity desire is part of the whole man and, therefore, Vala is complemented by Jerusalem, who is the form of Albion's love and openness to others and (for this reason) Albion's Emanation. To the extent that Albion opens his world to others, Jerusalem gives access to Christ. In the terms of Blake's primarily sexual metaphor, one can therefore say that Jerusalem is the bride of Christ. Each act of relationship depends in part on desire and it is, therefore, effected by Luvah and Vala. This allows us to say two things: first, that Vala is a bride of Albion—even though this being is at the same time an Emanation, wife, and daughter of Luvah; second, that Albion's bride in Eternity is, properly speaking, both Vala and Jerusalem.

In the fallen world that we see in Blake's vision of 'death eternal', this situation has been radically altered because Albion has killed Luvah (22: 31, E168) in order to make Vala his sole possession. Desire is for this reason no longer an identity within the whole man, but appears within his Spectre. For Albion-in-withdrawal desire has become a Narcissistic love; he now embraces the shape of the self which is retained by the Spectre. Similarly, Jerusalem appears only within Vala, the outline of the self. Albion says in horror:

> For I see Luvah whom I slew. I behold him in my Spectre
> As I behold Jerusalem in thee O Vala dark and cold.
>
> (22: 31-2, E168)

This retention by the Spectre of the outline of desire, of the form of the self (Vala), results in the disintegration of Jerusalem. Vala becomes an iron band which now encloses Albion:

> Art thou Vala? replied Albion, image of my repose
> O how I tremble! how my members pour down milky fear!
> A dewy garment covers me all over, all manhood is gone!
> At thy word & at thy look death enrobes me about
> From head to feet, a garment of death & eternal fear
> Is not that Sun thy husband & that Moon thy glimmering Veil?
> Are not the Stars of heaven thy Children! art thou not Babylon?
> Art thou Nature Mother of all! is Jerusalem thy Daughter
> Why have thou elevate inward: O dweller of outward chambers
> From grot & cave beneath the Moon dim region of death
> Where I laid my Plow in the hot noon, where my hot team fed
> Where implements of War are forged, the Plow to go over the Nations
> In pain girding me round like a rib of iron in heaven!
>
> (30[34]: 2-14, E176)

In this fallen world Vala is, as Albion perceives, the form of the world established by Los and Enitharmon. She is, in fact, married to Los (the sun), while Enitharmon (the moon) gives substance to her veil (line 7). Jerusalem is now seen as a harlot because she suggests a realm where relationship opposes and deconstructs the fixed moralities and codes of Vala.

Emblematic of the contentions that arise between these three figures in the fallen world is Albion's response to the suggestion of forgiveness. Jerusalem says to Vala:

> O Vala what is Sin? that thou shudderest and weepest
> At sight of thy once lov'd Jerusalem! What is Sin but a little
> Error & fault that is soon forgiven; but mercy is not a Sin
> Nor pity nor love nor kind forgiveness! O! if I have Sinned
> Forgive & pity me! O! unfold thy Veil in mercy & love . . .
>
> (20: 22-6, E165)

and she asks Albion:

> Why should Punishment Weave the Veil with Iron Wheels of War
> When Forgiveness might it Weave with Wings of Cherubim.
>
> (22: 34-5, E168)

To forgive, however, is to be no longer in the power of Vala. It is no longer to attempt to raise an ethics on the ground of nature,

## 136  Visionary Construction

but to allow the other to return. In withdrawal Albion cannot believe this; he responds to Jerusalem and Vala with a lamentation over his own culpability. He persists in judging himself and others (21: 1-4, 11-12, E166). To forgive would be for Albion to leave his constituted world and face the other whom he has injured. Instead, Albion decides to follow the less difficult path, of death. Less difficult, because it is merely a further step along the path of withdrawal. We therefore see Albion bear 'the Veil whole away' and hear him utter 'his last words' (23: 20, 26, E168). Finally we see him announce his death:

> If God was Merciful this could not be: O Lamb of God
> Thou art a delusion and Jerusalem is my Sin! O my Children
> I have educated you in the crucifying cruelties of Demonstration
> Till you have assum'd the Providence of God & slain your Father
> Dost thou appear before me who liest dead in Luvahs Sepulcher
> Dost thou forgive me! thou who wast Dead & art Alive?
> Look not so merciful upon me O thou Slain Lamb of God
> I die! I die in thy arms tho Hope is banishd from me.
> 
> (24: 53-60, E170)

It is this picture of Albion retreating into death even as Christ embraces him which closes Blake's vision of 'the land of death eternal'. At the same time it takes us back to the very beginning of the poem where we heard Christ affirm that he was in Albion's bosom and Albion was in his, and saw Albion turn 'away . . . down the valleys dark' from a Christ he thought was a 'Phantom of the over heated brain!' Blake's vision of ontological time is therefore complete. We can follow its dilation to the outline of identity and then watch it contract back to the moment in which Blake awakes from sleep. The form of this vision is seen, it is important to add, 'as we our ordered race have run'.

The ontological time of the fallen world is therefore made up of both the positive space created in Los's friendship to Albion and the negative space which is opened by Albion's withdrawal. The fallen world therefore oscillates between Calvary and Auschwitz, Jägerstätter and Hitler. This is why the opening chapter of *Jerusalem* is addressed to the Public. It is in the space and time which is opened by the ontological time of Los that history charts its course. It is in this space that there unfolds a string which will lead us back to Jerusalem.

# 4. Beginning

> The last years of the eighteenth century are broken by a discontinuity similar to that which destroyed Renaissance thought . . . a discontinuity as enigmatic in its principle, in its original rupture, as that which separates the Paracelsian circles from the Cartesian order. Where did this unexpected mobility of epistemological arrangement suddenly come from . . . ? Only thought re-apprehending itself at the root of its own history could provide a foundation, entirely free of doubt, for what the solitary truth of this event was in itself.
>
> Michel Foucault[1]

## TWO KINDS OF TIME

There is, as Foucault suggests, something enigmatic about the moments in which a culture, or discursive space, is founded or transformed. Many writers speak of an analogous difficulty in philosophy, where beginnings are peculiarly elusive.[2] Part of the reason for this difficulty is, no doubt, that we limit our world 'To the Time & Space fixed by the Corporeal Vegetative Eye' (VLJ, E563); we see only the Lockean time that is constituted by the reasoning memory. There are two reasons why from this perspective the question of origins must remain particularly elusive. First, for the Vegetative Man, time appears as 'a very Aged Man' (VLJ, E563). The birth of this being lies on the far side of what our memory can retain and is, therefore, out of reach. Second, sequential time appears only within the space opened by ontological time and this latter time is not accessible to the reasoning memory. Its appearance in vision, as we have seen in *Milton* and the first chapter of *Jerusalem*, depends upon a looking 'thro' the bounds established by the reasoning memory. Foucault writes that we would be able to understand the ruptures and transitions in history only if 'thought' could reapprehend 'itself at the root of its own history'. An inability to make this radical move is why philosophy fails again and again to find an origin which is without presuppositions and why Urizen's attempts in *The Four Zoas* to fathom the length and breadth of his world end in failure.

Yet it is precisely this kind of reapprehension that Blake is attempting to describe in the first chapter of *Jerusalem*. The time elaborated on these plates is ontological time. It is akin to the time that the poet measures in 'Four Quartets': 'time not our time . . . a time | Older than the time of chronometers',[3] or that which is described by Heidegger when he writes of 'the moment when time opens out and extends'.[4] It is because the ontological time described in the first chapter of *Jerusalem* is the moment from which the time of the fallen world 'opens out and extends' that it is only at the end of this chapter that we see sequential time appear:

> Thundring the Veil rushes from his hand Vegetating Knot by Knot, Day by Day, Night by Night; loud roll the indignant Atlantic Waves & the Erythrean, turning up the bottoms of the Deeps.
> (24: 61-3, E170)

This is also why it is only in the preface to the second chapter of *Jerusalem* that the poem turns to the question of beginnings.

In speaking of ontological time as the ground of sequential time it is important not to confuse it with the ground or first premiss that Urizen is attempting to discover. Urizen hopes to reach a point outside of history where 'self sustaining' (FZ 72: 24, E349) he can, like the Augustinian God, survey the totality of the universe. Such a position is clearly not reached in a vision of ontological time, for this beginning does not establish a zero point beyond which there is nothing. Blake himself writes that

> Many suppose that before [Adam] < the Creation > All was Solitude & Chaos This is the most pernicious Idea that can enter the Mind as it takes away all sublimity from the Bible & Limits All Existence to Creation & to Chaos. (VLJ, E563)

The moment of ontological time which lies beneath our history is itself a part of the history of Eternity and, therefore, far from being a point outside of existence it is a moment in the spring of eternal life. It is, however, a moment which has become fixed and motionless. We can therefore locate two very different histories. One is the fixed and repetitive cycle of fallen history which moves from Adam to Luther and remains within the ontological time of loss. The other is a history of liberty in which ontological time is transformed.

One can also say that Urizen's quest is, as the phrase 'self sustaining' suggests, the project of an individual subject. In *Jerusalem*, however, the narrator's vision of ontological time is attained at the precise point that the closed world of the self is punctured. The precondition for this vision, therefore, is a radical decentring of the self. As I have argued, the identity of Los and Albion is formed in relationship with each other, and in relationship with mortals. As Blake writes in the preface to the first chapter: 'We who dwell on Earth can do nothing of ourselves, every thing is conducted by Spirits, no less than Digestion or Sleep' (3, E145). There is no recourse in this line to either a transcendental subject or the psychological activity of a mortal self, for the Spirits can no more than mortals do anything of themselves. Instead, the word 'conducted' suggests a world where events appear in a relationship akin to that by which a conductor gives form to the music played by a number of disparate individuals; or an aqueduct conducts water to a destination. For the individual self ontological time is therefore what is, in a fundamental sense, always out of his/her grasp. It can be seen only in a vision which, by displacing the authority of the vegetative self and puncturing its world, makes its search for an origin within sequential time appear both irrelevant and misconceived.

The poem's description of ontological time allows it now to handle sequential time and the question of a beginning with a striking fluidity and profundity. If the ontic time of the Vegetated Man were our only reference point, then the fragmentation of Albion and his separation from Jerusalem would mean that she was no longer the Emanation of Albion. Politics would have no other reference point than this fact, or the 'once was' of memory. This history of the fallen world, where the Starry Heavens have fled from the whole man and Jerusalem is separated from Albion, is, however, located within a time which, while it forms the ground for this history, also permits a counter-movement towards relationship. The sculptures of Los's halls exist in the tension between the wheel of Religion and the call of Christ. Against the fragmentation of the fallen world, for example, where 'the Starry Heavens are fled from the mighty Limbs of Albion', Blake is therefore able to affirm that 'Jerusalem was & is the Emanation of the Giant Albion' and that the 'Inhabitants of Earth' (despite their obvious fragmentation) are united 'in One Religion' (E171).

The relationship between ontological and sequential times is, perhaps, most strikingly evident in the lyric which forms the bulk of the preface to the second chapter. The poem begins in the past tense with an assertion that 'The fields from Islington to Marybone | To Primrose Hill and Saint Johns Wood' (1-2, E171) were once the site of Jerusalem, and that England was a land where the woman Jerusalem, Christ, and Jerusalem's children could all be seen. Our consternation at these claims is increased by the third verse. Without warning the poem changes to the present tense and its narrator confidently reports the presence of Jerusalem in today's England:

> She walks upon our meadows green:
> The Lamb of God walks by her side:
> And every English Child is seen,
> Children of Jesus & his Bride,
>
> Forgiving trespasses and sins
> Lest Babylon with cruel Og,
> With Moral & Self-righteous Law
> Should Crucify in Satans Synagogue!
>
> (27: 17-24, E172)

The unease generated by these lines is heightened in the following lines where we see, apparently in the same time and space as the immediately antecedent verses, a number of Builders at work reconstructing a city (Golgonooza) on the site of a 'mighty Ruin'. This ruin turns out to be what is left of Jerusalem, for the poem now recounts a history in which Albion withdraws, his Spectre appears, Jerusalem falls and is born in a land far from the fields of Albion, the world is torn by warfare and violence, and the Human Form becomes a mortal worm. We have, therefore, two parallel accounts of the relationship between, and nature of, the past and the present. In the first Jerusalem was and is still seen on Albion's fields. In the second, Jerusalem was once seen in England, but now is separated from Albion by a vast distance.

Within the time and space of the vegetative man these accounts contradict each other and we must choose between them; however, the poem indicates in a number of places that the different realities that they suggest exist in the same world. The 'golden Builders,' for example, work in England where Jerusalem can still be seen. Similarly, the account of the fall of Albion and the withering up of 'Jerusalems Gates' (line 51) ends with words which bring us back to the first account. Jerusalem is no more, Albion has been fragmented, but what was, still is:

> The Divine Vision still was seen
> Still was the Human Form, Divine
> Weeping in weak & mortal clay
> O Jesus still the Form was thine.

> And thine the Human Face & thine
> The Human Hands & Feet & Breath
> Entering thro' the Gates of Birth
> And passing thro' the Gates of Death.
>
> (27: 57-64, E173)

These different realities and opposing trajectories structure the ontological time of the fallen world and, therefore, place us immediately in a situation of choice.

The present in which we exist as mortals is therefore forged in the intersection between these competing claims and realities. In being bound in this way we receive the freedom to elaborate a history. In the ontological time of loss, Blake, for example, stands at the point of intersection between withdrawal and embrace. He is not simply the person who wakes to the presence of Christ, but the person who falls once more into sleep, the individual who--as he admits in this poem—slew Jesus (65-6, E173). It is for this reason that the account of fallen history is followed by lines in which Blake announces his vocation for the third time. The first occurred immediately after his initial glimpse of ontological time and the second after the positive form and space held by Los had been elaborated. He is able to reaffirm it once again, with a perhaps deepened sense of what such a vocation implies, after the entire vision of chapter one and the preface's reiteration in brief of that vision have been completed. A decision such as this forges a path (in sequential time) through the space opened by ontological time.

Blake's vision of ontological time allows him to see the Fall not as something which occurred in the distant past, but as something which is occurring in every moment. Despite the fact that he stands in the 'tide of Time', Blake's commitment can therefore be not to a memory of what has been but to present reality:

> Come to my arms & never more
> Depart; but dwell for ever here:
> Create my Spirit to thy Love:
> Subdue my Spectre to thy Fear.
>
> Spectre of Albion! warlike Fiend!
> In clouds of blood & ruin roll'd:
> I here reclaim thee as my own
> My Selfhood! Satan! armd in gold.
>
> In my Exchanges every Land
> Shall walk, & mine in every Land,
> Mutual shall build Jerusalem:
> Both heart in heart & hand in hand.
>
> (27: 69-76, 85-8, E173)

BEGINNING

The history recounted in the second chapter of *Jerusalem* therefore begins not with the first but the second moment of time; it is preceded by the ontological time from which it unfolds. It therefore begins *in situ*:

> Every ornament of perfection, and every labour of love,
> In all the Garden of Eden, & in all the golden mountains
> Was become an envied horror, and a remembrance of jealousy:
> And every Act a Crime, and Albion the punisher & judge.
> 
> (28: 1-4, E174)

In the lines which follow this passage we hear Albion speaking from his 'secret seat' (28: 5, E174) and watch his Spectre, Satan, appear before his face (29[33]: 1-28, E175). We also hear a conversation between Vala and Albion (29[33]: 29-30[34]: 16, E176) and listen to Los as he stands before his forge (30[34]: 17-42, E176-7). The opening plates therefore recall the relationships which we saw in the first chapter. The lines in which the position of Los with regard to Albion is described, for example, closely parallel passages in the first chapter. This parallelism is inevitable in a world where sequential and ontological time depend upon each other. However, these opening lines differ radically from the first chapter because the situation that they describe is given a precise location in sequential time. The second chapter will deal with sequential rather than ontological time:

> Los stood at his Anvil: he heard the contentions of Vala
> He heavd his thundring Bellows upon the valleys of Middlesex
> He opend his Furnaces before Vala, then Albion frownd in anger
> On his Rock: ere yet the Starry Heavens were fled away
> From his awful Members.
> 
> (30[34]: 17-21, E176)

The beginning of the history which is traced within the time opened by Los's friendship to Albion-in-withdrawal is prior to the flight of the 'Starry Heavens'. At this stage in the history of withdrawal, Albion is still able to see, and feel angry about, the work of Los. In ontological time Blake sees:

> The Humanity in deadly sleep
> And its fallen Emanation. The Spectre & its cruel Shadow...
> 
> (15: 6-7, E159)

and the past, present, and future existing before him all at once. In sequential time we see the first event of this history and we can trace a path from the turning away in anger of Albion from Los to their eventual reunion.

At the very beginning of sequential time, on the edge of the world opened by the ontological time of loss, Los attempts to give form to Albion and in this way confront him with his actions. This attempt by the Eternal Prophet to awaken Albion is described as the progressive binding of Reuben and the subsequent sending of him across the Jordan. Reuben's identity is never described at great length; instead, the reader is presented with a plethora of associations, names, and brief definitions. We are forced to piece together our image of him in a way which, as we shall see, is entirely appropriate for this character.

Damon writes that Reuben symbolizes the 'average sensuous man' and he quotes Louis Ginzberg who translates his name as 'See the normal man.'[5] Reuben's biblical identity strengthens this suggestion for he is 'the founder of the eldest of the twelve tribes of Israel'. Reuben therefore stands for all of the tribes and, in Blake's cosmography, for all mankind. His name, 'the normal man', is, however, meant in an ironic sense for Reuben stands for the members of Albion when they have been torn from relationship. In *Jerusalem* he is for this reason characterized as a homeless wanderer, whose voice can be heard 'from street to street | In all the cities of the Nations Paris Madrid Amsterdam' (84: 13-14, E243).

It is important to note that these descriptions of Reuben refer to his identity after he has been bound by Los. At the moment of Albion's withdrawal, Reuben simply goes to sleep:

> Reuben slept in Bashan like one dead in the valley
> Cut off from Albions mountains & from all the Earths summits
> Between Succoth & Zaretan beside the Stone of Bohan.
> (30[34]: 43-5, E177)

The withdrawal of the whole man is *ipso facto* the precipitation of his members into the solipsism of sleep. Bashan is the land on 'the northern part of Palestine east of the Jordan'; Succoth and Zaretan were cities in this region. The clay ground which separates these two cities once 'furnished the materials for the casting of the metal ornaments to adorn Solomon's Temple'.[6] The location of the slumbering Reuben is therefore strikingly apt. In Eternity the 'average man' gives form to the giant Albion in a manner which is analogous to the way in which the clay found in the land between Succoth and Zaretan was used to form the ornaments for Solomon's temple. When Albion withdraws, however, Albion's body fragments and sinks back into silent and formless clay. Reuben is cut off from Albion and closed in a 'deathlike sleep'.

The biblical Reuben is, in addition to being the founder of the eldest tribe of Israel, 'the eldest son of Jacob', who was 'dispossessed because he seduced his father's concubine, Bilhah'.[7] In Blake's terms this story suggests that Reuben has been dominated by the female will. Where Albion attempts to appropriate the Emanation of a portion of his being and make it the whole, Reuben seduces his father's wife. Reuben and Albion therefore both regulate their desire with reference to a female figure and, as a result, withdraw from a more universal identity (symbolized in the biblical story by Reuben's birthright) to one which is centred on themselves alone. This same dynamic is also suggested in the identification of Reuben as Merlin. In the *Morte dé Arthur* Merlin's love for the Lady of the Lake results in his enclosure in a cave.[8] Merlin is, like the biblical and Blakean Reuben, separated from the whole man and reduced to an isolated self because he has been dominated by the female will.

Los responds to Albion's withdrawal and the separation of Bashan and Reuben from Canaan and the mountains of Albion, by giving form to the 'average man'. First Reuben's nostrils are bent 'down to the Earth'; then his eyes are rolled 'into two narrow circles' (30[34]: 47, 53, E177); his tongue is folded 'Between Lips of mire & clay'; and finally his ear is bent 'in a spiral circle outward' (32[36]: 6, 13, E178). The binding of Reuben is, of course, a prophetic and not an aesthetic activity. Los is attempting to awaken Albion to his plight and in order to do this he gives form to Albion's withdrawal. The narrow circles of the eye, the nose bent to the ground, the ear bent outwards and the tongue closed in a cavern of clay, all establish the outline of the caverned and fragmented man.

As each sense is formed and bound, Los sends Reuben across the river Jordan to Canaan in order to confront Albion with his error. Los is, unfortunately, doing the right thing at the wrong time. The land of Canaan has become 'the land of the Hittite' and a place where the children of Jerusalem are slain. Albion has no intention of returning to relationship. He is now called the Canaanite only because he is dominated by the females of the land. With this kind of audience Los's prophetic activity has startling results:

every-one that saw him
Fled! they fled at his horrible Form: they hid in caves
And dens, they looked on one-another & became what they beheld.
(30[34]: 48-50, E177)

Northrop Frye writes that the clause 'They became what they beheld' refers to

> the familiar doctrine that we see the world as monstrous because our minds are contorted. And the creation of Reuben fills those who see it with horror or ridicule because the natural man, a life proceeding to death, is to the visionary eye the nightmare life-in-death that thicks man's blood with cold. Even for us, who are used to it, there is no more terrifying vision than a ghost, or spectre, a human form at once dead and alive.[9]

In fact, Reuben fills the inhabitants of Canaan with horror, not because he represents the Spectre while they possess the visionary eye, but because his appearance confronts them with the reality of their situation. It is only in their response to Reuben that the Canaanites are transformed. They 'become what they behold' because they try not to behold him and consequently retreat into caves and dens. In other words, it is by not looking at Reuben, by denying the reality of their own condition, that the people of Canaan take on Reuben's 'horrible Form'. The word 'behold' therefore refers not simply to Reuben but to their fellows as well ('they looked on one-another'), who are now also closed within the cavern of the self. Rather than arguing, with Karl Kiralis, that as a 'Vegetative Man' Reuben was 'not ready for the Promised Land' and that this is why he decides 'to remain on the east side of the Jordan',[10] we can say that Reuben returns to Bashan because the inhabitants of Canaan are not ready to embrace him.

The failure of Los's attempts to awaken Albion places the Divine Family well within the ontological time of loss. They must now determine how best to respond to Albion's withdrawal. There are, unfortunately, only two possible responses: ridicule or concern; wrath or love. Amongst the Eternal ones, for example, some merely give expression to a sense of scandal. They argue that the members of Albion are now 'Vegetable only fit for burning'. (32[36]: 48, E179). Others in 'Great Eternity' attempt to understand Albion's world of withdrawal and they look forward to the time of his redemption when 'Length Bredth Highth again Obey the Divine Vision Hallelujah' (32: 56, E179). Los gives expression to the first response on plate 33[37] when he steps 'forth from the Divine Family' (33[37]: 1, E179) and speaks in wrath to Albion. It is important to see that his anger is quite justified, for Los is (as a result of Albion's withdrawal) beginning to feel the painful division that we observed in the previous chapter. In addition, Los must bear the brunt of Albion's wrath:

> I feel my Spectre rising upon me! Albion! arouze thyself!
> Why dost thou thunder with frozen Spectrous wrath against us?
> 
> (33[37]: 2-3, E179)

This response, however, threatens to cut all bonds of relationship; it encloses Los within his constituted world, and it serves to make Albion more indignant and even less receptive to the voice of others. Its potential fruit is, therefore, complete annihilation:

> So Los spoke: But when he saw blue death in Albions feet,
> Again he join'd the Divine Body, following merciful;
> While Albion fled more indignant! revengeful covering
> His face and bosom with petrific hardness, and his hands
> And feet, lest any should enter his bosom & embrace
> His hidden heart.
> 
> (33[37]: 10-34[38]: 3, E179)

When Los sees the effects of his anger he takes up the second response, and returns to the 'Divine Body'. Here can be found the presence of Christ:

> but mild the Saviour follow'd him,
> Displaying the Eternal Vision! the Divine Similitude!
> In loves and tears of brothers, sisters, sons, fathers, and friends
> Which if Man ceases to behold, he ceases to exist.
> 
> (34[38]: 10-13, E179-80)

In facing Albion, Los (and the Divine Family) is continually keeping before him the call of relationship, which is the Eternal Vision and the voice and presence of Christ.

This second response also has undesirable consequences, for to follow Albion as he withdraws is to enter, step by step, the world of withdrawal. This is what occurs to Albion's 'brothers, sisters, sons, fathers, and friends'. London, for example, finds that as a result of his friendship to Albion his blood is now 'vegetating' and rolling 'dreadful thro' the Furnaces of Los, and the Mills of Satan' (34[38]: 36, 37, E180). At its most extreme the attempt to remain in relationship with one who has withdrawn is to suffer martyrdom and death, to give one's life in the hope of reaching the tyrant. It is, however, only in self-giving such as this that the very ground upon which we stand is formed, the Divine Vision is sustained, and Los is able to find a ground on which to build Golgonooza.

A SEQUENTIAL CHAIN

The next steps in the sequential history of withdrawal are Albion's arrival at and then his passage through 'the Gate of Los' (35[39]: 11, E181). Albion is, at this point, still able to speak to Los, and Los is 'not yet infected with the Error & Illusion' (35[39]: 27, E181). Albion's steps backwards into withdrawal are met by a movement of his friends forwards. The four Zoas and 'the Twenty-four' come to his side, and 'the Divine Family' and 'Jesus the Saviour' appear (36[40]: 45-7, E182). This movement towards Albion nevertheless occurs within the space and time of withdrawal. To remain with Albion is to become a victim of his laws and to enter the world of Los and Enitharmon. Selsey's friendship with Albion, for example, induces him to allow himself 'to be call'd the son of Los the terrible vision' (36[40]: 52, E182), and Winchester permits his Emanations

> to be call'd Enitharmons daughters, and be born
> In vegetable mould: created by the Hammer and Loom
> In Bowlahoola & Allamanda where the Dead wail night & day.
> (36[40]: 55-7, E183)

At this point in sequential time Los is able to see the 'Twenty-eight' (the four Zoas and the twenty four cities) in 'Deaths dark caves ... in deep humiliation | And tortures of self condemnation' (37[41]: 23-5, E183), and he can see the Zoas

> Drinking the shuddering fears & loves of Albions Families
> Destroying by selfish affections the things that they most admire
> Drinking & eating, & pitying & weeping, as at a trajic scene.
> The soul drinks murder & revenge, & applauds its own holiness ...
> (37[41]: 27-30, E183)

but he cannot clearly see that there is no other possibility open to these beings. The Zoas cry:

> If we are wrathful Albion will destroy Jerusalem with rooty Groves
> If we are merciful, ourselves must suffer destruction on his Oaks!
> (38[43]: 8-9, E184)

Their confession of helplessness makes Los angry. Unlike the Zoas, Los is able to see that God will act only in their own persons; however, he is nevertheless unable to formulate an adequate alternative to the Zoas' passivity. His response at this point in the history of withdrawal is simply not to 'endure this thing!' (38[43]: 71, E186). He attempts, with the aid of the Zoas whom he has roused from inactivity with a passionate declamation of the world that is being brought into existence (38[43]: 12-79, E184-6), to carry Albion 'back | Against his will thro Los's Gate to Eden' (39[44]: 2-3, E186). One must admit that this response is better than the Zoas' passivity; however, to hope that kind violence will induce Albion to return is misguided. Los is attempting to bend Albion to *his* will, and the result is a further step into the world of withdrawal. The ocean which separates Albion from freedom now becomes

> a boundless Ocean bottomless,
> Of grey obscurity, filld with clouds & rocks & whirling waters
> And Albions Sons ascending & descending in the horrid Void.
>
> (39[44]: 15-17, E186)

All of the responses of the friends of Albion to his withdrawal have brought them closer to 'the Ulro'. They are now on the point of becoming 'Sexual, & . . . Created, and Vegetated, and Born' (39[44]: 22, E186); in other words, of being reduced to loss. 'Feeling the damps of death', the friends therefore,

> with one accord delegated Los
> Conjuring him by the Highest that he should Watch over them
> Till Jesus shall appear: & they gave their power to Los
> Naming him the Spirit of Prophecy, calling him Elijah
>
> Strucken with Albions disease they become what they behold;
> They assimilate with Albion in pity & compassion;
> Their Emanations return not: their Spectres rage in the Deep
> The Slumbers of Death came over them around the Couch of Death
> Before the Gate of Los & in the depths of Non Entity
> Among the Furnaces of Los: among the Oaks of Albion.
>
> (39[44]: 28-37, E187)

At this distance from relationship we hear the voice of Bath who, 'faint as the voice of the Dead in the House of Death' (39[44]: 44, E187), asks Oxford to try once more to reach Albion.[11] Albion, however, simply cannot hear either Oxford or Bath (40[45]: 35, E188).

All of the twenty-eight now embrace 'Eternal Death' and so enter the world of Los and Enitharmon, 'for Albions sake' (40[45]: 39, E188). Lincoln, Durham, and Carlisle become 'Councellors of Los,' Ely becomes a 'Scribe of Los,' Oxford faints (41[46]: 5, 6, 17, E188) and the world of Eternity is reduced to the confrontation between the righteousness of Albion and the righteousness, justice, and mercy of Los (pl. 42, E189-91). The penultimate moment in this history of withdrawal is the appearance of the 'Divine Vision' as a Sun (43[29]: 1, E191, which 'inclosd the Human Family' (43[29]: 27, E191). Humanity has now entered the world built by Los and Enitharmon. It remains only for Los to take his lamp and explore the inert mass that Albion has become, and for Albion to utter his last words.

## NARRATIVE AND VISION

The eclipse of the divine family by the sun of the fallen world brings Albion to a point of almost complete collapse. The only people to escape this catastrophe are 'the Emanation of Los & his | Spectre' (44[30]: 1-2, E193), who are able to survive because they collectively retain the shape of Albion in withdrawal: Albion's friends, family, valleys, cities, and fields have been reduced to the shape of loss that is held by this pair. They are called fugitives because, in order to complete his withdrawal, Albion must withdraw from the reality of his actions. His anger is, therefore, now directed against the reality held by these figures and, for this reason, against them as well. After giving an account of Albion's collapse, Enitharmon and the Spectre are embraced by Los (44[30]: 16-17, E193). This embrace completes the outline of the fallen world.

In a traditional narrative this development would indicate some kind of terminus from which readers could look back and survey the entire expanse of the history that has been narrated. They would retain this history as a consecutive series of appearances, and their ability to do this would perhaps generate a feeling that the story had been mastered or assimilated. There is, indeed, a temptation to do this in a discussion of the second chapter of *Jerusalem*, for the narrative that I have traced can be supplemented by a host of details which support the reader's sense of a fluid and engaging narrative progression. For example, Albion's regression into a state of withdrawal can be elaborated at some length. First he merely speaks 'from his secret seat' (28: 5, E174), but as he steps further and further away from relationship and is forced to spend more of his energy in retreating from the reality of his actions, he becomes more animated. He frowns 'in anger' (30[34]: 19, E176) and later flees 'more indignant' and 'revengeful' (33[37]: 12, E179), and on plate 42 he sends Hand

## 150  Visionary Construction

and Hyle to seize Los (42: 47, E190). The terminus of these increasingly desperate responses is the collapse described by the two fugitives and the announcement by Albion that 'Hope is banish'd from me' (47: 18, E196). Similarly, there is throughout the second chapter a slowly dawning realization of Albion's plight and a corresponding commitment to Albion on the part of the Divine Family. One can note a progression from the event in which a world of withdrawal appears, to Los's prophetic activity, and then to the gradual realization that if Albion is to be saved from Eternal death his friends and family must remain in relationship with him, even if the price of sustaining this bond is martyrdom and death. To concentrate on this progression alone would mean, however, that we were focusing our attention on ontic and not sequential time. Moreover, the terminus of this narrative is the occasion for a far-reaching disturbance to the history that we have been tracing. We can see the nature of this disturbance on plate 42.

The confrontation between Albion and Los which is described on this plate takes the reader further into sequential time. Anger and revenge have now turned into open combat. However, the account of this development concludes with lines which introduce a curious dislocation into the history that we have been following:

And Los drew his Seven Furnaces around Albions Altars
And as Albion built his frozen Altars, Los built the Mundane Shell,
In the Four Regions of Humanity East & West & North & South,
Till Norwood & Finchley & Blackheath & Hounslow, coverd the whole Earth.
This is the Net & Veil of Vala, among the Souls of the Dead.

(42: 77-81, E190-1)

The conjunction with which this passage begins suggests that the lines which follow will tell us of an act which is coterminous with, or consequent to, the conflict between Los and Albion. The second line of this passage, however, refers to the construction of Albion's Altars and the Mundane Shell, both of which are activities which began well before this point in the poem. In this chapter Albion began to build his Altars on the very first plate (28: 21, E174), while the construction of the Mundane Shell appeared to be complete in ontological time (13: 53-4, E157). Or, to take another example, 'The Net & Veil of Vala' cannot be reduced to something which can be built at a particular point in history, because it is the very shape of the temporal and spatial world which is held and given form by

Los. In these lines sequential time opens to reveal a relationship with a process which underlies all of time, with ontological time.

This opening is not, of course, limited to these lines. Throughout the second chapter the sequential narrative is continually subverted by lines which introduce a tension between the time of the 'vegetative Man' (in which the poem unfolds) and the time of vision. The binding of Reuben is, for example, not a simple event which occurs within a linear history, but one which helps to build the space in which this history is unfolded. We are told that Los rages for 'Sixty Winters' in the 'Divisions of Reuben,' and that this activity builds 'the Moon of Ulro, plank by plank & rib by rib' (32[36]: 4-5, E178). More dramatically, on plate 34[38], the poet affirms that all of the events of sequential time are present to him. When the Divine Family display the 'Divine Similitude' to Albion, Blake asserts that he sees 'them in the Vision of God upon my pleasant valleys' (34[38]: 28, E180). Similarly, London does not give himself for Albion at some point in the past, but in the moment in which Blake wakes from sleep:

So spoke London, immortal Guardian! I heard in Lambeths shades:
In Felpham I heard and saw the Visions of Albion
I write in South Molton Street, what I both see and hear
In regions of Humanity, in Londons opening streets.

(34[38]: 40-3, E180)

The history narrated in the second chapter opens again and again to ontological time in order to exhort the reader to adopt the stance of vision. As I have argued, Albion-in-withdrawal is given form as the six thousand year history of the fallen world. This means that he can be described as a single form (the subject of the first chapter) and as a six thousand year sequential history (the subject of the second, third, and fourth chapters). These two descriptions are not mutually exclusive. For example, when an individual experiences the death of a friend he enters a time of loss. This time can be described as a state and as a sequential history, for the entry into the ontological time of loss opens a sequential time which, beginning from the event of loss, traces a path from the struggle against recognizing the fact of loss, to anger at the person who has died, to acceptance of and then a final reconciliation to the fact of loss. The ontological time of loss and the sequential history of loss clearly emerge in relationship with each other. This series of stages and emotions maps the very shape and body of the time of loss.

Similarly, Albion-in-withdrawal exists along the dimensions of both ontological and sequential time. This is why in the first chapter of *Jerusalem* Golgonooza was described as a structure with a temporal extension. It contains 'all that has existed in the space of six thousand years' (13: 59, E157). However, in order to see this interrelationship we must see 'thro' the surface of the text; we must understand that *Jerusalem* is an 'Allegory addressed to the Intellectual Powers'.

A discussion of the first and second chapters of *Jerusalem* is therefore in the unenviable position of having to describe a relationship between two things which are both subject and object of any sentence which adequately describes the relationship between them. The sequential form of the book and, indeed, of all exposition and discourse, means that a vision of relationship can be described only against the grain of the language. It is, on the one hand, true (as I have maintained) that ontological time forms the space within which the events of sequential time are traced. At the end of the first chapter, for example, we see the intervals of sequential time vegetate 'Knot by | Knot, Day by Day, Night by Night' (24: 61-2, E170). However, on the other hand, it is also true that the events of sequential time form the space of ontological time. This is why there are events described in the second chapter which could radically alter the texture of ontological time. On plate 36, for example, the fall of Albion away from the time of loss and into 'the torments of Eternal Death' (25, E182) is averted only by an event in sequential history. Sequential time and ontological time emerge in relationship with each other; together they form the body of Albion-in-withdrawal.

To go no further than the recognition of the dependence of sequential and ontological time on each other is still to do scant justice to the extraordinary lines quoted above. The narrator asserts that the voice of London can be heard in his present, just as in lines twenty-seven and twenty-eight of the same plate he sees 'the Divine Family follow Albion' not in the distant past but in the 'Vision of God upon' his 'pleasant valleys'. These lines take the reader back to the beginning of the chapter and of the poem, to a moment of vision which does not need to be recollected because it can be found in the present. They suggest that all of the events of sequential time can be seen and heard (along with those of ontological time) 'in regions of Humanity, in Londons opening streets'. What Blake sees and hears in the present and in the past are the 'Visions of Albion' of which London and the sequential history of the second chapter are a part.

In the time and space of the 'Vegetative Man' we are being carried on in an ordered race of time (our reading of the poem, for example, has advanced almost to the half-way mark); however, in vision we wake with Blake (whether standing in 'the fields from Islington to Marybone', 'in London's opening streets', in Felpham, Lambeth, South Molton Street, the 'pleasant valleys', or in the unspecified location in the opening lines of the poem, to a vision of the whole man. This is because in vision the closed world of the self is punctured and, rather than seeing time as Lockean time, we are able to see it as the body of a single man: in vision we see and hear 'In regions of Humanity'. This body, although spatialized and temporalized by Los as the six thousand year extent of fallen history, is a moment in the eternal life of Albion, albeit a moment in which he has become enclosed. The attempt by Los and the Divine Family to follow Albion, although located in the second chapter of *Jerusalem*, is, in vision, coterminous with Christ's call to Albion at the beginning of the first chapter. Reading against the grain of the poem's onward movement (or, perhaps more accurately, seeing 'thro' the text) we find a single centre, a moment of vision in which we stand before the whole man.

There is, of course, no suggestion that the time and space opened by the vegetative man are not real. Instead, the poem is attempting to describe the complex interrelationship which exists between what I have called ontic, sequential, and ontological time. The reader is still standing with Blake in the moment of awakening, and before Jerusalem's gate; however, the vicissitudes of fallen perception mean that we must report this vision by foregrounding first one and then another of its aspects. In chapter one we saw the shape of ontological time; in chapter two begins a sequential history. In vision these two chapters and their subjects describe the shape of a single moment.

ONE HISTORY, OR TWO?

Perhaps the most severe disturbance to the time and space of the 'Vegetative Man' occurs as a result of the rearrangement of the second chapter in the third and fourth of the five copies of *Jerusalem* that Blake printed. In this second ordering the terminus of the history that we have been recounting becomes its beginning: the collapse of Albion, the flight of the Spectre and the Emanation to Los, and the exploration of Albion's interior begin the chapter. 'How can the terminus of a sequence be its beginning?', one is tempted to complain. It would seem a much less disturbing rearrangement if we could argue that Blake had changed his mind about the 'proper' ordering of the chapter, but the fifth extant copy printed by Blake reverts to the order of the first and the second. The second chapter of *Jerusalem* insists on turning on itself and making its ending its beginning. The problem is made even more intriguing by the appropriateness of *both* orderings. In reading copies A, C, and F, the escape of the fugitives from the débâcle of Albion's collapse and the subsequent solidification of his body is a very convincing conclusion to his withdrawal. However, when one turns to copies D and E, the same events seem to provide a very satisfying and, indeed, powerful beginning. This flexibility of beginning and end, far from being inexplicable or merely arbitrary, is a result of the relationship between ontological and sequential time.[12]

Albion's withdrawal from relationship immediately places him in the ontological time and space of withdrawal. He is therefore immediately placed inside a world of loss. The 'spiritual' or ontological form of this world is described in the expanding circles of the first chapter of *Jerusalem*. The shape or outer surface of this world is held by Enitharmon and the Spectre of Urthona.

From the perspective of the 'Vegetative Man', we view the world held by Enitharmon and the Spectre both as a physical space in which we exist and as a 'tide of Time' which flows from creation to apocalypse. But if the relationship between ontological time and sequential time (the relationship between the withdrawal of Albion from Christ and the six thousand year history in which this withdrawal is spatialized and temporalized) is one of mutual determination, then we can say that while it is true that the history recounted in the second chapter leads us to the world of loss, it is equally true to argue that this latter world precedes the movement of sequential time. In vision we glimpse this expanse of time and space as the body of a single being. In other words, *in vision* the world that is given outline in the embrace between the Spectre and Enitharmon can be seen to be present in the moment in which the history of withdrawal begins, and can be seen to be present in the moment in which that history is completed. This is why, for example, in copies A, B, and D the solidified and static form which Los explores at the end of the chapter is in fact present at the beginning. Before this solidified form has been discovered in the narrative, Albion describes himself as 'a barren Land' (29: 16, E174) and the narrator describes the condensation of the 'hills & valleys' of Albion's members into 'solid rocks'. Albion is covered with snow and ice (28: 13, E172) and locked within 'an endless labyrinth of woe' (28: 19, E172).

Within the constraints of story-telling within the fallen world, this relationship between ontological and sequential time generates two quite distinct narratives. In the first, sequential time builds and establishes the space of withdrawal; in the second, sequential history is traced within the terrain opened by Albion's withdrawal. For the poet who attempts to elaborate this vision within the fallen world, this produces something of a quandary. It would seem that he/she must choose between the first or the second arrangement, but to do so is to assimilate the world held by the Spectre and Enitharmon to the dimensions of ontic time. Blake's alternate orderings of the second chapter of *Jerusalem* (and the suggestion that even within individual copies the beginning and the end of the chapter can be reversed) is an attempt to overcome this dilemma. They suggest that the solidified body of Albion (the world held in Los's embrace of the Spectre and of Enitharmon) underlies all of time. The alternate orderings of the second chapter underline that *Jerusalem* is vision. The poem exhorts us to look 'thro' the linear surface of the poem to the moment of vision with which the poem begins.

Perhaps the most interesting example of Blake's 'Allegory' can be seen in the radical differences between the account of the relationship between Los and the Spectre given in the first chapter, and that given in the second. In the first chapter the Spectre is called a host of unpleasant names. In the second chapter he is described in a very different fashion. We are told, in fact, that Los's Spectre 'is named Urthona' (44[30]: 4, E193) and that he, with Enitharmon, is worthy of praise and capable of considerable insight:

> Being not irritated by insult bearing insulting benevolences
> They percieved that corporeal friends are spiritual enemies
> They saw the Sexual Religion in its embryon Uncircumcision
> And the Divine hand was upon them bearing them thro darkness
> Back safe to their Humanity as doves to their windows:
> Therefore the Sons of Eden praise Urthonas Spectre in Songs
> Because he kept the Divine Vision in time of trouble.
>
> (44[30]: 9-15, E193)

In ontological time we witnessed the painful division of the Spectre and Emanation from Los; yet in the second chapter the Spectre and Emanation seem to have a radically different aetiology and, rather than dividing from Los, they are embraced and taken in by him (44[30]: 16-17, E193). We will consider the question of aetiology first.[13]

On plate 44 the Spectre is called 'Urthonas Spectre' (44[30]: 14, E193) as well as Los's Spectre (44[30]: 1-2, E193). Enitharmon is described as the Emanation of Los (44[30]: 1, E193); however, to the extent that Los is himself Urthona in the state of loss, she quite clearly bears some relationship to this prelapsarian figure. As in earlier poems, Enitharmon and the Spectre can therefore be said to trace their line of descent back to a fallen and an unfallen Zoa.

In the first chapter of *Jerusalem* we see the ontological time and shape of the entire fallen world. From this perspective the actual fall of the Spectre, Los, and Enitharmon from Urthona is clearly of no importance. Within the fallen world what is of paramount importance is the division of the Spectre and Enitharmon from Los. In the second chapter the situation is very different, for we read a sequential account of the Fall. As a result we see Urthona enter the modality of Los, and the Spectre and Enitharmon approach and then enter the bosom of Los. From the perspective of sequential time we can see that 'the Sons of Eden praise Urthonas Spectre in Songs' because he retains the shape of Albion-in-withdrawal (he holds before Albion the shape of Eternity—life-in-renewal with the Saviour) and in this way keeps 'the Divine Vision in time of Trouble'. Unlike the sons of Albion he is 'not irritated by insult' and is able to bear 'insulting benevolences' because he is the shape of Albion's withdrawal. (The passage quoted above in fact suggests that the Spectre and the Emanation are themselves 'bearing insulting benevolences'.) They are also able to see 'that corporeal friends are spiritual enemies' because although Albion's actions give form to their world, he is nevertheless opposed to their existence. They must become fugitives lest they also fall victim to his laws and are assimilated.

The saving work of the Spectre does not mean that he is no longer a deadly threat to Los. He is still Los's 'Pride & Self-righteousness' because the Spectre and the Emanation form the outline of Los's achievements, his prophetic art. There is therefore the temptation for Los to remain within the world that he has created rather than open again and again to Albion. Los must embrace this saving demon if he is to live at all, suffer the continual division of the Spectre from his side and, at the same time, bend the Spectre to his will in an attempt to force him to retain the form of his openness to Albion-in-withdrawal. We can therefore say that the division recounted in the first chapter presumes the embrace and unification which is described in the second. The narrative of the second chapter returns once again to its beginning and a circle is formed in which ontological and sequential time can be seen as the shape of a single moment. The fallen world is composed of both division and embrace.[14] The present, the point at which the linear narrative of the second chapter now arrives, is forged in the space between these two realities.

# 5. The Geography of the Present

> See, I have set before thee this day life and good, and death and evil ... I call heaven and earth to record this day against you, *that* I have set before you life and death, blessing and cursing: therefore choose life, that both thou and thy seed may live.
>
> Deut. 30: 15, 19.

## ALL AND NOTHING

We normally think of the present as a moment of time which is pressed between the competing claims of the past and future. The present in this sense can be simply defined as the *now*; however, its position at the point of fracture between the continents of what has been and what is to come already prefigures the difficulty experienced in any attempt to grasp this fleeting phantom. We glance at our watch and observe that it is *now* fifteen minutes past eleven, but even as it is announced this *now* has been displaced by another, it has vanished in the stream of time. In fact, as Heidegger points out, when we talk of the *now* we mean not one but a series of such moments, each self-contained and separate from the others, which are extended in a sequential chain.[1] It is the sequence of such moments which makes up Newtonian or Lockean time.

The present can, however, be understood in a second sense, and one which is at the very least equi-primordial with the first. In this second understanding the present is taken to mean simply that which is present. The sun, the moon, the sky, Los, Albion, London and, indeed, even our sense of time as a progression of *nows*, are all present. The present is a *pastiche* or a chorus of different presences, a manifold of beings who are all turned towards us and are all soliciting our attention. Literary forms such as narrative are strikingly inadequate to this time, for there is no perspective from which this present could be ordered without fragmenting and diminishing what presents itself as a seamless totality.

The present as the *now* is held and structured by the individual. In this second present, however, the organizing principle is displaced from the individual to the world which precedes and supports him. The closest approximation that we have to this time is that offered by dance. In watching a dance we observe a manifold of dancers who all solicit our attention. We do not extract from this multiplicity and watch one figure to the exclusion of all others; instead, the dance is constituted in the relationship between the dancers and their various appeals. It is true, of course, that the steps of the dance unfold in serial progression; however, it is not this sequence in itself which forms the totality of the dance. When we respond to dance we perceive it as a rhythmic whole, a body, in which each dancer and each step have their appropriate weight. It is the interconnection and interpenetration of steps and of dancers that produces the experience which is present to us.[2]

It would, however, be wrong to choose too quickly between these different presents. Even in this brief description it is clear that dance, even as it foregrounds the relationships which hold between the various dancers and their movements, depends upon a sequential progression in order to be elaborated. The present in this sense has its own direction and its own canny logic which give it a particular trajectory and a movement with respect to the past and the future. Similarly, the evanescent *now* suggests, although it is not foregrounded, a dance of presences. The oscillation between these two poles, and the tension between them, is characteristic of the present in which we live. We live in a moment which is always on the verge of vanishing and yet which, at certain times, can almost overwhelm us with the richness and clarity of its manifold appeals. In the first understanding we have a wheel turning another wheel, one present inevitably bringing a second into our purview. In the second we have a series of interlocking presences (depicted by Blake on plate 22), which all face and solicit the reader's attention. We are caught in a present which is on the one hand established by our reasoning memory and yet which is, on the other hand, the site of all encounters with others. The third chapter of *Jerusalem* takes us into this contradictory realm.

RAHAB AND LOS: WITHDRAWAL AND FRAGMENTATION

In the previous chapter each plate was linked to the next by syntax and by a largely uninterrupted narrative progression. The illuminations were similarly woven into this progression. The first ten plates of the third chapter of *Jerusalem* are by contrast broken into discrete elements. The reader finds, for example, that narrative and syntactical links between these elements are either non-existent or slight and that the illuminations are to some extent freed from the cloth of the text. The poem now moves with the logic of dance or music and for this reason the individual dancers are clearly delineated.

The first and, from her perspective, the dominating feature of the present is 'Vala dressed as Rahab',[3] who appears in the upper half of plate 53. From the vantage point of her throne, this figure surveys the entire extent of the third chapter. Vala is, of course, a fitting conclusion to the history narrated in the previous chapter, for in withdrawing from relationship Albion enters a world in which he is dominated by the passive power.

The history which results in the reign of Vala/Rahab is also a history of the various attempts to recall Albion. The lower half of the plate therefore goes on to detail the result in the present of this redemptive history. It is interesting to observe the subtle transmutation that occurs to this history as it arrives at this plate. The process of withdrawal has now become a fact which is simply and even brutally present. Albion is no longer engaged in the process of withdrawal; he has withdrawn and therefore Los now weeps 'vehemently' over his fate (53: 2, E202). In the previous chapter Los had not yet been 'infected with the Error & Illusion' (35[39]: 27, E181). On this plate 'the roots of Albions Tree' have 'enterd the Soul of Los' (53: 4, E202). Similarly, the 'Twentyfour Friends of Albion' and the 'awful Four' (53: 22, E203) are now lying on their couches and the 'Giant forms' of 'the Children of Los' are 'time after time' condensed into 'Nations & Peoples & Tongues' (53: 7-8, E202). The work of Los and the sufferings of Albion's friends now open the space of Generation (53: 27-8, E203). In the present we therefore see, ranged against the power and sovereignty of Rahab, the saving work and the sufferings of Los. This first element of the dance therefore pits Rahab against Los; the state of withdrawal which Albion has entered is juxtaposed with the form established by Los:

> Here on the banks of the Thames, Los builded Golgonooza,
> Outside of the Gates of the Human Heart, beneath Beulah
> In the midst of the rocks of the Altars of Albion. In fears
> He builded it, in rage & in fury. It is the Spiritual Fourfold
> London: continually building & continually decaying desolate!
>
> (53: 15-19, E203)

This fundamental antagonism between Los and Rahab does not appear in a vacuum. The site of their antagonism is, of course, the inert body of the fallen man, which is located at the nadir of his fall from Eternity. The body and history of the fallen man underlie, and are therefore part of, what is present. They are, however, a much less dominating or intense presence than Los and Rahab. The history of the Fall and the condition of Albion are for this reason described in extraordinary brevity. This rather complex element is detailed in the following plate.

In the first five lines of plate 54 we glimpse the Eternity from which Albion fell. In the next three lines the fact of Albion's fall is narrated. The poem then takes another six lines to describe Albion's present condition:

> The silent broodings of deadly revenge springing from the
> All powerful parental affection, fills Albion from head to foot
> Seeing his Sons assimilate with Luvah, bound in the bonds
> Of spiritual Hate, from which springs Sexual Love as iron chains:
> He tosses like a cloud outstretchd among Jerusalems Ruins
> Which overspread all the Earth, he groans among his ruind porches.
>
> (54: 9-14, E203)

Each of these passages is separated from its neighbours by double spacing. The second and third are also divided by a line of birds which seem to separate Eternity and the Fall from the fallen condition. The first and the third are in the present tense because they are present realities, while the second is narrated in the past tense because it is a fact which has occurred and is therefore present in the fallen world in the modality of memory. The illumination which follows this tripartite division summarizes Albion's condition. He has rolled himself into a globe and can no longer see the myriads of Eternity which surround him. Eternity and Albion are separated by the fact of enclosure.

The strong rectangular design and firm defining lines of the illumination entitled 'This World' seem to check the descent from Eternity to the fallen world. In the lines which follow, Albion does not fall into non-entity; instead we see the internal conflicts which characterize a world in which the individual is 'bound in the bonds | Of spiritual Hate, from which springs Sexual Love as iron chains' (54: 11-12, E203). In the lines immediately beneath this design we see the Spectre rise over Albion and hear his claims to be God. Albion responds to his presumption by attempting to draw England back into his bosom and away from the power of the Spectre. This cannot be done because in withdrawal his Emanation is continually separating from him. As a result his Emanation becomes the long Serpent of the temporally extended fallen world. Under these lines, in the lowest portion of the plate, we see Albion's four Zoas, who are apparently closed within the ground. Lines 15–32 and the illumination of the Zoas therefore provide the reader with an anatomy of the state of withdrawal that Albion has reached. At the same time these final elements take part in a movement which threatens to breach the equilibrium established by 'This World' and which hopes to draw Eternity itself into its orbit.

The domination of Albion by the Spectre implies a movement which proceeds from the bottom of the page to the top, from the fragmentation of Albion depicted at the bottom of the plate and the consequent assumption of power by the Spectre, to the outline of 'This World'. The globe in which Reason, Desire, Pity, and Wrath have been separated from each other is in fact the very shape of the present and of the world that is held by the Spectre. The globe forms the apex of a triangle whose feet stand in the bottom corners of the plate; it forms the uppermost point of a movement which threatens to push aside the myriads of Eternity and assimilate what is at this moment out of its reach: the realities which exist beyond the line of birds, within the space of Eternity. The regression of Albion from Eternity is therefore met by the ascent of the Spectre; his fragmentation is coterminous with the retaining work of the reasoning memory. 'This World', the present in which we all exist, stands at the intersection of this regression and this ascent. The pasts which lead to this point are contained in the present in the same way that a comet retains a link with the fiery tail which marks the path back from the comet to the sun. It is important to note that 'This World' is also the site of the conflict between Los and Rahab which was introduced in the previous plate. At this point in the dance we can see the present as a struggle between these two figures which is enacted at the point where Albion's regression and the Spectre's ascent intersect.

THE INHABITANTS OF ETERNITY AND THE FALL

On the following plate the poem's perspective changes quite abruptly and the reader's attention is directed to the response of 'those who disregard all Mortal Things' (55: 1, E204) to the fall of Albion. From within the fallen world it is true that Albion's fall appears to have always already occurred and therefore, from this perspective, that a response that was contemporaneous with this event could not be an element in the present. In previous chapters, however, I have argued that the six thousand years of fallen history defines the shape of Albion-in-withdrawal. For the inhabitants of Eternity the fall of

Albion (and therefore the full extent of fallen history) is the *moment* (in our time, six thousand years long) of Albion's withdrawal. The response of these beings to Albion's withdrawal is therefore present to each moment of fallen history.

'Those who disregard all Mortal Things' are the inhabitants of Eden rather than Beulah. It is a sign of the extraordinary nature of Albion's withdrawal that even these beings are in danger of being drawn after him. The sight of 'a Mighty-One | Among the Flowers of Beulah still retain his awful strength' (55: 1-2, E204) is so disturbing that a number check their movements and are tempted to descend and see what has occurred (55: 3-5, E204). To follow Albion is, as we have seen, to become enclosed in the fallen world. Even to look at Albion-in-withdrawal necessitates a moderation of the Eternals' flames. This is the case put forward by a second group who argue that the inhabitants of Eden should have nothing 'to do with the Dead' (55: 6, E204). This same group then goes on to argue that the 'Veil which Satan puts between Eve & Adam' (55: 11, E204) has been forbidden by 'the Eternal Man'. In the fallen world this kind of argument would generally be resolved by discussion and then rational agreement that one or other of the positions was correct. In Eden a third group suggests that a collective decision be reached by allowing 'him who only Is' to make a decision (55: 17-18, E204).

This adjudication takes the form of 'Mental Warfare' in the course of which these beings allow the very texture of their world to be thrown into question, in the apparent belief that in this openness truth will appear. The result of this warfare is not unanimity and certainly not dissolution in a general will. Nor is it a simple acceptance of one position. Instead, the inhabitants of Eden reach a majority decision which is related to and yet transcends both the desire to see 'these changes' in Albion and the knowledge that they must in some way keep themselves separate from Albion's vortex. They decide on a 'Separation', but one which keeps open the possibility of a return, by Albion, to Eternity and, at the same time, ensures that the divine will be able to reach into the depths of hell.

The inhabitants of Eden enact this decision by preserving 'the Human Organs . . . in their perfect Integrity' (55: 36, E205). This preservation parallels the formation of 'the Two Limits, Satan and Adam, | In Albions bosom' (31[35]: 1-2, E177); it establishes a world which has a 'limit of Opakeness, and a limit of Contraction', but no 'Limit of Expansion!' and 'no Limit of Translucence' (42: 29, 35, E189). The formation of these limits is an event which can be said to occur within each moment of history (and therefore within the present) because it is an act carried out from Eternity. The inhabitants of Eden respond to Albion as a 'whole man'; they are not themselves enclosed within the limits they establish or lost within the 'tide of Time'. This can be seen in the next step that is taken by these figures.

This work of preservation is the necessary precondition for the naming of the 'Seven Eyes of God'. The 'Eyes of God' define a progression which traverses the distance between the worms and the gods, from Lucifer to Jesus; they therefore provide the means by which time and Eternity can meet again. All of these eyes are present to the inhabitants of Eden: 'Lucifer, Molech, Elohim, Shadai, Pahad, Jehovah, Jesus' (55: 32, E205), all appear before their eyes. It is only the eighth eye, the one which permits Albion to re-enter Eternity, that remains hidden in Albion's forests. The Edenic Assembly have provided limits to Albion's fall, but until he returns they can only see him as an inert globe. For those of us caught in the 'tide of Time', Albion is elongated into a linear history; for the inhabitants of Eden he appears as the globe depicted on the previous plate. Fallen history is therefore intersected by an act of creation which gives it form. As a result, each moment of the expanse which stretches from Lucifer to Jesus is charged with an extraordinary surplus and excess.

The decision by 'those who disregard all Mortal things' to set limits to the Fall is an important event; however, by itself it is of no avail. The inhabitants of Eden are drawing a line around Albion and in this way attempting to give him definition, but the line of identity exists only within relationship and Albion is continually withdrawing from any such thing. It is as if one side of a line which we had drawn was being continually erased. Such a procedure would, of course, even if the erasure proceeded in extraordinarily small increments, quickly reduce the line to nothingness. The Eternals need a person within the fallen world who is able to give Albion form. Plate 55 therefore concludes with the question of 'Who will go forth for us! & Who shall we send before our face?' (55: 69, E205).

In moving from this plate to the next there is a sudden and almost dizzy change of perspective. Rather than standing with the Eternals as they survey the expanse of Albion-in-withdrawal, we now enter the heat of a particular struggle in a single moment of fallen time. The dislocation caused by this transition is heightened by the clear denomination of the second plate as a response to the former. The plates face each other, both lack all but marginal illumination, and the first word of the second locates it in the temporal moment immediately following the Edenic call. This is, of course, not to suggest that this is the only moment in fallen time in which the inhabitants of Eden are answered. The Edenic call is to each moment of fallen time. In the midst of Albion's fall, in the heart of the present, we can therefore always hear a voice calling to us to respond. The cry for a being to 'go forth for us!' is a constant element in the fallen world; it is our response which must rise again and again to meet it.

The particular moment in which we observe Los's response to the Edenic Assembly is the present, the present of Blake's own day. The principal antagonists in this time are the Deists, to whom the third chapter of *Jerusalem* is addressed. The motivating forces behind this time and religion are the female powers, the Daughters of Albion in particular, who give substance to the form which is the ground for 'Natural Religion', 'Natural Philosophy', and 'Natural Morality'. This gives us a further means of locating the present of this chapter,[4] for the female powers achieve supremacy when Albion's fall is completed and the power of the Spectre is assured.

To briefly recount the dynamic that is at work here: in the process of withdrawal it is initially the Spectre who overtly struggles with the active power and with Los. As this struggle proceeds a world is precipitated in which the active power is enclosed. This universe is held in the hermaphroditic embrace between the Spectre and the Emanation. When this process begins it appears that it is the Spectre who is in control; however, to the extent that he gains power over Albion it is the Daughters that achieve supremacy. The Spectre's power is limited to the retention and manipulation of what is and, therefore, as the Fall proceeds it appears that the power that retains the world is himself determined by what he has retained. The female gains in power to the precise extent that the Spectre is able to gain dominion over the active power. In the third chapter we now stand with Los in a world where the female has power over the male from cradle to grave (56: 3–4, E206): it is the physical and passive form of the world which now determines the active power:

> This World is all a Cradle for the erred wandering Phantom:
> Rock'd by Year, Month, Day & Hour; and every two Moments
> Between, dwells a Daughter of Beulah, to feed the Human
> Vegetable.
>
> (56: 8–10, E206)

From the perspective of the figures who weave the cradle of the natural world and the flesh of the body, their work encloses nothing more than a 'Worm' and a 'Clod of Clay'. When Los asks them where the creatures which they have now 'enwoven with so much tears & care' (56: 23, E206) were found, they can recollect no more than a sense of loss:

> O it was lost for ever! and we found it not: it came
> And wept at our wintry Door: Look! look! behold! Gwendolen
> Is become a Clod of Clay! Merlin is a Worm of the Valley!
>
> (56: 26-8, E206)

In this present, Los's response to the Edenic assembly is realized as a complex struggle against the force of enclosure represented by the Daughters of Albion. This is evocatively described as a dialectic between the songs and utterances of Los and those of the Daughters. Los cannot simply reject the Daughters for the form of the fallen world is a 'Cradle' and a 'Garment' for 'the Human Vegetable'. Instead, he adopts a relationship to them which is in many ways similar to the one he holds with his Spectre. After the first interchange Los asserts that the Daughters must obey his command. The form of the fallen world holds the form of Albion-in-withdrawal; it is therefore a crucial component in the work of Albion's watchman (56: 31, E206).

The Daughters are less than eager to comply with Los's wishes. They reply by telling him that they

> tremble at the light therefore: hiding fearful
> The Divine Vision with Curtain & Veil & fleshly Tabernacle.
>
> (56: 39-40, E206)

The Daughters tremble because to obey Los's dictate is to open the possibility that Albion will return. They realize, like Enitharmon at the end of the fourth chapter, that the regeneration of the active power will radically alter the world in which they gain their power. Los replies to their response 'swift as the rattling thunder upon the mountains':

> Look back into the Church Paul! Look! Three Women around
> The Cross! O Albion why didst thou a Female Will Create?
>
> (56: 42-3, E206)

There are at least three ways of reading the exhortation in line 42. The Church Paul, as Bloom notes, is one of the churches in the cycle from Adam to Luther. However, as Damon notes, the same phrase could refer to St Paul's in London[5] and the exhortation could be addressed to all those present in this city. Equally plausible is the possibility that the phrase is directed to Paul himself, who is being exhorted to look back into the Christian church which he is helping to found. There is, in fact, no real need to choose between these possibilities. Whether Los is addressing the historical Paul, the inhabitants of London and England, or the beings who live in the church which Blake called Paul, the import of Los's cry is the same. Los is attempting to draw our attention to the forces of enclosure which are always already turning our visions of others into dogma. Paul and the church called Paul are archetypal examples of the enclosure that invariably follows a particular appearance of the divine. The same process can, of course, be found in the London of Blake's (or our own) day. It is this call, and the movement away from enclosure and towards relationship that it implies, which forms the substance of Los's response to the call of 'those who disregard all Mortal Things'. It is in this prophetic work of Los—in his struggle with the Daughters and his attempt to make them obey his dictate—that the call for a being who 'will go forth for us' is answered.

The relationships between the presences delineated in the first four plates of this chapter are both intimate and complex. The opposition between Los and Rahab, which stands as the terminus of the history recounted in the second chapter, exists at the point of intersection between the fall of Albion into withdrawal and the Spectre's ascent to power. The point of intersection, 'This World', is itself defined by the response of 'those who disregard all Mortal Things' to Albion's withdrawal and Los's response to their call. There is, however, still one important strand of the present which has not entered the dance.

In the previous chapter we observed the process in which Albion's family and friends gave their lives for him. Their martyrdom resulted in the formation of a ground for fallen life. It is therefore not surprising that the fifth plate of this chapter goes on to detail the presence of this ground in the time of Deism. The cities of 'Bath & Canterbury & York & Edinburgh' still raise their voices, but we can now no longer hear what they are saying. In the present their eloquence has been drowned by the surging waters of the Atlantic Ocean, which separates Albion from freedom (America). The Ocean weeps over the death of his own children (57: 5-6, E207).[6] The voices of Albion's friends have not been heeded and for this reason their now muted cry is juxtaposed with a brief account of the Fall and of the 'Wonder' experienced by 'all in Eternity!' as 'the Divine Vision' opens 'The Center into an Expanse' (57: 12-18, E207).

The illumination upon which the text for this plate has been superimposed, however, subtly contradicts the completeness (if not the accuracy) of this description. The voices of the friends of Albion have, indeed, been muted, but the gift of their lives has turned the rocky globe of destiny (which we saw on plate 57) into a 'soft green earth with cities and churches'[7] and on this ground, thanks to the work of Los, the Daughters of Albion have become the Daughters of Los, and here they are able to create a world of generation.

Taken together, these presences and the relationships which hold between them form a map which outlines the geography of the present. The time which is delineated in this way is, at first, strangely unfamiliar, because we are all accustomed to describing the present in terms of what is corporeally present; but to limit ourselves to this is to confine ourselves within the world defined by Vala. In these plates Blake has shifted the locus of his description from the material facts of the present to the *acts, events,* and *relationships* which together form the dance and the place in which the natural, material world is found. To dwell in the present described in the first plates is to experience the dance between Los, Rahab, Albion, the Spectre, 'those who disregard all Mortal things' and the friends of Albion. Taken together the relationships between these beings define the axes along which fallen life is elaborated. It now remains for the poem to describe the minute particulars of the present which opens between these axes.

THE SHAPE OF THE PRESENT

The next two plates contain a series of short descriptions, definitions and illuminations which fill in our picture of the present. In most cases the nature of the terrain which is described can be inferred from the axes which have been established in the previous plates. We see, for example, the 'Two Contraries War against each other in fury & blood' (58: 15, E207); 'The Daughters of Albion. divide & unite in jealousy & cruelty' (58: 5, E207); 'The Inhabitants of Albion' as 'their Brain' is 'cut round beneath the temples' (58: 6-7, E207); and Los as he produces 'a World of Generation from the World of Death' (58: 18, E207).

The fallen world in which we live is 'a Mighty Temple' (58: 22, E207) and an 'awful Building' (58: 21, E207) which, thanks to the efforts of Los, delivers Albion from nonentity. The entire expanse of the fallen world that opens between the axes described on previous plates can therefore be described in relation to Los:

> China & India & Siberia are his temples for entertainment
> Poland & Russia & Sweden, his soft retired chambers
> France & Spain & Italy & Denmark & Holland & Germany
> Are the temples among his pillars. Britain is Los's Forge;
> America North & South are his baths of living waters.
>
> (58: 39-43, E208)

However, earlier in this plate we are told that Urizen directs the construction of this 'awful Building' and that he is the person delivering Form out of confusion' (58: 21, 22, E207). The passage quoted above continues with the assertion that Los's world, the world of the present, is 'the Ancient World of Urizen in the Satanic Void' (58: 44, E208). Moreover, this same passage describes the world of generation which is created from the body of death by Los as a production which emerges from out of the disintegration of the Zoas and as a result of the efforts of the Spectres of Albion to 'Rear their dark Rocks among the Stars of God':

> The Four Zoa's rush around on all sides in dire ruin
> Furious in pride of Selfhood the terrible Spectres of Albion
> Rear their dark Rocks among the Stars of God: stupendous
> Works! A World of Generation continually Creating; out of
> The Hermaphroditic Satanic World of rocky destiny.
>
> (58: 47-51, E208)

The vision of ontological time described in the first chapter and the inclusion of Rahab and Albion-in-withdrawal amongst the elements in the opening plates of this chapter have, of course, to a certain extent prepared us for this characterization of the present. The shape of the fallen world is formed in the relationship between Los and the fallen Albion. On the one hand Los gives form to Albion; on the other hand it is also true that Albion brings Los (loss) into being. The first chapter, as we have argued, was therefore structured around the interaction between Los, Enitharmon, and the Spectre on the one hand, and Albion, Vala, and Jerusalem on the other. The structure of this passage in fact reflects the interrelationship between these two poles of the fallen world quite closely. It moves from

## 170   Visionary Construction

the assertion that Urizen is architect of the 'Mighty Temple' to a characterization of the fallen world as a building centred on Los. It then suggests that the fallen world belongs to Urizen and that the Spectres of Albion have a part in producing it. Finally it swings back to Los and we see that he has produced his world from Albion's withdrawal:

> For the Veil of Vala which Albion cast into the Atlantic Deep
> To catch the Souls of the Dead: began to Vegetate & Petrify
> Around the Earth of Albion. among the Roots of his Tree
> This Los formed into the Gates & mighty Wall, between the Oak
> Of Weeping & the Palm of Suffering beneath Albions Tomb.
> 
> (59: 2-6, E208)

Nevertheless, despite the prefiguration of this passage by earlier passages in the poem, what remains surprising is the prominence of Urizen and the characterization of the fallen world as his 'Ancient World'. The relationship between Los and Urizen which is suggested by these lines is reminiscent of the account in *The Four Zoas* of the fall of the Zoas to a universe created by Los and Enitharmon. It is almost as if we have entered a different poem; or as if the leaning tower of Pisa were to be found in Spain rather than Italy. Plate 59 goes on to make this connection with *The Four Zoas* even more explicit. We now learn that Verulam, London, York, and Edinburgh are the 'English names' of the four Zoas (59: 14, E208) and we read a brief précis of the history recounted in the earlier poem:

> But when Luvah assumed the World of Urizen Southward
> And Albion was slain upon his Mountains & in his Tent.
> All fell towards the Center, sinking downwards in dire ruin,
> In the South remains a burning Fire: in the East. a Void
> In the West, a World of raging Waters: in the North; solid Darkness
> Unfathomable without end: but in the midst of these
> Is Built eternally the sublime Universe of Los & Enitharmon.
> 
> (59: 15-21, E208-9)

This history contrasts strangely with the account of the four Zoas that is given in the second chapter of *Jerusalem*. It brings us to the same world encountered towards the end of the sixth Night of *The Four Zoas*, where the Zoas cast forth their 'monstrous births' (74: 27, E351) around the world of Los and Enitharmon.

The narrative of *The Four Zoas* is a dream of nine Nights. It is, therefore, a poem which attempts to describe the Fall, the fallen world, and the moment of regeneration from the perspective of sleep. By contrast, *Jerusalem* begins with and is centred in a moment of vision and awakening. This does not mean that the world of sleep and the world of awakening are radically incommensurate, for both sleep and awakening are possibilities within the time of Los. Although it is beyond the scope of this essay to argue this point in detail, we can therefore say that just as the moment of awakening can be glimpsed in *The Four Zoas*, so too the history narrated within that earlier poem can be glimpsed in the moment of vision. The description in *Jerusalem* of the terrain which opens up along the axes of the present therefore includes the trace of a narrative which if it were to be elaborated (by falling to sleep rather than waking) would completely disrupt the poem. For the moment this narrative remains in the background and the poem completes its description of the minute particulars of the present:

> Other Daughters of Los, labouring at Looms less fine
> Create the Silk-worm & the Spider & the Catterpiller
> To assist in their most grievous work of pity & compassion
> And others Create the wooly Lamb & the downy Fowl
> To assist in the work: the Lamb bleats: the Sea-fowl cries
> Men understand not the distress & the labour & sorrow
> That in the Interior Worlds is carried on in fear & trembling
> Weaving the shuddring fears & loves of Albions Families.
>
> (59: 45–52, E209)

With the description of the work undertaken by the daughters of Los, the first movement of the third chapter is almost complete. We stand within, and indeed are part of, a fabric woven out of a manifold of presences and relationships.

VISION

In the preceding plates the poem seemed to check its own movement by breaking into a series of relatively short definitions and descriptions. The voices which characterized the earlier plates of this chapter are resolved into the even voice of the narrator, whose attention moves across the surface design of the fabric which is woven by the Daughters of Los. It is almost as if there were a lull in the poem. This slowing of pace is, however, the prelude for an expansion, almost an explosion, of voice, and for the climax of this section of the third chapter. In the final element of the dance of the present three plates are drawn together and voices other than the narrator's now almost completely predominate. We hear the voices of 'the

Slaves' singing 'the Song of the Lamb ... in evening time' (60: 38, E210); the call of Jerusalem and the response to her call by Christ; and the voices of Mary, Joseph, and an Angel. So powerful is this irruption of voice and vision that the fabric which has been described in the preceding plates now seems to take a step backwards and become the background for these voices; it now defines the space in which they resonate. Within the present of the fallen world we are now confronted with voices which give expression to the emotions of both suffering and hope.

Jerusalem is 'closd in the Dungeons of Babylon' (60: 39, E210) where she sits at

> the Mills, her hair unbound her feet naked
> Cut with the flints: her tears run down, her reason grows like
> The Wheel of Hand. incessant turning day & night without rest
> Insane she raves upon the winds hoarse, inarticulate.
>
> (60: 41–4, E210)

Nevertheless, even from this position she is able to see the form of Christ and hear his voice (60: 50-1, E211):

> For thou also sufferest with me altho I behold thee not;
> And altho I sin & blaspheme thy holy name, thou pitiest me;
> Because thou knowest I am deluded by the turning mills.
> And by these visions of pity & love because of Albions death.
>
> (60: 61–4, E211)

Christ responds to her affirmation by drawing her attention to the figures of 'Joseph & Mary', who appear in 'the Visions of Elohim Jehovah' (61: 1, E211). Jehovah is a type of the Urizenic god, while the Elohim are associated with the creation of this world and therefore with Los. We can therefore say that Christ is drawing her attention to something which is perceived within the very fabric of the fallen world, a possibility which appears within the world formed by Los and Urizen. Jerusalem does not see Mary and Joseph in the joy of the annunciation, or in rapt wonder at the mystery of a virgin birth, but in the midst of an argument which follows on from Mary's infidelity. Joseph is at first angry, but this anger subsides into forgiveness:

Ah my Mary: said Joseph: weeping over & embracing her closely in
His arms: Doth he forgive Jerusalem & not exact Purity from her who is
Polluted. I heard his voice in my sleep & his Angel in my dream:
Saying, Doth Jehovah Forgive a Debt only on condition that it shall
Be Payed? Doth he Forgive Pollution only on conditions of Purity
That Debt is not Forgiven! That Pollution is not Forgiven

Such is the Forgiveness of the Gods, the Moral Virtues of the
Heathen, whose tender Mercies are Cruelty. But Jehovahs Salvation
Is without Money & without Price, in the Continual Forgiveness of Sins
In the Perpetual Mutual Sacrifice in Great Eternity! for behold!
There is none that liveth & Sinneth not! And this is the Covenant
Of Jehovah: If you Forgive one another, so shall Jehovah Forgive You:
That He Himself may Dwell among You. Fear not then to take
To thee Mary thy Wife, for she is with Child by the Holy Ghost.

(61: 14-27, E211-12)

Melanie Bandy argues that we should understand the Holy Ghost to be the libidinal energy which belongs to Mary. She writes that 'In this act, because she followed her energies, Mary was truly with child by the Holy Ghost.'[8] In Blake's œuvre, however, the Holy Ghost is never simply associated with energy. In the preface to the fourth chapter of *Jerusalem*—a preface which exhorts us 'to abstain from fleshly desires that we may lose no time from the Work of the Lord'—Blake associates the Holy Spirit with 'an Intellectual Fountain' (E231), and on plate 91 Los informs us that the 'Genius' of each man 'is the Holy Ghost in Man' (91: 9, E251). In Blake's annotations to Thornton we read that in Heaven the Holy Ghost is called by the name of Jesus (E668).

The whole thrust of this passage is not that Mary has done nothing wrong and that therefore there is no need for forgiveness, but that from Joseph's perspective she is 'impure'. It matters little whether one believes that adultery is a sin or not. The point at issue here is that, for Joseph, Mary has sinned against the laws that he has adopted. If Mary had not sinned, then there would clearly be no need to speak to Joseph of forgiveness. The assertion, by the Angel, that Mary is with child by the Holy Spirit in fact follows on from the argument that 'Jehovahs Salvation | Is . . . in the continual Forgiveness of sins' and from the contention that the covenant that Jehovah makes with the fallen world is 'If you Forgive one-another, so shall Jehovah Forgive You.' It is, as I have argued in my discussion of *Milton*, in the time of embrace (and therefore forgiveness) that the closed world of the self is punctured and one attains an openness in which God can dwell. This is nothing less than the fissure in which—as we have seen in *Milton*—Christ is born into the fallen world. It is in this sense that it is true to say that Mary is 'with Child by the Holy Ghost' (61: 27, E212). It is in Joseph's forgiveness of Mary (and one could say, Mary's forgiveness of Joseph for his anger) that the child born of the adulterous woman becomes the Christ child. In the final line of the above passage, 'then' is the crucial word. Jehovah's covenant means that wherever there is forgiveness of sins God will dwell amongst us and Christ will be born into the fallen world.

The result of Joseph's forgiveness is a reintegration of male and female powers: he is no longer closed within a world formed by a fixed morality and in which his Emanation is an elusive object of desire; instead, Mary becomes a world which he is able to embrace:

> Then Mary burst forth into a Song! she flowed like a River of Many Streams in the arms of Joseph & gave forth her tears of joy Like many waters, and Emanating into gardens & palaces upon Euphrates & to forests & floods & animals wild & tame from Gihon to Hiddekel, & to corn fields & villages & inhabitants Upon Pison & Arnon & Jordan.
>
> (61: 28-33, E212)

This extraordinary reversal opens out to the reader, almost like a flower, from the fabric elaborated in the previous plates; it grows towards us from out of the spaces of the present. However, what is equally present to fallen humanity is the gap which separates the reality of vision from fallen reality. As Jerusalem's vision proceeds, it turns to this second reality: we see Christ crucified, Jerusalem herself faint 'over the Cross & Sepulcher', and Rome and Europe adopt the religion of the Druids. The vision is therefore reduced to the very condition of the person to whom it is appearing. At this point the vision turns outward and addresses Jerusalem. Christ says: 'Repose on me till the morning of the Grave. I am thy life' (62: 1, E212).

The vision of Joseph and Mary puts Jerusalem in an extraordinary position. She responds, both as a figure within the vision and a person to whom the vision is addressed, by saying that she can see the 'Body of death' and the 'Spiritual Risen Body' (62: 13, 14, E213): *both* are realities. She is even able to believe that she will see God in her flesh (62: 16, E213), but she does not know the path that will lead to this event. Christ's reply does not (for the moment) close this gap, but it opens within the present the force of hope. The present is itself a call to live the life that opens out in the tension between vision and the fallen world:

> Jesus replied. I am the Resurrection & the Life.
> I Die & pass the limits of possibility, as it appears
> To individual perception. Luvah must be Created
> And Vala; for I cannot leave them in the gnawing Grave.
> But will prepare a way for my banished-ones to return

# The Geography of the Present

> Come now with me into the villages. walk thro all the cities.
> Tho thou art taken to prison & judgement, starved in the streets
> I will command the cloud to give thee food & the hard rock
> To flow with milk & wine, tho thou seest me not a season
> Even a long season & a hard journey & a howling wilderness!
> Tho Valas cloud hide thee & Luvahs fires follow thee!
> Only believe & trust in me, Lo. I am always with thee!
>
> (62: 18-29, E213)

Hope is experienced against the background of, and can itself be concealed by, the 'closed order' of the fallen world. The world oscillates between hope and despair, openness and closure, transparence and opacity. This can be seen quite clearly in the contrast between the passage which opens and the passage which closes the three plates discussed above.

In the lines which begin plate 60 we see

> The clouds of Albions Druid Temples rage in the eastern heaven
> While Los sat terrified beholding Albions Spectre who is Luvah.
>
> (60: 1-2, E209)

In this instance, however, closure gives way to vision, for from

> within the Furnaces the Divine Vision appeard
> On Albions hills: often walking from the Furnaces in clouds
> And flames among the Druid Temples & the Starry Wheels.
>
> (60: 5-7, E210)

For the reader this disclosure is paralleled by the emergence of the vision of Mary and Joseph in the following plates. However, in the lines which close plate 62 there is an inverse movement. It begins with the assertion that 'Los beheld the Divine Vision among the flames of the Furnaces' and that for this reason 'he lived & breathed in hope' (62: 35-6, E213); however, it goes on to detail the loss of this vision:

> but his tears fell incessant
> Because his Children were closd from him apart: & Enitharmon
> Dividing in fierce pain: also the Vision of God was closd in clouds
> Of Albions Spectres, that Los in despair oft sat, & often ponderd
> On Death Eternal in fierce shudders upon the mountains of Albion
> Walking: & in the vales in howlings fierce, then to his Anvils
> Turning, anew began his labours, tho in terrible pains!
>
> (62: 36-42, E213)

Like Blake at the beginning of the poem, Los must wake again and again to vision; he must begin his labours 'anew' because the world (as we have seen in our vision of ontological time) is composed of a movement towards relationship and a movement towards closure. Just as Blake is overwhelmed by the 'rushing fires' that he sees in 'Londons darkness', so too the world that is formed in the dance of the present, and the vision of hope that is engendered by this world, are threatened by the rushing fires of enclosure. The present, like ontological time, is composed of two radically different movements and tendencies.

The exact point of fracture between these two tendencies can be seen on plate 62, where a giant figure, 'Albion's Spectre who is Luvah', arises behind the text and threatens to cast it (and the vision that it holds) aside. The figure at the base of this plate is both Blake and the reader, who are now confronted with a hiatus which opens before them in the very texture and structure of the present. In place of a dance of presences and a flowering of vision, we now see a sequential history of fragmentation which gathers momentum as it moves from the past towards the future. The iron links of this progression now permeate the poem. The plates are linked in a linear progression. The illuminations show us images of bondage and constriction. A serpent winds itself around the head of Luvah on plate 62 and around the body of a woman on plate 63. On plate 65 a chain has been drawn along the full length of the plate. At the base of plate 67 a man lies chained to the ground and a line of vegetation, 'part of the Polypus which covers all the earth', stretches along the length of plates 66, 69, and 71. A less extended growth can be seen in the margins of plates 67 and 68. The present, as I have argued at the beginning of this chapter, is not merely a manifold of presences, but a linear sequence of 'nows' which are held by the Spectre. In this sense the present is an instant in thrall to the overwhelming bulk of the past and the future. It is to this present that the poem now turns.

A SECOND NOW

The history that is recollected (and therefore appears within) this second present begins with an extremely condensed version of the events which initiate the Fall. In the opening lines it appears that Albion has already begun the process of withdrawal, for we are told that 'Jehovah stood among the Druids in the Valley of Annandale' and that the 'Four Zoas... tremble before the Spectre' (63: 1-3, E213). In the following lines we learn that Luvah slew Tharmas (the Zoa of unity) and that Albion responded to this event by bringing him 'To Justice in his own City of Paris' (63: 6, E214). This event provoked the vengeance of Vala (63: 7-8, E214), and resulted in the division of Reuben (63: 12, E214) and the closure of life within a static form (63: 18-22, E214).

At the time of the Fall Los was able to see all of these events, but he thought that they were no more than a vision of the *possibility* of withdrawal which is attendant upon the entry of a person into Beulah. Los therefore put aside what he had seen 'in the Looking-Glass of Enitharmon' (63: 38, E214).[9] Even when Los saw 'in Vala's hand the Druid Knife of Revenge & the Poison Cup | Of Jealousy' (63: 39-40, E214), he still thought that it was 'a Poetic Vision of the Atmospheres'. He only realized that something rather different had occurred when Canaan rolled apart from Albion and, as we have seen in more detail in the second chapter of the poem, when Reuben fled among the Caverns of Albion (63: 41-4, E215).

We have, in the course of a single plate, covered an extraordinary amount of ground. This brevity is to be expected at this stage of a linear history. The events narrated on plate 63 are present in the fallen world in two ways. First, like all beginnings, they are present in the dim reaches of memory. They are the almost forgotten prime cause which sets the chain of fallen time and history in motion. Second, they delineate a line of force which determines the present. We can therefore say that the history that appears in the present is both a construct created by the historian from what his/her reasoning memory is able to retain, and a line of force which determines the world in which the historian stands.

The present in which Blake stands is a time in which the Female Will has gained an awesome power and Deism, as the preface tells us, teaches Natural Religion and Natural Virtue. This is why the narrative jumped first to Los's initial response to the withdrawal of Albion and now takes a second leap to the appearance before Los of 'All the Daughters of Albion' as Vala and the vegetation of Vala in the Looms of Enitharmon (64: 6-11, E215). From within the time of Deism, the warfare of the Sons of Albion against Los, the efforts of Albion's family to recall him, the solicitation of the Divine Vision and the construction of limits by 'those who disregard all mortal Things' are all invisible. A history which made events such as these its landmarks would at best be seen as irrational, unsubstantiated, or subversive, for Deism constructs a history which attempts to suppress any challenge to its own hegemony.

The vegetation of Vala is, however, not simply an element in recollection; it is present in a second and, perhaps, more fundamental way. The vegetation of Vala forms part of a

## 178  Visionary Construction

sequential chain which leads to the present. It is therefore present in our world as a *material force*. This can be seen in the next step of this history, where Vala is embraced by the Spectre. This event results in the formation of the shell of the fallen world:

> A dark Hermaphrodite they stood frowning upon Londons River
> And the Distaff & Spindle in the hands of Vala with the Flax of
> Human Miseries turnd fierce with the Lives of Men along the Valley
> As Reuben fled before the Daughters of Albion Taxing the Nations.
>
> (64: 31-4, E215)

Although this event has occurred in the past, it quite obviously (like the vegetation of Vala) determines, and is therefore a presence within, the present. The line of force which passes from withdrawal to Vala, to the vegetation of Vala, and then to the embrace of Vala by the Spectre, sets bounds to the fallen world. The contrast here with the dance of the other present is quite striking. Earlier in this chapter we described a series of presences which solicited our attention. Here we have a sequential progression, a sequence of cogs, in which we have become weird marionettes, puppets who are subject to a force which lies outside of our control. As we move further into this section of the poem, this progression gains an inexorable force and ponderous momentum.

The embrace of Vala and the Spectre founds the world of moral righteousness which will henceforth determine the behaviour of humanity. The immediate result of this event is therefore the death of Luvah. The malefactor has been judged by and become a victim of the moral order. This event is not something which is concluded in the past; instead, the death of Luvah is present throughout the six thousand years of fallen history:

> They vote the death of Luvah, & they naild him to Albions Tree in Bath:
> They staind him with poisonous blue, they inwove him in cruel roots
> To die a death of Six thousand years bound round with vegetation
> The sun was black & the moon rolld a useless globe thro Britain!
>
> (65: 8-11, E216)

The song which is sung by the 'Spectre Sons of Albion round Luvahs Stone of Trial' (65: 56, E217) describes an event which has taken place in the past, but the world which this event brings into being and which the Spectres celebrate is clearly present:

> This is no warbling brook, nor shadow of a mirtle tree:
> But blood and wounds and dismal cries, and shadows of the oak:
> And hearts laid open to the light, by the broad grizly sword:
> And bowels hid in hammerd steel rip'd quivering on the ground.
> Call forth thy smiles of soft deceit: call forth thy cloudy tears:
> We hear thy sighs in trumpets shrill when morn shall blood renew.
>
> (65: 50-5, E217)

Similarly, the death of Luvah brings in a very present reality, for it marks the time when the Sons of Urizen leave 'the plow & harrow' and take up 'the chariot of war & the battle-ax' (65: 12, 14, E216) and when 'the Arts of Life' are changed into 'the Arts of Death' (65: 16, E216). The vegetation of Vala and her embrace with the Spectre are events which have occurred in the past; however, they are present to us as forces which determine the structure of our world. This is why in this history we can see the present prefigured in the past. The line from the past to the present can be seen most clearly in the fate of the Spectre Sons of Albion.

### THE HAND OF VALA

From the perspective of the 'Spectre Sons of Albion', it is Luvah who has pitted his strength against the unity imposed by Albion and consequently caused them to be separated from their humanity. These figures therefore take vengeance on Luvah. This response achieves the opposite of what they had intended:

> Astonishd: terrified & in pain & torment. Sudden they behold
> Their own Parent the Emanation of their murderd Enemy
> Become their Emanation and their Temple and Tabernacle
> They knew not. this Vala was their beloved Mother Vala Albions Wife.
> Terrified at the sight of the Victim: at his distorted sinews!
> The tremblings of Vala vibrate thro' the limbs of Albions Sons:
> While they rejoice over Luvah in mockery & bitter scorn:
> Sudden they become like what they behold in howlings & deadly pain.
> Spasms smite their features, sinews & limbs: pale they look on one
>   another.
> They turn, contorted: their iron necks bend unwilling towards
> Luvah: their lips tremble: their muscular fibres are crampd & smitten
> They become like what they behold!
>
> (65: 68-79, E217-18)

The separation of the Spectre Sons from their humanity means that they are no longer part of a world which emerges in relationship; instead, like the reasoning memory, they must form a world by the assimilation of others. As Blake writes: 'a Spectre has no Emanation but what he imbibes from decieving | A Victim!' (65: 59–60, E217). In political terms this takes the form of imperialism. Rather than recognizing that Luvah's revolt is at the very least codetermined by the imposition of a fixed order by Albion, they attempt to appropriate the world of Luvah. We therefore see the Spectre Sons 'Drinking' Luvah's 'Emanation in intoxicating bliss' (65: 58, E217). Luvah has become 'the Victim of the Spectres of Albion' (66: 15, E218). For Luvah and for Albion the attempt to assimilate the world to their own perspective resulted in enclosure within the world of their own desires. For both figures Vala (along with the Spectre) therefore became the regent of their world. Similarly, the judgement of Luvah by the Spectre Sons encloses them in a world which is bounded by their own desires. This is why they find, to their astonishment, that Vala is now their Emanation. The Spectre Sons are themselves enclosed within the world bounded by Vala and as a result they themselves become her victims. Their bodies are therefore irresistibly drawn towards the plight of Luvah (the victim). In this complex reworking of the Oedipus myth, the Spectre Sons simply do not realize that they are themselves born from Albion's fragmentation—that 'this Vala was their beloved Mother Vala Albions Wife' (65: 71, E217). They are therefore unable to see that to attempt to reduce Luvah to their perspective (to possess his fallen Emanation) is for them to be enclosed by Vala.

The vengeance taken by the Spectre Sons repeats the structure of withdrawal implicit in Luvah's murder of Tharmas and Albion's judgement of Luvah. In each case it results in entry into the state of Satan:

> Satan is the State of Death, & not a Human existence
> But Luvah is named Satan, because he has enterd that State
> A World where Man is by Nature the enemy of Man.
> 
> (49: 67–9, E199)

In this state Luvah, human desire, is enclosed within its own perimeters. All who take vengeance or assimilate the world to their perspectives take up this position in which apparent mastery is quickly superseded by enclosure and domination by the female. The world established by the Spectre Sons is therefore 'A building of eternal death' and at its heart we find Vala 'turning the iron Spindle of destruction' (66: 9–10, E218).

It is now the Daughters of Albion who 'sit naked upon the Stone of trial' (66: 19, E218) and mock the victim,

> Saying: Behold
> The King of Canaan whose are seven hundred chariots of iron!
> They take off his vesture whole with their Knives of flint:
> But they cut asunder his inner garments: searching with
> Their cruel fingers for his heart, & they enter in pomp,
> In many tears; & there they erect a temple & an altar.
>
> (66: 24-9, E218)

All those who see these things become like Luvah. 'Amidst delights of revenge' (66: 39, E218) they take on the form of Vala and are enclosed within the cavern of the self. The Divine Vision becomes no more than 'a globe of blood wandering distant in an unknown night' (66: 44, E219) and humanity becomes a formless Polypus, a mass of individuals

> By Invisible Hatreds adjoind, they seem remote and separate
> From each other; and yet are a Mighty Polypus in the Deep!
> As the Misletoe grows on the Oak, so Albions Tree on Eternity: Lo!
> He who will not comingle in Love, must be adjoind by Hate.
>
> (66: 53-6, E219)

It is these 'Invisible Hatreds' that link the portions of this history and make it a force which determines the present. As a result of this history 'The Human form began to be alterd by the Daughters of Albion | And the perceptions to be dissipated into the Indefinite' (66: 46-7, E219):

> The Stars flee remote: the heaven is iron, the earth is sulphur,
> And all the mountains & hills shrink up like a withering gourd,
> As the Senses of Men shrink together under the Knife of flint,
> In the hands of Albions Daughters, among the Druid Temples.
> By those who drink their blood & the blood of their Covenant.
>
> (66: 81-67: 1, E219-20)

### THE CLIMAX

As the first movement of the third chapter reached its climax, it seemed to disrupt its own progression. The manifold of presences was suddenly ruptured by the twin forces of vision and hope. The second movement of this chapter also ends with an expansion, but of a very different kind. The narrative that we have been following has described a progression which moves from the murder of Tharmas by Luvah and Albion's subsequent judgement of Luvah, to Vala's hermaphroditic embrace with Luvah, through the vengeance taken by the Spectre Sons of Albion and its results, to the reduction of the world to 'a Mighty

Polypus in the Deep!' Throughout this history we can see Vala extend her iron hand. The judgement of Luvah by Albion results in the vegetation of Vala, which is in turn the precondition for Vala's embrace of the Spectre and the consequent fabrication of the doxa or nature of the fallen world. The vengeance of the Spectre Sons assimilates them to her world and the same transformation is effected amongst all those who are party to revenge.

This history that is recounted on these plates tells us, therefore, of a gradual accretion of life to Vala. One can see its progress as being analogous to a trickle of water which turns into a stream and then into a raging torrent. Vala extends her power until all of life has become a Polypus. The climax of this history is reached on plates 67-9 in which we see an extraordinary expansion of her power. At this point the entire world is structured by the Daughters of Albion and the male power is no more than a growth from the female. The narrative seems to pick up speed, events are described in greater detail and the poem generates the feeling that a gigantic force is looming over the present. The vision of plates 60-2 has now been almost entirely eclipsed by this counter-movement.

The account of the climax of Vala's power begins with the creation of a 'Double Female' (67: 3, E220). In previous plates the Daughters of Albion have centred in Vala, but now they congregate as Rahab and Tirzah. This intensification of female power results in the extension of the 'Great Polypus of Generation' until it covers 'the earth' (67: 34, E220). These developments bring us to the world described in the preface to this chapter. They take us to the edge of Blake's present, where nature, as the passive power, has achieved dominion over the active powers. As Basil Willey writes:

'Nature' has been a controlling idea in Western thought ever since antiquity, but it has probably never been so universally active as it was from the Renaissance to the end of the eighteenth century. Nature was the grand alternative to all that man had made of man; upon her solid ground therefore—upon the *tabula rasa* prepared by the true philosophy—must all the religion, the ethics, the politics, the law, and the art of the future be constructed.[10]

In this century nature was the corner stone of both revolution and reaction.[11] Blake calls this philosophy 'the Atheistical Epicurean Philosophy of Albions Tree' and in so doing he indicates that it has its genesis within the very being of fallen man. The power of the female in the eighteenth century is not an aberration within fallen history; in fact, the roots of Vala's power can be traced back to the acts of murder and judgement which establish the fallen world. This is why a Deist philosophy can be described as Epicurean, for already in the late fourth and early third centuries before the birth of Christ, Epicurus was arguing that 'Sensation is infallible' and that it is 'our sole ultimate guarantee of truth'. The Epicurean philosophy therefore owes allegiance to Vala, for it tends to close humanity within the shell of what appears to the self.[12]

Yet the vehemence of Blake's attack against Deism in the eighteenth century is at times the occasion for some consternation. Basil Willey claims that

> The historic rôle of 'Nature' at this time was to introduce, not further confusion, but its precise opposites,—peace, concord, toleration, and progress in the affairs of men, and, in poetry and art, perspicuity, order, unity, and proportion.[13]

As a result Bloom, for example, even goes so far as to argue that

> There is not much accuracy, one fears, in Blake's indictment of historical Deism, and indeed by 'the Deists' he does not mean Toland, Collins, Tindal and the other controversialists who argued for a religion of Nature against the Anglican orthodoxy of *their* day (E939).

If Blake were to choose between Anglican orthodoxy and the deism of Toland *et al.*, it is possible that he would have more sympathy with the 'devils'. Nevertheless, in the poetry after *The Book of Urizen*, both reaction and revolution are seen to be contained by a single history. To argue for a religion of nature against a more orthodox nature is to repeat the acts of the Spectre Sons of Albion in their struggle against Vala. The argument of nature against nature is, indeed, the paradigmatic form of the dynamism which propels fallen history and invariably turns the revolutionary into the tyrant and then into the new victim. *Jerusalem* makes the mechanism which animates this history remarkably clear. As the narrator tells us:

> The Twelve Daughters in Rahab & Tirzah have circumscribd the Brain
> Beneath & pierced it thro the midst with a golden pin.
> 
> (67: 41-2, E220)

In this condition the human individual is closed within the shell of his constituted world, and therefore animated by sexual desire, by the yearning for a presence which will fill the lack which is the foundation of the psyche. While the self remains under the power of the Daughters, this yearning can never be fulfilled and it is therefore sublimated in warfare:

> I am drunk with unsatiated love
> I must rush again to War: for the Virgin has frownd & refusd.
>
> (68: 62-3, E222)

For the Warriors it seems that the veil which physically and epistemologically surrounds them can be broken only by violence, rape, and warfare: 'They cry to one another, "If you dare rend their Veil with your Spear; you are healed of Love!"' (68: 42, E222). As we have seen with regard to the Spectre Sons, an act of violence such as this only places them more firmly than ever within the world of Vala. Deism and all religions of nature are to be opposed because they preclude the entry into relationship which is the foundation of Eternity.

The gradual assimilation of being to the world of the female powers results in the reduction of the male to a single identity:

> Then all the Males combined into One Male & every one
> Became a ravening eating Cancer growing in the Female
> A Polypus of Roots of Reasoning Doubt Despair & Death.
> Going forth & returning from Albions Rocks to Canaan:
> Devouring Jerusalem from every Nation of the Earth.
>
> (69: 1-5, E223)

This giant form is a parody of Albion's humanity, for its unity is not founded on relationship, but on a formless aggregate of individuals. It is a Polypus which stands 'at variance with Itself | In all its Members: in eternal torment of love & jealousy' (69: 6-7, E223). This 'enormous Form' is called 'Hand'.

We use our hands to touch others, to mould inert matter and so give shape to something, and to perform complex tasks such as eating and drinking. The hand is often expressive of the entire person. In writing we speak of a person's hand and even in speech the hand is often peculiarly expressive of the speaker's intentions. The hand which is described on plates 69 and 70 is, by contrast, one which pits itself against the whole person. It is no longer a vehicle of expression, nor does it exist in a contrary relationship with the individual; instead, it is animated by a will directed against Albion: Hand is 'Plotting to devour Albions Body of Humanity & Love' (70: 9, E224). Hand appears as a force in his own right, but within his heart is hidden Rahab-Vala. He is in fact a 'Cancer growing in the Female' (69: 2, E223).[14]

The description of the genesis of the giant form of Hand brings us to the now in which we live. The events of the history that we have been tracing are present in recollection and in the touch of Vala's iron hand which stretches along the lines of this history to determine the bounds of the world in which we live. This history is closed and the present reached with the announcement that 'The Starry Heavens all were fled from the mighty limbs of Albion' (70: 32, E224).

THE GEOGRAPHY OF THE PRESENT

In the first two movements of the third chapter of *Jerusalem* the present is defined in radically contradictory terms. It is a manifold of presences which solicit our attention and structure the world, and it is a space which is determined by a linear history. It is, however, possible to describe the present in a third way. The dance of presences and the fallen history are themselves made possible by the ground that is established by Los. We can describe this ground in two ways: positively, by describing the relationships which compose it, and negatively, by an account of what this world once was. One could say, perhaps, that this third description of the present is the interior shape of the present that is composed of both the dance of presences and the iron history of Vala.

The third movement of the third chapter of *Jerusalem* therefore begins with a long and detailed account of the prelapsarian names and locations of 'Albions Twelve Sons, & of his Twelve Daughters' (71: 10, E225). This world of relationship has been destroyed; it exists in this context only as a negative determinant of the present:

> But now Albion is darkened & Jerusalem lies in ruins:
> Above the Mountains of Albion, above the head of Los.
>
> (71: 54-5, E226)

The present of the fallen world can now be located in relationship to Los. Los's position beneath the ruins of Jerusalem and the 'darkened' Albion is not unexpected, for in the second chapter we saw the 'Family Divine' delegate their powers to Los,

> Conjuring him by the Highest that he should Watch over them
> Till Jesus shall appear.
>
> (39[44]: 29-30, E187)

Nevertheless, his position with regard to Albion has changed significantly from that described in the second chapter. From this point in time his attempts to recall Albion can be seen as a failure; in fact, the situation has become so dire that he fears that a direct appeal will cause Albion to turn completely from the Divine Vision:

> And Los shouted with ceaseless shoutings & his tears poured down
> His immortal cheeks, rearing his hands to heaven for aid Divine!
> But he spoke not to Albion: fearing lest Albion should turn his Back
> Against the Divine Vision: & fall over the Precipice of Eternal Death.
> But he receded before Albion & before Vala weaving the Veil
> With the iron shuttle of War among the rooted Oaks of Albion.
>
> (71: 56-61, E226)

Nevertheless, it is only through Los's attentiveness to Albion-in-withdrawal that Albion and Vala are saved from the 'fall over the Precipice of Eternal Death'. As we have seen in previous chapters, Los's world emerges in relationship with Albion and Vala.

In the next plate we learn of the four—'Rintrah & Palamabron & Theotormon & Bromion' (72: 11, E226)—who help Los guard the four walls of Jerusalem. The poem then turns to an enumeration of the different counties of Ireland, which form the 'Land of Erin' (72: 27, E227). Erin is a space of embodiment and therefore a space of meeting. In this *locale*, as we have argued in the first chapter, we can be open to the call and the solicitations of others: we can hear and touch and feel. The Thirty-two Counties of Ireland (and therefore the Land of Erin) are centred

> in London & in Golgonooza. from whence
> They are Created continually East & West & North & South
> And from them are Created all the Nations of the Earth
> Europe & Asia & Africa & America, in fury Fourfold!
>
> (72: 28-31, E227)

These plates therefore assert that Los grounds two quite contradictory movements. He supports the linear unfolding of Vala by remaining attentive to Albion, and he creates, as a manifold of cotemporaneous presences, the Land of Erin and 'all the Nations of the Earth'.

For the reader this recognition that Los grounds two such radically divergent movements results in a sudden and startling reorientation. Previously we have seen the present as a time which is divided between a linear history and a dance of presences. It is now affirmed that it is Los who grounds both the dance of the present and the unfolding might of Vala. It is in Los that these two movements gain being. Vala and Erin, contraction and expansion, enclosure in the world of the self and the embrace of others, are different moments of the world formed by Los and Enitharmon. As Blake writes:

> And the Four Gates of Los surround the Universe Within and Without; & whatever is visible in the Vegetable Earth, the same Is visible in the Mundane Shell; reversd in mountain & vale.
>
> (72: 45-7, E227)

We have, of course, already seen the part that Los and his daughters play in the dance of the present and glimpsed his horrified reaction to the consolidation of Vala's power; however, Los is also present in a more fundamental sense. It is Los's relationship with Albion in ontological time (which was described in detail in the first chapter of *Jerusalem*) which opens both of these aspects of fallen existence. Los creates a world which, by providing a limit to the Fall, gives form to Vala. On the other hand, this same world opens the possibility of resurrection and regeneration described in plates 60-2. The best description of this duality in Los's world is contained on plate 73:

> Where Luvahs World of Opakeness grew to a period: It
> Became a Limit, a Rocky hardness without form & void
> Accumulating without end: here Los. who is of the Elohim
> Opens the Furnaces of affliction in the Emanation
> Fixing The Sexual into an ever-prolific Generation
> Naming the Limit of Opakeness Satan & the Limit of Contraction
> Adam, who is Peleg & Joktan: & Esau & Jacob: & Saul & David.
>
> (73: 22-8, E228)

Luvah's world is given form by Los. At the same time 'the Kings & Nobles of the Earth & all their Glories', which are 'Created by Rahab & Tirzah in Ulro', are preserved from 'Eternal Death' and so given existence in the world that Los creates around them (73: 38-40, E228-9). Los gives form to Vala by providing limits to the Fall, but this work is complemented by the turning of Los again and again to Albion. The passage quoted above continues:

> Voltaire insinuates that these Limits are the cruel work of God
> Mocking the Remover of Limits & the Resurrection of the Dead
> Setting up Kings in wrath: in holiness of Natural Religion

188  *Visionary Construction*

> Which Los with his mighty Hammer demolishes time on time
> In miracles & wonders in the Four-fold Desart of Albion
> Permanently Creating to be in Time Reveald & Demolishd.
>
> (73: 29-34, E228)

There is one more change of perspective which the chapter demands of the reader. The vision of Los as the ground of the present of the fallen world is itself the precondition for a further reorientation. In the penultimate plate the reader seems to begin on yet another history, this time exceptionally condensed, of the Fall. Before this account has proceeded very far it is interrupted by the narrator who suddenly speaks in the first person:

> Teach me O Holy Spirit the Testimony of Jesus! let me
> Comprehend wonderous things out of the Divine Law
> I behold Babylon in the opening Street of London, I behold
> Jerusalem in ruins wandering about from house to house
> This I behold the shudderings of death attend my steps
> I walk up and down in Six Thousand Years: their Events are present before me
> To tell how Los in grief & anger, whirling round his Hammer on high
> Drave the Sons & Daughters of Albion from their ancient mountains.
>
> (74: 14-21, E229)

This passage completes our picture of the present. On the one hand this time in which we live contains a dance of presences which solicit our attention; on the other hand, we can discern Vala's iron hand and cruel necessities which turn their force on the present. Both of these presences are grounded in the universe established by Los and which provides the overall shape of the present. From the point of view of vision, however, there is a fourth present: *all the events of six thousand years are present to Blake*. This extraordinary claim radically re-situates the reader.

During the course of our discussion of the third chapter of *Jerusalem*, we have simply observed the unfolding of the three elements which make up the present. In the process we have, perhaps, been drifting away from the moment of vision. As the chapter closes, we are recalled to the point at which the poem began. The delineation of Los as the ground of the present demanded that we see dance and linear history as aspects of a single existence. The claim that all of the events of history are present to the narrator demands that we see the *now* that has been the predominant concern of this chapter as a portion of the whole man. We are in this way taken back to the very beginning of the poem, to the opening streets of London, in which Blake woke to his vision of Albion/Christ. In other words, in vision we are still standing in the moment in which the poem begins. The sequential history narrated in the second and third chapter forms the shape of ontological time. Together, ontological and sequential time form the body of Albion-in-withdrawal and, as we shall argue in the next chapter, the body of Christ. It is only in the fallen world and within the limitations imposed by the materials of the fallen world that the vision of Albion/Christ must be represented in a linear fashion. It is the moment of awakening with which the poem begins which allows the narrator to walk up and down in history. In the lines which follow we see him perform this task with an extraordinary confidence and *élan*.

In ontological time we saw the relationship of Los to Albion as a structure which extended along the entire length of fallen time. Within this structure Los walks up and down and in this way remains in relationship with each fragment of the fallen and now spatially extended Albion. It is this history, made permanent by Los, which is seen by the narrator. The Twenty-seven heavens of 'Rahab Babylon the Great' (75: 1, E230)

> Appear in strong delusive light of Time & Space drawn out
> In shadowy pomp by the Eternal Prophet created evermore
>
> For Los in Six Thousand Years walks up & down continually
> That not one Moment of Time be lost & every revolution
> Of Space he makes permanent in Bowlahoola & Cathedron.
>
> (75: 5-9, E230)

In support of this claim the narrator details this history from Adam to Luther and describes the action of Jesus who,

> breaking thro' the Central Zones of Death & Hell
> Opens Eternity in Time & Space; triumphant in Mercy.
>
> (76: 21-2, E231)

Once again the reader can see the duality of the fallen world. Humanity is caught within an endless cycle of time (stretching from Adam to Luther) which, nevertheless, contains the possibility of regeneration:

> Thus are the Heavens formd by Los within the Mundane Shell
> And where Luther ends Adam begins again in Eternal Circle
> To awake the Prisoners of Death; to bring Albion again
> With Luvah into light eternal, in his eternal day.
>
> (76: 23-6, E231)

## 190 Visionary Construction

This possibility of regeneration has not been embraced and so the chapter concludes with a reiteration of the statement that 'now the Starry Heavens are fled from the mighty limbs of Albion' (76: 27, E231). The narrator and the reader of *Jerusalem* exist in a present in which vision calls us to 'Awake!', 'expand!' and in which we are swept along in a sequential progression away from the point at which this voice is heard.

# 6. Winding the Golden String into a Ball

How can his knowledge protect his desire for truth from illusion?
How can he wait without idols to worship, without
Their overwhelming persuasion that somewhere, over the high hill,
Under the roots of the oak, in the depths of the sea,
Is a womb or a tomb wherein he may halt to express some attainment?

W. H. Auden[1]

### THE GOLDEN STRING

In the first lines of the preface to the fourth chapter the cries of the Spectre Sons, and the voices of Vala, Rahab, Los, and Hand, are replaced by a simple, almost childlike voice offering the reader 'the end of a golden string'. All that we need to do, this voice affirms, is to 'wind it into a ball' and it will lead us 'in at Heavens gate, | Built in Jerusalems wall' (77, E231). As if to confirm that such a course of action is possible a small figure is drawn at the top of this plate who is rolling a string into a ball. The 'end' that is being offered to the reader is on one level readily identified.[2] It is the fourth chapter, the end of the ontic and sequential progression that we have been following, the future which stands at the end of the line stretching from the past and through the present. It is also the 'end' of the line of force unfolded by Vala and, by analogy, the end of the lives (collective and individual) of the worm of sixty winters. The location of 'Heavens gate' and the 'wall' in which it can be found is also quite clear. By following the poem's progression backwards, by winding the sequential, linear string of words into a ball, we arrive back at the frontispiece and stand with Los before the gate built in the 'wall' of the poem. This return would radically alter our position with regard to the doorway depicted on this plate, for our entry would no longer be deferred by the sequential unfolding of the poem and of time; instead, by winding the string of time into a ball we would return along the lines, and yet against the current, of that force which forbids us entry. The entry of Los and the reader into Jerusalem (and thus into heaven) could therefore be effected and it would indeed be true, as the preface to this chapter affirms, that 'Hell is opend to Heaven' (77: 34, E233).

Although the string offered to the reader can be readily identified, the means by which we are to turn and wind it into a ball is certainly not clear. Each attempt of the will to move the self against the current of time can meet only with failure, for such a course of action is itself a regression and withdrawal. The attempts of Los to draw Albion back against his will to the point where he began, for example, merely extend the space of Ulro. There is no path back through time to an innocence which has not encountered experience. Yet the path back to *Jerusalem*'s gate must be discovered if we are to enter this city and embrace Albion. And the path that leads to this point does seem to be in some way backwards 'thro' the text, for the figure whom we see winding up a length of string is walking against the current of the text. It is as if the reader has been confronted with a Zen koan and in order to pass beyond it he/she must change his/her orientation.[3] Till this occurs we are (like Los) in the same plight as the bird depicted on plate 78. We are an Icarus without wings, a Daedalus who cannot pick up the string that lies at his feet. From this melancholy position the rising sun (seen on the left of the illumination) can only be seen as a sun setting far in the west.[4]

A Zen master would, perhaps, point out at this stage of our discussion that the question of how to wind the 'golden string' into a ball is a little premature. We cannot hope to accomplish this task until we have the 'end' of the string in our hands. The beaked figure is, in fact, looking in the wrong direction. We must, first of all, pick up the 'end' ourselves; we must turn to the fourth and final chapter of *Jerusalem*.

THE CLOSE OF HISTORY

The fourth chapter begins with a continuation of the history which stretches from the withdrawal of Albion (second chapter) to the state entered as a result of that withdrawal (third chapter). It details the trajectory taken by this history as it passes into the future. This future is not described in the mode of possibility, nor is it proclaimed as the future predicted by the 'honest man' as he gazes at the present; instead, it is a history which is placed in the narrator's past. This tense is appropriate because the final chapter of *Jerusalem* details a history which the narrator has seen in vision and which he is therefore able to announce as having already occurred. This time is a portion of the temporally and spatially extended body of Albion-in-withdrawal.

The ability of the narrator to see 'past, present and future existing all at once' does not imply a philosophy of fatalism. The present is determined in the sense that limits to the possible are set by Albion's fall. We are all immersed within a time and space which predates us; we are hurried on in the 'tide' of a time which extends on either side of our individual lives. However, within this time mortals are radically free. Free, because within the possibilities opened by this time we are able to choose the course of our life. Radically free, because regeneration is a member of the set of options opened by the fallen world.

The fourth chapter begins by locating the poem's readers within the moment of history that they have reached. Now, 'The Spectres of Albions Twelve Sons' attempt to 'devour' the sleeping body of Albion (78: 1-3, E233), their armies 'surround the Forty-two Gates of Erin', they give the name of Rahab to 'their Mother Vala' and elevate her to a position from which she has 'power over the Earth' (78: 12-16, E233-4). This attenuation of the power of Vala brings Jerusalem to the verge of non-existence:

> Disorganizd; an evanescent shade, scarce seen or heard among
> Her childrens Druid Temples.
> 
> (78: 28-9, E234)

The world summarized by the opening plate gains moving expression in the voice of Jerusalem—heard from within 'the darkness of Philisthea' (78: 30, E234)—as she laments over the condition to which she and Albion have been reduced (78: 31-79: 7, E234). At the climax of her speech Jerusalem addresses herself directly to Vala and asks her to say why her

>                               shuttles
> Drop with the gore of the slain; why Euphrates is red with blood
> Wherefore in dreadful majesty & beauty outside appears
> Thy Masculine from thy Feminine hardening against the heavens
> To devour the Human!
> 
> (79: 68-72, E236)

Vala's reply to this question is a striking instance of an attempt to validate the present order by offering a (highly selective) account of the past.

Vala is, of course, inextricably involved in the Fall. She forms the veil that separates self from other and therefore she is involved in any struggle of one against another. Vala's history attempts to diminish this role. For example, we are told that it is Luvah who initially commands her 'to murder Albion | In unreviving Death', (80: 16-17, E236), but we do not hear what Vala's response was to this request. Instead, Vala describes a struggle between Luvah and Albion. Quite clearly Vala must have participated in this struggle, for at its conclusion both she and Luvah are dead. Vala, nevertheless, while admitting that there were two corpses, claims to have revived both bodies to life in her bosom (80: 20, E236). This event involves a complete inversion of the personality, for now the active power emerges from the passive. In previous chapters we have seen how this phenomenon resulted in the death of the whole man; similarly, at this point in Vala's narrative she tells us that Luvah framed a knife and placed it in 'his daughters hand!' (80: 23, E236). Vala speaks of Luvah's daughter as if she were someone separate from herself and she does not tell us that the knife is offered as a means of fulfilling her father's demand that she 'murder Albion'. Instead, after observing, with some measure of shock and guilt, that a death of this kind 'was never known | Before in Albions land' (80: 23-4, E236), she tells Jerusalem that she keeps Albion in this state so that he does not return and kill Luvah (80: 27-31, E236).

Vala's fear is not really that Albion might murder Luvah, for as her narrative has already implied this event would only increase her own power. The real danger is that Albion could return in response to the call of Jesus, and a return of this kind would remove both Albion and Luvah from the dynamic in which Vala gains her strength. Vala's lamentations are therefore an attempt to describe to Jerusalem why what is, must be; and they are a strategy designed to entice forgiveness itself into 'Luvahs Tents' (80: 31, E236). Far from implying any conversion in Vala herself (as Bloom suggests)[5] Vala's 'lamenting songs' (80: 8, E236) are an integral part of her work. As she sings, a body is woven for 'Jerusalem . . . according to her will' (80: 35, E237). Moreover, her songs produce in Los the emotions of both anger and pity (80: 41, E237).

Vala's world, despite its appearance of strength, is therefore at one point extraordinarily vulnerable. As Vala admits: 'if once a Delusion be found | Woman must perish & the Heavens of Heavens remain no more' (80: 14-15, E236). Until this occurs Albion is confined beneath the delusion that Vala's veil, the nature constructed by the Daughters of Albion, is reality. Once the contingent nature of this veil has been shown, Albion is free once more to enter into relationship. Vala's fear that Albion will return in response to the call of Christ is, however, accompanied by a second and perhaps more immediate danger to the Daughters and to Vala: Vala's power is threatened by the very logic of its own unfolding. In order to understand this threat we must briefly recapitulate our discussion of the mechanism which propels fallen history.

In the course of the history recounted in the previous chapter, we saw the Spectre draw 'Vala into his bosom magnificent' (64: 25, E215). In this embrace the Spectre seems at first to be the dominant partner, but when the Spectre next enters this history it is as the Spectre Sons of Albion who are born from Vala. We can gloss this phenomenon by observing that the adoption of a creed is an embrace by a male (retaining) power of a passive power. As a result of this embrace the believer is formed by these ideas and he becomes, metaphorically at least, an infant. Locke, for example, begins the *Essay* with an account of the embrace by his reasoning memory of a particular nature. Once this embrace has been accomplished, however, the initiative swings to the passive power and this nature generates a series of rules for the conduct of life. Locke is born from the nature that he has embraced. Similarly, the embrace of Vala by the Spectre of Albion means that he is born from Vala.

In being born from Vala, however, the Spectre is formed as a Warrior, a self-enclosed identity who attempts to assimilate others to his perspective. It is therefore inevitable that as he grows in strength he should come to realize that he is enclosed by the Nature that has borne him. In the third chapter, for example, we find that the Spectre Sons of Albion struggle against the being that encloses them. This process in which the children of the Fall oppose a particular nature with another nature is the very stuff of generation. As I have argued, this struggle ensures that a particular nature is overthrown at the expense of becoming assimilated to the overall rule of Vala. Although the struggle against Vala results in her reinstatement, this dynamic means that the Daughters are subject to a continual consumation. The progression from youth to old age, from the Ptolemaic to the Galilean system, from Adam to Luther, all result in the transformation of the cradle of grass woven by the Daughters.

For much of history this consummation does not threaten Vala herself; in fact, it is what ensures that she can remain indefinite. However, at the end of time the situation is rather different. The consummation of particular natures gradually reveals them to be aspects of a single nature, that of Rahab/Vala. Moreover, at this point Vala has assimilated all of existence to her perspective and as a result 'the Twelve Daughters of Albion' are united in the 'Double Female' called 'Rahab & Tirzah' (67: 2-3, E220). This global form gives birth to the Spectres as 'One Male', which can now be seen as 'a ravening eating Cancer growing in the Female' (69: 1-2, E223). On this more unified and global level the struggles of earlier levels are repeated, but now the wrath of the Warriors can be directed against Vala herself, and therefore it can potentially threaten the entire world formed by the Daughters.

Given this vulnerability of the Daughters to Jesus and to the Warriors that they weave, their overall strategy is, quite understandably, to remain indefinite. An indefinite delusion is one which cannot be disproved. This is why almost any 'doxa' can appear attractive and seem to represent the truth if it is presented in generalities. Rahab therefore not only resists definition but makes lack of definition an element in the morality that she propounds:

> And Rahab like a dismal & indefinite hovering Cloud
> Refusd to take a definite form. she hoverd over all the Earth
> Calling the definite, sin: defacing every definite form.
>
> (80: 51-3, E237)

There are, fortunately, quite definite limits to how indefinite Rahab can be. On the one hand her power is safeguarded by refusing to accept definite form; on the other hand if her sovereignty is to have any meaning at all she must weave a definite form and in this way herself become definite. The power of Rahab is, it seems, in an inverse relation to her security. As Gwendolen will assert later in the poem: 'Men are caught by Love: Woman is caught by Pride' (81: 6, E238). It is pride in their own form and power that causes the female delusion to be discovered.

For much of history Rahab is able to remain indefinite because her Daughters take definite form. The change from one world fabricated by the Daughters to the next even gives the impression that we live in an open-ended world; it generates the illusion that we are in some way moving closer to reality. However, behind all of this movement the basic principle which animates all of these 'systems'—that of Rahab/Vala and the Female Will—remains indistinct and unformulated. This resolution of the conflict between the desires for security and for power works well for Rahab, but only at the expense of re-introducing the conflict at a different level. If the twelve Daughters who form the figure of Vala were collectively to decide to remain indefinite, then there would be no observable appearance to the self and therefore neither the Daughters nor Rahab could have any power. The Daughters are therefore subject to the consummation that Rahab wishes to avoid. Moreover, as the Daughters collectively form the identity of Vala/Rahab, each identification of the Daughters is a partial identification of Vala/Rahab. For the Daughters the problem is, given that they must have a definite form, how to keep the identities that they have woven enclosed within their world. Towards the end of time (when the Double Female has been identified as a single form) this question involves not simply their own survival, but the survival of Rahab/Vala as well. This is the dilemma faced by Gwendolen on plates 81 and 82.

Gwendolen is the female counterpart to Hyle and she gives him a form of 'self-interest & selfish natural virtue'; she gives him the form of a Warrior (80: 67-79, E237-8). The difficulty is that as Gwendolen gives Hyle form (as, for example, a religion or ideology forms its subscribers) so too she is revealed (80: 71-2, E237) and therefore herself becomes a target for the wrath of the Warrior that she has created. The question for Gwendolen is therefore, 'what shall we do to keep | These awful forms in our soft bands' (80: 84-5, E238). Gwendolen's concern is not simply for her own safety, but for the existence of all of the Daughters. She says:

> I have heard Jerusalems groans; from Vala's cries & lamentations
> I gather our eternal fate: Outcasts from life and love:
> Unless we find a way to bind these awful Forms to our
> Embrace we shall perish annihilate, discoverd our Delusions.
>
> (82: 1-4, E239)

To achieve this end Gwendolen proposes a strategy which, she hopes, will make her world deaf to the voice of Jesus and proof against the advances of the Warriors.

TO BIND THE INFANT IN THE BANDS OF LOVE

Gwendolen attempts to render her delusions secure and 'keep' the awful forms in her 'soft bands' with the twin forces of fear and desire. On the one hand she punishes all who transgress her moral code. On the other hand she becomes a form that is 'perfect in beauty' (81: 5, E238). Gwendolen hopes that as a result of this strategy the Warrior will be transformed into a child who cannot leave the side of the mother who has given him birth. Hyle will become totally subservient to the nature that Gwendolen represents (81: 8–16, E239).

In its essence this strategy is not new; in the fallen world the passive power always attempts to form a shell which encloses existence. At this point in time, however, when the forms of the Double Female and the Male have been identified, it is possible to envisage a movement on the part of the female which would bring the male in its entirety under the control of the female. If Gwendolen were to be successful then the cycles of generation would be averted: the son would never be able to leave the mother who has given him birth. As Gwendolen exclaims: 'the mighty Hyle is become a weeping infant; | Soon shall the Spectres of the Dead follow my weaving threads' (82: 8–9, E239).[6]

It is, of course, not enough simply to reduce Hyle to an infant; Gwendolen must entice her other sisters to perform the same feat, for only then will Rahab/Vala be secure from the Warriors and from Jesus. Gwendolen therefore fabricates a falsehood which she hopes will draw her sisters to 'Babylon on Euphrates' (82: 18, E239). This falsehood asserts that Los will turn away from Albion, leave him desolate, and create a world of surfaces. Gwendolen says to her sisters:

> I heard Enitharmon say to Los: Let the Daughters of Albion
> Be scatterd abroad and let the name of Albion be forgotten:
> Divide them into three; name them Amalek Canaan & Moab:
> Let Albion remain a desolation without an inhabitant:
> And let the Looms of Enitharmon & the Furnaces of Los
> Create Jerusalem, & Babylon & Egypt & Moab & Amalek,
> And Helle & Hesperia & Hindostan & China & Japan.
>
> (82: 22–8, E239)

If Los were to 'let the name of Albion be forgotten' and simply create the fallen world, then Golgonooza would fall, for this city is created in the continual turning of Los to Albion. In its place we would have nothing more than the phenomenal world, the world which the Daughters create between the Mundane Shell and the earth. Without foundation this world would dissolve, but the Daughters do not realize this. Gwendolen's falsehood is attractive because it seems to them that if Los accepts that Albion will never return and agrees to let his 'name . . . be forgotten', then existence itself would finally be enclosed by the Daughters. Rather than being subject to the vicissitudes of Generation and threatened by the advances of the Warriors and the possible return of Albion and Christ, the Daughters would be able to make their delusions permanent.

So far Gwendolen has spoken only in generalities. The proof of her contentions is, of course, her ability actually to transform Hyle into a harmless infant. Gwendolen claims that Hyle has given her 'sweet delight by his torments beneath [her] Veil' (82: 39, E240) and that she has fed him with 'the fruit of Albions Tree' and 'sweet milk' drawn from the 'contentions of the mighty for Sacrifice of Captives' (82: 40-1, E240). She also claims to have carried him in her womb and nourished him with the milk of her world; however, the being that she has formed is a 'Winding Worm' and not an infant. This creature now threatens Gwendolen with an anger and wrath many times more powerful than that of the Warriors:

> So saying: She drew aside her Veil from Mam-Tor to Dovedale
> Discovering her own perfect beauty to the Daughters of Albion
> And Hyle a winding Worm beneath [her Loom upon the scales.
> Hyle was become a winding Worm:] & not a weeping Infant.
> Trembling & pitying she screamed & fled upon the wind:
> Hyle was a winding Worm and herself perfect in beauty:
> The desarts tremble at his wrath: they shrink themselves in fear.
>
> (82: 45-51, E240)

Gwendolen's attempt to reduce humanity to a form which is completely determined by the Daughters quite clearly results in the fabrication of death itself. The limit of opacity established by Eternity at the time of the Fall cannot be overstepped by the Daughters without stepping into the void of non-existence.

The Daughters are attracted by Gwendolen's beauty—Cambel, for example, trembles with jealousy (82: 52, E240)—because it represents the perfection of their world and powers. However, the evident failure of this beauty to reduce Hyle to an infant leaves them with only one course of action. It is only in the furnaces of Los and within the spaces of Generation that they will be able to reduce the Warriors to infants and so gain respite from their advances. Cambel, for example, is now drawn into the furnaces of Los and there she labours

> To form the mighty form of Hand according to her will.
> In the Furnaces of Los & in the Wine-press treading day & night
> Naked among the human clusters: bringing wine of anguish
> To feed the afflicted in the Furnaces: she minded not
> The raging flames, tho she returnd [consumd day after day
> A redning skeleton in howling woe:] instead of beauty

Defo[r]mity: she gave her beauty to another: bearing abroad
Her struggling torment in her iron arms: and like a chain,
Binding his wrists & ankles with the iron arms of love.

(82: 63-71, E240)

Once again, the phenomenon described here is not new. Throughout fallen history the Daughters have been drawn again and again into the furnaces of Los. What is unprecedented, however, is that the Daughters as a whole, at this point in history, perceive that it is only in Los's furnaces that they can avert death:

Gwendolen saw the Infant in her siste[r]s arms; she howld
Over the forests with bitter tears, and over the winding Worm
Repentant: and she also in the eddying wind of Los's Bellows
Began her dolorous task of love in the Wine-press of Luvah
To form the Worm into a form of love by tears & pain.
The Sisters saw! trembling ran thro their Looms! soften[in]g mild
Towards London: then they saw the Furna[c]es opend, & in tears
Began to give their souls away in the Furna[c]es of affliction.

(82: 72-9, E240)

Bloom argues that Los is comforted by the events which occur at this point in the poem because he is able to observe 'a genuine change of heart in the camp of the enemy, which is a presage of the greater change to come' (E943). In fact the Daughters have not changed their colours. They are still principally concerned with their own survival and the maintenance of their power. They have entered the furnaces of Los simply because they realize that there is no other way to avoid the 'winding Worm' uncovered by Gwendolen. They are therefore still concerned to form an infant who is subservient to their will—Cambel binds the child's 'wrists & ankles with the iron arms of love' (82: 71, E240)—but they realize that the most efficacious way of doing this is through the furnaces of Generation, and also that they will have to pay a price for their safety. They will not be able to remain 'perfect in Beauty', but must themselves enter the world of Generation and give their beauty to others. Los is comforted by this development because the Daughters do not choose the path of death. They are directed, albeit for selfish and, even in their own terms, quite misguided reasons, into the world of Generation. This is why the relief that Los feels because the danger has been averted is followed by a long speech in which he evinces a weariness with his long sojourn in the fallen world.

By entering the furnaces of Los, the Daughters are able to avoid the winding Worm and, for a short period of time, reduce their Warriors to infants. However, as plate 84 makes clear, this stratagem achieves only a postponement of their crisis. In generation they are able to make Hand a child, but this event then becomes the portent of his return as an adult in an ever more frightening form:

> The night falls thick Hand comes from Albion in his strength
> He combines into a Mighty-one the Double Molech & Chemosh
> Marching thro Egypt in his fury the East is pale at his course
> The Nations of India, the Wild Tartar that never knew Man
> Starts from his lofty places & casts down his tents & flees away
> But we woo him all the night in songs.
>
> (84: 20-5, E243)

## A FORM FOR THE FALLEN WORLD

The birth and rebirth of the Warriors in ever more powerful and threatening forms precipitates yet another change in strategy on the part of the Daughters. They now call on Los for help:

> O Los come forth O Los
> Divide us from these terrors & give us power them to subdue
> Arise upon thy Watches let us see thy Globe of fire
> On Albions Rocks & let thy voice be heard upon Euphrates.
>
> (84: 25-8, E243)

Once again it is important to see that this call does not represent a change of heart, for as the Daughters sing 'in lamentation' they unite 'into One | With Rahab as she turnd the iron Spindle of destruction' (84: 29-30, E243). The Daughters hope that Los will offer them a means of finally gaining victory over their Spectre Sons.

The invocation of Los is accompanied by an embrace of the falsehood uttered on plate 82 by Gwendolen:

> Terrified at the Sons of Albion they took the Falshood which
> Gwendolen hid in her left hand. it grew &, grew till it
> Became a Space & an Allegory around the Winding Worm
> They namd it Canaan & built for it a tender Moon.
>
> (84: 31-85: 2, E243)

This represents a striking change within the fallen world. As I have argued in previous chapters, there are two worlds within the universe of loss. The first, Golgonooza, is built by Los. The second is built by the Daughters (and held by the Sons) of Albion. Although they exist within the same ontological time, these worlds have radically different tendencies. The first is the spiritual London, Golgonooza, while the second, Babylon, is founded on moral virtue. Politics would, of course, be a lot simpler if Los could simply reject the world fabricated by the Daughters; unfortunately, this world establishes a garment, a body, and a cradle for Albion-in-withdrawal. In order to remain in relationship with Albion, Los must continually demand that the Daughters obey his will; the indefinite world of death must be given a form in the forge of friendship. At a number of places in *Jerusalem* we have seen Los attempting to check the momentum of this world of death and open it to Albion (cf. 56: 41-3, E206). And in the second chapter Erin exhorts the Daughters of Beulah to

> Remove from Albion, far remove these terrible surfaces.
> They are beginning to form Heavens & Hells in immense
> Circles: the Hells for food to the Heavens: food of torment,
> Food of despair.
>
> (49: 60-3, E199)

By calling on Los the Daughters suddenly eliminate the distance between surface and substance, and as a result the gap which separates them from the Daughters of Los is removed. The Daughters still weave a shadowy surface superadded to the real surface, but this surface is now congruent with that formed by Los. This is why the call to Los is accompanied by Gwendolen's falsehood. The Daughters call Los, not because they have been suddenly converted to a religion of compassion, but because they believe that Los intends to turn from Albion, leave him without an inhabitant, and in the place of Golgonooza create a world of enclosure. If he were to accomplish this reversal Los would become the foundation for the world fabricated by the Daughters. The substance of the fallen world would be swallowed up by its surface.

This development is at first rather shocking in its uncompromising judgement of the systems with which we order and structure our lives. As we pass from one of the worlds fabricated by the Daughters to the next (from the Copernican to the Newtonian or Einsteinian universe) we often have the sense that our conceptual grasp of the world is becoming more and more refined. It is, however, only in the failure of these philosophies, in the moments in which they become congruent with loss, when the absurdities of their claims to be able to enclose the world within their bounds become manifest, that we see their ontological reality, which is loss. It is our own failure to communicate, or realize our own potentialities or ideals, that figures forth for us the shape of our own fallen identities.

The invocation of Los and the embrace of Gwendolen's falsehood therefore has the effect of fabricating a body of loss. Albion's surface, his body, now assumes the shape of loss/Los. This is why the land of Canaan—the physical not the spiritual promised land—now appears around the winding Worm. Now death itself has a body and a shape; Albion is no longer encased in the shifting (and therefore mysterious) natures which are fabricated by the Daughters; instead he is clothed in the shape of loss, which is his reality.

WINDING THE BODY OF ALBION INTO A BALL

The conjunction of the form fabricated by the Daughters of Albion and the world constructed by Los seems to be a rather puzzling event. We have argued that in withdrawal, at the very beginning of fallen time, Albion enters the time and space of loss; yet this world is precisely the one to which the daughters are reduced as they call to Los for assistance and embrace Gwendolen's falsehood. In order to understand the relationship between the beginning and the end of fallen time we must keep in mind the two directions in which the text is pulling us. From the perspective of the reasoning memory Generation is perceived as a linear progression which passes from the past to the future. In vision, however, history is seen as the shape of Albion-in-withdrawal. In fact, sequential history is the temporal extension given to Albion-in-withdrawal. At the end of fallen history, therefore, we do not really have any more than we began with: 'All things Begin & End in Albions Ancient Druid Rocky Shore'. At the end of the third chapter the narrator tells us that

> Where Luvahs World of Opakeness grew to a period: It
> Became a Limit, A Rocky hardness without form & void
> Accumulating without end: here Los. who is of the Elohim
> Opens the Furnaces of affliction in the Emanation
> Fixing the Sexual into an ever-prolific Generation.
>
> (73: 22-6, E228)

But 'Luvahs World of Opakeness' grows 'to a period' in both the first and the last moments of time.

From the perspective of ontic time the end of time is simply the last 'now' in a long succession of such instants. In vision this last moment can be seen to complete the form of Albion-in-withdrawal and, therefore, to return us to the beginning of the poem and the beginning of the time of withdrawal. In the fourth chapter of *Jerusalem*, 'Luvahs World' once more draws 'to a period' and Los must open the furnaces of affliction. Los smiles at this development because the completed form of Albion-in-withdrawal represents the completion of his own form (that of loss) and he is therefore able to glimpse Enitharmon. Hoping that he will be able to embrace her once more he again extends the form of Albion-in-withdrawal into a six thousand year history:

> Los smild with joy thinking on Enitharmon & he brought
> Reuben from his twelvefold wandrings & led him into it
> Planting the Seeds of the Twelve Tribes & Moses & David
> And gave a Time & Revolution to the Space Six Thousand Years
> He calld it Divine Analogy, for in Beulah the Feminine
> Emanations Create Space. the Masculine Create Time, & plant
> The Seeds of beauty in the Space: listning to their lamentation.
>
>                                   (85: 3-9, E243)

In the course of this six thousand years the Daughters will once again weave a shadowy surface superadded to the real surface, and in this history Reuben will be scattered; but at this stage in the poem (at the very end and beginning of time), when the form of Albion-in-withdrawal is completed and reaffirmed by Los, the scattered fragments of Albion have a form or container in which they can be put. Albion therefore has a form which can, as we shall see, be the ground for a movement into Eternity. The tomb can be a womb (as the lines from the frontispiece affirm); the fallen world can become the shell which is put off by the growth of the seed. The world of loss can be seen as a 'Divine Analogy' of the spaces created by the Daughters of Beulah. Both are spaces which form the ground for a return to the 'Wars of Life Eternal'. The recognition that the line of fallen time forms a circle, and that this circle is the outline of Albion-in-withdrawal, is the moment in which the reader sees the long line of *Jerusalem* (the poem, the city, and the woman) wound into a ball. Fallen time and space have become a womb for Albion. This new development is celebrated by Los in the 'Song of Los, the Song that he sings on his Watch' (85: 21, E244).

The Book of Los ends with the fabrication by Los of 'a Human Illusion | In darkness and deep clouds involvd' (5: 56-7, E94). Similarly, The Song of Los encloses the history of America and Europe in an eternal circle. By contrast, although the form which now encloses Albion is still a production of loss, Los can now see within its spaces the Emanation of Albion, Jerusalem (86: 1-3, E244). In previous plates we have seen Jerusalem only as she exists within the dungeons and under the power of Vala. Now, with the completion of the tomb/womb in which Albion is enclosed, we are able to see her 'Form . . . In the opacous Bosom of the Sleeper' (86: 1-2, E244). Jerusalem, as I have argued, can be seen as vision itself, as a sequential history which is anchored in vision, and as an 'orderd race' which is held in the reasoning memory. Rather than being mutually exclusive, these 'levels' make up the whole poem. Jerusalem is similarly layered: she includes the reality of vision, for she has 'Gates of pearl' which reflect 'Eternity' (86: 4-5, E244); her spaces retain a relationship with their ground, for her Wings form a 'canopy' in which Eternity dwells (86: 9-10, E244); and, finally, she is a form in which 'the Spectres' of her 'Dead' can be seen. As the Emanation of Albion Jerusalem/Jerusalem is, like the fallen world, 'Three-fold | In Head & Heart & Reins' (86: 2-3, E244). Jerusalem is therefore a city/Emanation/poem which is open, and it holds within its spaces the possibility of change. As Los testifies:

> I see the River of Life & Tree of Life
> I see the New Jerusalem descending out of Heaven
> Between thy Wings of gold & silver featherd immortal
> Clear as the rainbow, as the cloud of the Suns tabernacle.
> (86: 18-21, E244-5)

Nevertheless, as the presence in her form of the 'Spectres' of her 'Dead' suggests, Jerusalem/Jerusalem is inextricably involved with the fallen world. The tension between transparence and opacity, the vision of Jerusalem and the rush of time which draws us apart from her, can be seen at this point in the poem as well. At the beginning of his song Los must exhort the Daughters to refrain from building 'an Earthly Kingdom' (the syntax of lines 27-32 suggests that this call is addressed to Jerusalem/Jerusalem as well), and the Song itself is an exhortation to Jerusalem to 'Come forth' from Babylon (85: 30, 32, E244). Jerusalem/Jerusalem exists in the midst of a movement towards disintegration. The epiphany of Jerusalem as the body of the fallen world and the Emanation of Albion is therefore followed by the vision of this same body as the Antichrist.

## WINDING THE BODY OF LOS INTO A BALL

The completion of the body of Albion-in-withdrawal is at the same time the completion of the body and Emanation of Los. On plate 85 Los had a premonition of this event, but now as Los's work draws to a close his Emanation, Enitharmon, divides completely from him (86: 50–87: 2, E245–6). This separation is the prelude to an attempt by Enitharmon to gain power over Los. As with the Daughters of Albion Enitharmon's power is threatened by Los's friendship with Albion, for it is in the crucible of this relationship that Christ appears. Her power is also threatened by Los's capacity to create new forms for the fallen world. Enitharmon therefore attempts to enclose Los within the form of the fallen world, and when he suggests that she can work alternate with him she replies:

> No! I will sieze thy Fibres & weave
> Them: not as thou wilt but as I will, for I will Create
> A round Womb beneath my bosom lest I also be overwoven
> With Love; be thou assured I never will be thy slave
> Let Mans delight be Love; but Womans delight be Pride
> In Eden our loves were the same here they are opposite
> I have Loves of my own I will weave them in Albions Spectre.
>
> (87: 12–18, E246)

If Enitharmon were to be successful and the passive power could determine the identity of the active, then Los's world would become opaque and the relationship that Los has up to this point sustained with Albion-in-withdrawal would be lost. This would mean that Christ himself would be in thrall to Enitharmon and the Daughters of Albion, for it is only in Los's openness to Albion that the Divine Vision appears within the fallen world. Enitharmon's strategy to achieve this end resembles that adopted by the Daughters of Albion. By enforcing a strict moral code she hopes to be able to ensure that the female is never embraced and, therefore, that the bounds of the given are not breached. Enitharmon confidently asserts:

> This is Womans World, nor need she any
> Spectre to defend her from Man. I will Create secret places
> And the masculine names of the places Merlin & Arthur
> A triple Female Tabernacle for Moral Law I weave
> That he who loves Jesus may loathe terrified Female love
> Till God himself become a Male subservient to the Female.
>
> (88: 16–21, E247)

Enitharmon, however, is herself the form of the universe of Los. In framing a moral code of this kind, and refusing Los's embrace, she gives clear and precise definition to this world. Enitharmon's fabrication of a form which encloses Los therefore works against her intentions, for (by creating a 'Female Womb') it outlines a body for Los. Moreover, as I have argued, the space of Canaan and the 'Allegoric Night', which now surround Albion-in-withdrawal, are produced when the world woven by the Daughters of Albion coincides with that created by Los. In giving concrete expression to the form of Los, Enitharmon is in fact completing the definition of this space and this night. The 'Allegoric Night' now stretches throughout the fallen universe, and Enitharmon is portrayed, paradoxically, as a mother who sustains Los:

> O perverse to thyself, contrarious
> To thy own purposes; for when she began to weave
> Shooting out in sweet pleasure her bosom in milky Love
> Flowd into the aching fibres of Los. yet contending against him
> In pride sending his Fibres over to her objects of jealousy
> In the little lovely Allegoric Night of Albions Daughters
> Which stretchd abroad, expanding east & west & north & south
> Thro' all the World of Erin & of Los & all their Children.
>
> (88: 26-33, E247)

We can therefore say that the delineation of Enitharmon as a separate identity and her attempt to enclose Los within a single form winds the body of Los into a ball.

The completion of the body of Los and of the body of Albion-in-withdrawal results in the consolidation of Albion's error. As I have argued in my discussion of the first chapter of *Jerusalem*, the form of the fallen world exists in the interaction between the world of death eternal and the world of Golgonooza, between the Daughters of Albion and the Daughters of Los, surface and substance, body and spirit. As a result of the developments discussed above—the coincidence of the world woven by the Daughters and that created by Los; the completion of the form of Albion-in-withdrawal; and the completion of the world of Los —the fallen world gains a single, rigid form. Error has now been consolidated.

One can imagine this form as the outline of a world, or as a horizon, which is shared (although they stand on opposite sides) by both Albion and Los. This extraordinary body is the very form of withdrawal and is therefore what now keeps Albion and Los apart. It is, in other words, a Covering Cherub which closes Los and Albion apart from relationship and therefore from Eden:

> Thus was the Covering Cherub reveald majestic image
> Of Selfhood, Body put off, the Antichrist accursed
> Coverd with precious stones, a Human Dragon terrible
> And bright, stretchd over Europe & Asia gorgeous.
>
> (89: 9-12, E248)

One of the striking features of these events (the appearance of the Daughters' 'Allegoric Night', the separation of Enitharmon and the consolidation of Error in the Covering Cherub) is that they seem to occur in the first and last moments of fallen history. The appearance of Enitharmon as a 'Globe of blood' which trembles beneath Los's bosom suggests the similar division in *The Book of Urizen* which was the *prelude* to Los's enclosure in his own remembered world and which was the *precondition* for the construction of a world of loss. When Enitharmon is completely separated, she and Los appear 'like two Infants', who wander away from Enion in the desert (86: 62-3, E246). This, and the terrible struggle between them for dominance which ensues (86: 63-4, E246), recalls the very first appearance of Los and Enitharmon in the world that is precipitated in *The Four Zoas* as a result of the Fall. In the passage quoted above, the Covering Cherub stands between Albion/Los and Eden. The linear narrative therefore locates his appearance at the very end of time, but the image itself suggests the Covering Cherub that stands at the beginning of time and banishes Adam and Eve to a fallen history. Immediately before these lines, we read that at this point in history

> The Four Zoa's in all their faded majesty burst out in fury
> And fire. Jerusalem took the Cup which foamd in Vala's hand
> Like the red Sun upon the mountains in the bloody day
> Upon the Hermaphroditic Wine-presses of Love & Wrath.
>
> (88: 55-8, E247)

It is as if Vala, Jerusalem, and the Zoas are about to repeat the events of the Fall once again. The same phenomenon can be seen in the plates which follow on from the appearance of the Covering Cherub. Plate 90, for example, includes the description of an event which occurs at the very beginning of time: 'The Feminine separates from the Masculine & both from Man, | Ceasing to be His Emanations, Life to Themselves assuming!' (90: 1-2, E249). On this plate we also hear once again of how 'the Twelve Sons | Of Albion drank & imbibed the Life & eternal

Form of Luvah' and Reuben is cut apart by Hand 'and double Boadicea' (86: 16-17, 23-5, E249-50).

In terms of ontic time the appearance of Canaan, the separation of Enitharmon from Los and the appearance of the Covering Cherub occur in the last moments of that time. In the vision of Jerusalem, however, they can be seen to complete the form of Albion-in-withdrawal. Los extends the withdrawal of Albion into a history of six thousand years duration, but the completion of this history merely gives temporal/spatial form to the moment of withdrawal. The completion of fallen history brings us back to its beginning. We can also say that the last moment of time is the first moment of history in a second sense. This end and beginning returns us to a moment which, were it not for Los, would plunge Albion into eternal death. In order to preserve the body of Albion-in-withdrawal, the last moment of fallen time must be followed by the extension of Albion-in-withdrawal once again. The history of the fallen world moves in eternal cycle from Adam to Luther. The end and beginning of the vision of Jerusalem describe the limits of the six thousand year body of fallen history which preserves the form of Albion-in-withdrawal. They define the outline of the vision which opens from the first plate of the poem.

### WINDING THE BODY OF THE WORLD INTO A BALL

Albion and Los are now face to face. The body of the fallen world (and the body of the poem) can be described as the body of Los, Enitharmon; the Emanation of Albion, Jerusalem; and the Covering Cherub which keeps Los and Albion apart from each other and closes Eternity off from them. The situation is similar to that described by Rilke in the poem from *The Book of Hours* beginning, 'You, neighbour God, if sometime in the night'. Los and Albion, like Rilke's poet and God, are neighbours:

> Between us there is but a narrow wall,
> and by sheer chance; for it would take
> merely a call from your lips or from mine
> to break it down.[7]

On the one hand, the body of the fallen world gives definition to both Los and Albion-in-withdrawal; on the other hand, it is the necessary ground of Los's openness to Albion-in-withdrawal. Moreover, as Christ is manifest in the fallen world in Los's relationship to Albion-in-his-absence, it is in this body that

Christ himself is born. Christ must be born (as Los tells Enitharmon in the eighth Night of *The Four Zoas*) 'as a Man | Is born on Earth ... of Fair Jerusalem | In mysterys woven mantle & in the Robes of Luvah' (104: 33–5, E378). Christ is therefore born as a child of Vala (the form of the fallen world) and as the husband of Jerusalem (62: 6–15, E213).

From within a linear narrative Christ appears at a particular point in history. In vision, however, Christ can be seen as the Alpha and Omega of history. It is within Los's relationship to Albion in his absence that Christ is born, but this relationship is conducted across the full extent of fallen history. Christ therefore is at the heart of fallen time and, as I have argued, at the very centre of the vision of *Jerusalem*. History itself is the body which Christ has assumed in order to cast off. This is why Generation can be described as both the '[*Image*] of regeneration' and the point where the dead desire to place the 'Abomination of Desolation':

> O holy Generation! [*Image*] of regeneration!
> O point of mutual forgiveness between Enemies!
> Birthplace of the Lamb of God incomprehensible!
> The Dead despise & scorn thee, & cast thee out as accursed:
> Seeing the Lamb of God in thy gardens & thy palaces:
> Where they desire to place the Abomination of Desolation.
>
> (7: 65–70, E150)

If Generation is to be the 'point of mutual forgiveness between Enemies', Los must remain in relationship with Albion. In previous plates he has refused the allurements of the Daughters of Albion. It is now the Spectre who attempts to lead Los away from Albion.

The completion of the fallen world gives the Spectre an alphabet of forms with which he can perform the most astonishing mental gymnastics:

> The Spectre builded stupendous Works, taking the Starry Heavens
> Like to a curtain & folding them according to his will
> Repeating the Smaragdine Table of Hermes to draw Los down
> Into the Indefinite, refusing to believe without demonstration.
>
> (91: 32–5, E251)

At this point in time the Spectre is able to confront Los's hope for what is not yet (the return of Albion) with the force and persuasiveness of what *is* (the fallen world). It is, of course, quite clear that all this activity remains within the world of Los; the Spectre is able to fold the 'Starry Heavens ...

according to his will', but he is unable to leave the fallen world. This is of no real concern to the Spectre for, by drawing Los into the 'Indefinite,' he hopes to circumscribe the possibility of Albion's return and so render this world impregnable. In fact, it is the very concreteness of his world that he hopes will draw Los away from Albion. From the perspective of the reasoning memory the contest between what is and what is not yet must result in the victory of the visible over the invisible, and of the material reality of the present condition over the spiritual reality of what could be.

Part of the Spectre's persuasiveness resides in his ability to draw an apparent correspondence between the knowledge formed as a result of his manipulation of the veil of what *is* and the eternal realities. This claim is similar to Locke's claim to be able to generate the complex ideas of eternity and infinity by the arrangement and rearrangement of the simple ideas which appear to the self. If this is so then humanity can and should remain within the secure environment of what is. God is a God of nature, of the present, and he is an apologist for what is. By contrast, Los affirms that 'he who wishes to see a Vision; a perfect Whole | Must see it in its Minute Particulars' and, moreover, that 'every | Particular is a Man; a Divine Member of the Divine Jesus' (91: 20-1, 29-30, E177). In other words, we must see 'thro' the constituted world of the self. Paradoxically, it is the Spectre's knowledge that is indefinite, for it is founded on the data available to the reasoning memory. It is vision that appears in definite outline because it is vision of others.

Los deals with the temptation posed by the Spectre by 'subduing' his own self and unbinding the eye and ear of the Spectre (91: 44-6, E252). Los does not identify himself with nature, yet he does not destroy it. Instead, the nature held by the Spectre is radically displaced. The images which Blake uses to convey the extremity of this displacement are quite striking:

> Then he sent forth the Spectre all his pyramids were grains
> Of sand & his pillars: dust on the flys wing: & his starry
> Heavens; a moth of gold & silver mocking his anxious grasp
> Thus Los alterd his Spectre & every Ratio of his Reason
> He alterd time after time, with dire pain & many tears
> Till he had completely divided him into a separate space.
>
> (91: 47-52, E252)

As the result of Los's wounding of his self, the pyramid, with its secret chamber and impregnable walls, becomes a grain of sand. The form designed to convey the individual with all his wealth into the land beyond death therefore becomes an object which is both subject to the forces of mortality and is itself their agent. The pillars which once held up the roof of the Spectre's world are now merely dust on an instrument designed for flight. And the 'Starry Heavens' which the Spectre could fold and unfold according to his will are now outside his grasp.

With the Spectre divided into a separate space the fallen world can be seen as the ground for an appeal by Los (and Jesus in Los) to Albion-in-withdrawal. The poem therefore returns to its beginning, for this appeal (which can be heard on plate 96) is nothing less than the appeal which we saw on the opening plates of the poem. What remained implicit in the original vision has, however, at this point in the poem been elaborated. We can now see both Jesus and Albion as giant figures which stretch across the full extent of time. The moment of Albion's withdrawal can be seen as the six thousand year history given form by Los. It is this history which gives a body to the moment of withdrawal and so opens the possibility of Albion's return.

The world now stands, as Enitharmon recognizes, on the verge of regeneration:

> The Poets Song draws to its period & Enitharmon is no more.
> For if he be that Albion I can never weave him in my Looms
> But when he touches the first fibrous thread, like filmy dew
> My Looms will be no more & I annihilate vanish for ever
> Then thou wilt Create another Female according to thy Will.
>
> (92: 8-12, E252)

Albion can, however, not simply arise, for the body which Los and Christ face is nothing more than a body of death, an inert body of clay. It is now, therefore, that an event occurs which once again can be located in the first and last moment of time. With the completion of the body of Albion-in-withdrawal, life is breathed into this body of clay and Albion and Brittannia are able to arise. It is important to remember that this moment is not the instant of regeneration. It is, instead, merely the moment in which life is given to the inert body of Albion-in-withdrawal. In this moment Los is seen simply as 'the Great Spectre Los' who has preserved the form of Albion-in-withdrawal. As a result of this awakening, Albion (like Blake in the opening plate of the poem) is able to see in Los the call of Christ. However, while he remains within his fallen body this vision is threatened (just as it is on a mortal level) by the world of the self. As Albion says:

> O Lord what can I do! my Selfhood cruel
> Marches against thee deceitful from Sinai & from Edom
> Into the Wilderness of Judah to meet thee in his pride
> I behold the Visions of my deadly Sleep of Six Thousand Years
> Dazling around thy skirts like a Serpent of precious stones & gold
> I know it is my Self: O my Divine Creator & Redeemer.
>
> (96: 8-13, E255)

This moment is therefore one of extreme danger. As Jesus propounds the need for forgiveness, brotherhood and, in Albion's words, the 'Mysterious | Offering of Self for Another' (96: 20-1, E256), the Covering Cherub overshadows them (96: 18, E255) and then comes between them (96: 29, E256).

In the first lines of *Jerusalem*, Albion responded to Jesus's call by affirming that he was not '*One*' but '*Many*' and by judging Jesus to be no more than a 'Phantom of the over heated brain!' (4: 23-4, E146). At the end of *Jerusalem* the same call draws forth a very different response. As a result of the work of the poet/prophet, Error has now been consolidated and Albion is able to see his own role in the fabrication of the Covering Cherub which threatens to destroy Los and Jesus; on the other hand he can also clearly see and hear the call of Los and Jesus. It is finally their faithfulness and friendship, embodied in *Jerusalem* and in the body of the fallen world, that causes the startling reversal of lines 30-3:

> Albion stood in terror: not for himself but for his Friend
> Divine, & Self was lost in the contemplation of faith
> And wonder at the Divine Mercy & at Los's sublime honour.
>
> (96: 30-2, E256)

It is this radical change of comportment, and the leap which follows, that renders the abyss of the fallen world 'a Vision' and 'a Dream' (96: 36, E256). Albion's world is now opened to others and as a result

> the Furnaces became
> Fountains of Living Waters flowing from the Humanity Divine
> And all the Cities of Albion rose from their Slumbers, and All
> The Sons & Daughters of Albion on soft clouds Waking from Sleep
> Soon all around remote the Heavens burnt with flaming fires.
>
> (96: 36-40, E256)

The world of the self is now inverted and, rather than being the horizon of the world, it becomes the ground for the expansive life of Eternity. The world of Los and Enitharmon is no longer the horizon of what is, but the ground for a movement into relationship. At this point in the poem we see the possibility implicit in the opening vision of Jesus's call to Albion-in-withdrawal: Albion's return and regeneration. In the apocalypse which follows it is as if the structures of the self have been turned inside out. Rather than a closet, each Man has 'Four Faces' (98: 12, E257); the ear is no longer a 'whirlpool fierce to draw creations in' (*BT*6: 17, E6), but an organ which circumscribes and circumcises 'the excrementitious | Husk & Covering into Vacuum' and drives 'outward the Body of Death in an Eternal Death & Resurrection' (98: 18–20, E257). The solitary ruminations of the caverned man have been replaced with visionary conversation:

And they conversed together in Visionary forms dramatic which bright
Redounded from their Tongues in thunderous majesty, in Visions
In new Expanses, creating exemplars of Memory and of Intellect
Creating Space, Creating Time according to the wonders Divine
Of Human Imagination.

(98: 28–32, E257–8)

With this vision of apocalypse *Jerusalem*, and the vision seen by Blake as he wakes each morning, is completed.

ENDING

Northrop Frye argues that in *Jerusalem* the reader is not prepared for the apocalypse that occurs at the end of the fourth chapter:

We look back to see where the reversal of perspective occurred, but find nothing very tangible, and after so much churning, the mere silent appearance of the expected butter may seem almost an anticlimax.[8]

His opinion is echoed by numerous critics of the poem, although not necessarily with the same negative judgement. W. J. T. Mitchell writes that 'If we read back into the preceding episodes to find the event that has made the difference, we find only ambiguous signals, not efficient causes.'[9]

It is true, of course, that Albion's awakening depends upon the breath of the Divine, that his decision to enter the furnaces of affliction is freely taken and therefore not causally determined, and that Jesus's appearance represents the irruption in time of a force which proceeds from beyond its perimeter. Nevertheless, to compare the apocalypse of *Jerusalem* to the appearance of butter in cream, or to say that it is grounded in a 'leap of faith in the present moment', is profoundly misleading.

The apocalypse of Jerusalem details the point of encounter between Christ and Albion, Los and Albion, the eternal and the temporal, Albion and Brittannia, and Albion and his members. This is an encounter for which Los, and the entire poem, has been preparing the necessary, even if not the sufficient, conditions. In ontic time it is true that apocalypse appears at the very moment that Error is consolidated and the Antichrist appears. From this perspective it does indeed seem that regeneration bears no relationship to the history that precedes it, but, in vision, apocalypse can be seen to be an event which occurs throughout the six thousand year extent of the fallen body of Albion. From the perspective of vision, therefore, the entire poem has prepared for this event by delineating, in tireless detail, the body of fallen time which makes the leap of Albion's regeneration possible.

An apocalypse of this kind offers a series of conceptual difficulties to the critic. Eschatology is traditionally called

> the 'doctrine of the last things' or the 'doctrine of the end'. By these last things were meant events which will one day break upon man, history and the world at the end of time.[10]

But Albion is the six thousand year extent of fallen history and therefore his regeneration bears a relationship to each moment of time. When Albion awakes, for example, all of time is gathered into his body: he sees his 'deadly Sleep of Six Thousand Years . . . like a Serpent of precious stones & gold' and confesses that this form is his 'Self' (96: 11-13, E255). We must say that rather than occurring at the end of time apocalypse is enacted in each moment of the fallen world. How are we to characterize this relationship of apocalypse to the moments of fallen time?

From the perspective of ontic time the apocalypse is 'now' and 'not yet'. It is interesting to note that Christ speaks of the coming of the kingdom of God in similar terms. In Luke 17: 20-37, for example, he speaks of a kingdom which is both present and which approaches us from the imminent future.[11] This choice of tense clearly creates a series of vexing problems for interpretation. Norman Perrin writes, for example, that 'The question to be raised . . . is . . . whether it is legitimate to think of Jesus' use of Kingdom of God in terms of "present" and "future" at all.'[12] In Jerusalem this paradox appears because of the tension between vision and the perspective of the closeted self. For the closeted self time seems to vanish into an unreachable past and an unfathomable future. What exists is only what is present to the self. Love is 'love to the existent and the like' (*philia*).[13] For Blake, however, the linear expanse of fallen time is the body of the whole man, and similarly each moment of the time of an individual's life, although perceived by the reasoning memory as a worm sixty winters long, forms part of his identity. Vision sees this extensive body of humanity as a single identity and, moreover, as a moment in the life of Albion that has been frozen. This provokes an expansion of love to include that which is not present to the closeted self. Love becomes *agape*: 'love to the non-existent, love to the unlike, the unworthy, the worthless, to the lost, the transient and the dead'.[14] Vision is therefore able to see in the 'now' both the fact of enclosure and the possibility of regeneration, indeed, the *reality* of regeneration. The fallen world closes the self within a dull round of six thousand years duration and so postpones regeneration: the apocalypse is 'not yet'. But this round is a moment in the life of Albion, and therefore apocalypse and regeneration can be pictured as crowding in on all sides of the fleeting moment of withdrawal. The reality of apocalypse is 'now'. On the one hand 'Error or Creation will be Burned Up . . . the Moment Men cease to behold it' (*VLJ* E565). On the other hand 'Man is born a Spectre or Satan & is altogether an Evil, & requires a New Selfhood continually & must continually be changed into his direct Contrary' (E200). In casting off the enclosure of the self a last judgement passes upon the self, but this event must be repeated again and again, for the apocalypse is 'not yet'.

The final plate of the poem seems to contain two contradictory movements. On the one hand the plate itself 'faces back into the work'.[15] From this perspective the poem has become a serpent temple, a vast surface which still closes us off from Albion. All we see of the poem (now it has closed and we have left the moment of vision) is the surface of *Jerusalem*, the shape of the poem that has been retained by the reasoning memory. This form is retained in the relationship between the Spectre of Los and his Emanation. The former is seen on this plate with his back turned towards us. He is moving away from Los and towards the serpent temple, carrying a form which suggests the material, earthly sun. The latter, standing on the right hand side of the plate, has similarly turned her back to the reader. She is unfolding the veil of the night sky over the 'moon-ark of Generation'.[16] The world of the self would therefore seem to be quite intact. However, there has been a major rearrangement of forces within this world. On plate 6 Los turned away from the reader, and the Spectre formed a roof which closed Los within the world of the self. By contrast, on this final plate the world held by the Spectre and the Emanation is the ground for a movement forward. Los now faces the reader. The fallen form of Jerusalem/*Jerusalem* no longer forms the horizon of the self; instead it is the ground for a movement into relationship. This movement is that in which Christ can be seen in Los. It is interesting to note that this plate is turned at right angles to the ones which precede it. Los is stepping forth in a movement which proceeds both at right angles to the linear movement of *Jerusalem* and which takes him back against the stream of the poem to the doorway seen in its opening plates. It is this casting off of the world of the self which *Jerusalem* now exhorts the reader to attempt. It is the poem itself, the very vehicle which has taken us to this point, which now must be cast off. The poem must be not the horizon of our world but the ground for a leap into relationship. It is in this constant casting off of the world of the self that we are able to elaborate a history of freedom.

# 7. Los and Jesus

> Voltaire insinuates that these Limits are the cruel work of God
> Mocking the Remover of Limits & the Resurrection of the Dead
> Setting up Kings in wrath: in holiness of Natural Religion
> Which Los with his mighty Hammer demolishes time on time
> 
> (J 73: 29–32, E228)

Most discussions of Los proceed along a linear path and note the changes in Blake's conception of this figure as his œuvre proceeds.[1] However, one of the major thrusts of the poems that I have been discussing is that the linear time which appears to the closeted man is not the only or in fact the most fundamental experience of time. It therefore offers us only a partial view of Los.

From the perspective of 'sleep', Los creates and is himself enclosed within linear time. He is a worm elongated into a winter which is six thousand years long. Los is demiurge and fallen creator; he is a figure of flesh who must be born, whose world must be elaborated, and who must come to realize that the world in which he is domiciled is his creation. However, from the perspective of embrace, a very different Los can be seen. Los is now the eternal watchman and prophet. He is the ever-apparent Elias, who is able to open within the spaces of his creation and of his body a movement which continually opens the world of loss to others. Finally, in the time of awaking, the six thousand years of fallen history can be seen as a visionary construction which sustains a relationship to Albion-in-withdrawal. It is important to recognize that demiurge, watchman, and visionary prophet coexist with one another. Los, like Albion, is a figure who is extended throughout a six thousand year history; yet he is one man. Los forms the horizon of the fallen world; however, Los's embrace of the 'creation' that hems us in, and his continual opening of it to Albion-in-withdrawal, changes the prison into a seed. It is in this reversal, enacted by the 'new' Los within the body of the 'old', that Los becomes Sol and we reach the very limits of the fallen world. It is at this point that Los appears in the similitude of Jesus.

The appearance of Jesus within the fallen world represents the *raison d'être* of Los's prophetic work and defines the furthest reach of *Jerusalem*. Jesus appears at the precise point that self and other, time and Eternity, male and female, enter into relationship: in *Milton* he appears where Milton and Ololon, time and Eternity, are on the verge of embrace; and in *Jerusalem* he is seen and heard in the attentiveness of Los to Albion-in-withdrawal. Conversely, when Albion withdraws into the enclosure of the self, he loses sight of the Divine Vision. Jesus is therefore seen in the casting off of enclosure and the entry into relationship with another.

This is why Jesus is characterized in Blake's œuvre as an iconoclast and breaker of limits. In *Milton* we are told that Jesus has torn and 'now shall wholly purge away with Fire' the 'Sexual Garments' which hide 'the Human Lineaments as with an Ark & Curtains' (41: 25–7, E142–3); in *Jerusalem* Jesus is characterized as a person who rends 'the Infernal Veil . . . & the whole Druid Law removes away' (69: 38–9, E223), and later in the same poem he is described as a person who

>    breaking thro' the Central Zones of Death & Hell
> Opens Eternity in Time & Space; triumphant in Mercy.
>                               (75: 21–2, E231)

Jesus is the movement out of enclosure and into relationship (the spring of eternal life) which forms the very basis of life.

Jesus is therefore seen whenever individuals move into relationship. He is this movement into relationship, but, it is important to add, he is also *the body* of relationship. In the first Night of *The Four Zoas*, for example, when 'those in Great Eternity' meet 'in the council of God | As one Man' (21: 1–2, E310), they appear in two quite different forms. When they contract their Senses 'They behold Multitude', but when they expand their senses they

>                               behold as one
> As One Man all the Universal family & that one Man
> They call Jesus the Christ & they in him & he in them
> Live in Perfect harmony in Eden the land of life
> Consulting as One Man above the Mountain of Snowdon Sublime.
>                               (21: 3–7, E311)

Similarly, in Night the Eighth 'All in Great Eternity' meet 'in the Council of God | as one Man Even Jesus' (99: 1–2, E371), and when the 'Twenty-four' join together in *Jerusalem* to attempt to recall Albion, they appear as one in 'A Human Vision! | Human Divine, Jesus the Saviour, blessed for ever and ever' (36[40]: 46–7, E182).

It is therefore possible to distinguish between our corporeal body and the spiritual body of Jesus which appears in relationship. In the 'Laocoön' engraving, for example, Blake distinguishes between 'The Divine Body' and 'The Natural Man'. On the one hand he writes that 'What can be Created Can be Destroyed | Adam is only The Natural Man & not the Soul or Imagination', and on the other hand he affirms that 'The Eternal Body of Man is The IMAGINATION. | God himself | that is | The Divine Body | ... [Yeshua] JESUS we are his Members' (E273). This 'Eternal Body of Man' is a body of relationship; it is a dynamic, living form which is defined in the movement which circumscribes and circumcises 'the excrementitious | Husk & covering into Vacuum evaporating revealing the lineaments of Man | Driving outward the Body of Death in an Eternal Death & | Resurrection' (98: 18–20, E257).

One of the most striking claims that Blake makes for Los's creative work, and for his own work as well, is that this 'Divine Body' 'manifests itself in his Works of Art (In Eternity All is Vision)' (E273). We can gloss this by observing that Los's creation, and by implication the 'lesser' productions of prophets and poets such as Blake, is important for two closely linked reasons. First it gives a body to Albion-in-withdrawal and in this way consolidates Error. It is this negative task which opens the possibility that Albion will recognize his error and so be moved to cast it off. Second, by maintaining a relationship with Albion and by opening his created world again and again, Los makes it possible for Jesus's voice to be heard within the fallen world. In other words, Los creates the body of Error which makes it possible for Jesus to be *incarnated* and born within the body of the fallen world.

The body in which Jesus is incarnated is also the body in which he is crucified. The act of calling fallen humanity to a life of relationship defines him as the archetypal Transgressor. He belongs, as the Bard tells us, to the Class of the 'Reprobate' and he 'was Punish'd as a Transgressor' (13: 27, E107). Jesus is therefore both Transgressor and Victim, for what cannot be included within the fallen man's single law must be excluded. This is why in *Milton* Jesus is seen with 'The Clouds of Ololon folded' around his limbs 'as a Garment dipped in blood', and why in *The Four Zoas* he is seen in the robes of Luvah. On plate 95 of *Jerusalem* this double role can be seen in the attempt by Albion's Self to overcome Jesus by crucifying him (96: 8–13, E255). Golgonooza (the 'deadly Sleep of Six Thousand

Years' which is given substance by Los) is itself the new Golgotha, the point at which Christ is crucified once more.

The appearance of this many-sided figure to Albion in the last plates of *Jerusalem* underlines that the power which forms the ground for Albion's eternal life is outside the self. As Blake writes in *A Vision of the Last Judgment*, 'Eternal Things' all spring from

the Divine Humanity All beams from him [ <Because> *as he himself has said All dwells in him*] He is the Bread & the Wine he is the Water of Life. (*VLJ*, E561)

This does not mean that the individual is simply moulded by Jesus. In the opening plates of *Jerusalem* and in the passage quoted above, the relationship is reciprocal. Jesus dwells in us and we dwell in him. However, in this conception the world-forming imagination of the individual and of Albion is displaced from the centre of the universe.

In Blake's œuvre the autonomous imagination of the Romantics is subject to a visionary deconstruction with the result that in Los it is transformed into a process of visionary construction. The term Imagination is, however, reserved for the limit-breaking call of Jesus. Imagination in this sense is a person who leads us outside of ourselves and into relationship. In Blake's œuvre identity is formed in relationship and therefore we can also say that the Imagination is a person who, by calling us outside of ourselves, forms us. To be formed by Jesus is to allow the Spectrous world of the self to be moved by the call of another and so to allow one's own being to be recast. It is to turn the forms held in the memory into 'Visionary forms dramatic'. This is a labour which we are always only just beginning.

# Notes

### INTRODUCTION

1. G. E. Bentley, Jr. (ed.), *William Blake: The Critical Heritage* (London and Boston: Routledge & Kegan Paul, 1975), 69.
2. Ibid. 182.
3. Raymond Lister, 'W. B. Yeats as an Editor of William Blake', *Blake Studies*, suppl. to vol. 1 (1968-9), 136.
4. Margaret Rudd, *Organiz'd Innocence* (London: Routledge & Kegan Paul, 1956), 22.
5. Kathleen Raine, *Blake and Tradition*, The A. W. Mellon Lectures in the Fine Arts (1962), (London: Routledge & Kegan Paul, 1969), vol. i, p. xxviii. See also George Mills Harper, *The Neoplatonism of William Blake* (Chapel Hill: Univ. of North Carolina Press, and London: OUP, 1961).
6. David V. Erdman, *Blake: Prophet Against Empire* (1954; rev. edn. Princeton, NJ: Princeton Univ. Press, 1969), p. xii.
7. Northrop Frye, *Fearful Symmetry: A Study of William Blake* (Princeton, NJ: Princeton Univ. Press, 1947), 417.
8. Paul Ricoeur, 'What is a Text? Explanation and Interpretation', in David M. Rasmussen (ed.), *Mythic-Symbolic Language and Philosophical Anthropology* (The Hague: Martinus Nijhoff, 1971), 144.
9. Ricoeur contrasts a hermeneutics of suspicion with a hermeneutics of belief. See *Freud and Philosophy: An Essay on Interpretation*, trans. Denis Savage (New Haven: Yale Univ. Press, 1970). He writes: 'According to the one pole, hermeneutics is understood as the manifestation and restoration of a meaning addressed to me in the manner of a message, a proclamation, or as is sometimes said, a kerygma; according to the other pole, it is understood as a demystification, as a reduction of illusion . . .' (p. 27).
10. Quoted by Gayatri Chakravorty Spivak in Preface to her translation of *Of Grammatology*, by Jacques Derrida (Baltimore: Johns Hopkins Univ. Press, 1976), p. xxvi.
11. The word 'other' is often capitalized in contemporary philosophical, literary, and psychoanalytic writings. I have not followed this convention because it suggests a more abstract and impersonal 'other' than I wish to invoke here. For Blake, the 'other' is always a person: in Eternity even Rocks, Clouds, and Mountains are vocal (FZ 71: 4, E148), and in the apocalypse at the end of *Jerusalem* 'even Tree Metal Earth & Stone' are seen to have 'Human Forms' (99: 1, E258). I have refrained from capitalizing the word 'self' because to do so invokes the concept of the Jungian Self. A notion such as this is obviously very different from what Blake means by this word.

## 224  Notes to Introduction

12  Hans-Georg Gadamer, *Philosophical Hermeneutics*, trans. and ed. David E. Linge (Berkeley: Univ. of California Press, 1977), 9.
13  Maurice Merleau-Ponty, *The Prose of the World*, trans. John O'Neill, ed. Claude Lefort (Evanston: Northwestern Univ. Press, 1973), 13.
14  Quoted by Richard C. McCleary in Preface to his translation of *Signs*, by Maurice Merleau-Ponty (Evanston: Northwestern Univ. Press, 1964), p. xiv.
15  David V. Erdman, *The Illuminated Blake* (Garden City, NY: Doubleday, 1974). All citations of full-plate illustrations in Blake's illuminated poems refer to this volume.
16  All references to Blake's poetry and prose are taken from the newly revised edition of *The Complete Poetry and Prose of William Blake*, ed. David V. Erdman, commentary by Harold Bloom (Garden City, NY: Anchor Press–Doubleday, 1982) and will be inserted parenthetically in the text.
17  Samuel Taylor Coleridge, *Biographia Literaria*, ed. James Engell and W. Jackson Bate (London: Routledge & Kegan Paul, and Princeton, NJ: Princeton Univ. Press, 1983), in *The Collected Works of Samuel Taylor Coleridge*, ed. Kathleen Coburn, Bollingen Series 75, vii: pt. i, 304. (For recent critiques of the Romantic Imagination see e.g. Paul de Man, *The Rhetoric of Romanticism* (New York: Columbia Univ. Press, 1984); Nelson Hilton and Thomas A. Vogler (eds.), *Unnam'd Forms: Blake and Textuality* (Berkeley and Los Angeles: Univ. of California Press, 1986); Jerome McGann, *The Romantic Ideology: A Critical Investigation* (Chicago: Univ. of Chicago Press, 1983).
18  Frye, *Fearful Symmetry*, 19.
19  Ibid.
20  Ibid. 30.
21  Ibid.
22  Ibid. 412.
23  Ibid. 26, 27.
24  Ibid. 26.
25  The following list is far from exhaustive. I will have cause to quote numerous other examples of this phenomenon in the argument that follows.
26  Hazard Adams, *Blake and Yeats: The Contrary Vision* (Ithaca, NY: Cornell Univ. Press, 1955), 24.
27  Harold Bloom, *Blake's Apocalypse: A Study in Poetic Argument* (London: Victor Gollancz, 1963), 281.
28  Edward J. Rose, 'The Gate of Los: Vision and Symbol in Blake', *Texas Studies in Literature and Language*, 20 (1978), 6. Rose writes in 'The Symbolism of the Opened Center and Poetic Theory in Blake's *Jerusalem*', in *Studies in English Literature: 1500-1900*, 5 (1965), 587–606, that 'Self-fulfillment is the interior self-explosion into eternity; it is the opening of a center' (p. 601).

29 Robert F. Gleckner, *The Piper and the Bard: A Study of William Blake* (Detroit: Wayne State Univ. Press, 1959), 54.
30 Morris Eaves, 'The Title-page of *The Book of Urizen*', in Morton D. Paley and Michael Phillips (eds.), *William Blake: Essays in Honour of Sir Geoffrey Keynes* (Oxford: Clarendon Press, 1973), 229.
31 W. J. T. Mitchell, *Blake's Composite Art: A Study of the Illuminated Poetry* (Princeton, NJ: Princeton Univ. Press, 1978), 136.
32 Daniel Stempel, 'Blake, Foucault, and the Classical Episteme', *PMLA* 96 (1981), 405.
33 Anne K. Mellor, *Blake's Human Form Divine* (Berkeley: Univ. of California Press, 1974), 325.
34 Melanie F. Bandy, *Mind Forged Manacles: Evil in the Poetry of Blake and Shelley* (Tuscaloosa, Ala.: Univ. of Alabama Press, 1981), 24.
35 David E. James, *Written Within and Without: A Study of Blake's 'Milton'*, Europaische Hochschulschriften, 14th ser. (Frankfurt am Main: Peter Lang, 1978), 67.
36 Harald A. Kittel, '*The Book of Urizen* and *An Essay Concerning Human Understanding*', in Michael Phillips (ed.), *Interpreting Blake* (Cambridge: CUP, 1978), 114.
37 Morton D. Paley, *Energy and the Imagination: A Study of the Development of Blake's Thought* (London: OUP, 1970), 260.
38 Leonard W. Deen, *Conversing in Paradise: Poetic Genius and Identity-as-Community in Blake's Los* (Columbia: Univ. of Missouri Press, 1983), 20.
39 Minna Doskow, *William Blake's 'Jerusalem'* (Rutherford, Madison, Teaneck, NJ: Fairleigh Dickinson Press, 1982), 168.
40 Donald Ault, *Narrative Unbound: Re-Visioning William Blake's 'The Four Zoas'* (Barrytown: Station Hill Press, 1987), 22.
41 In Blake criticism, Los and Jesus are often confused. See e.g. Cecil Anthony Abrahams, *William Blake's Fourfold Man* (Bonn: Bouvier Verlag Herbert Grundmann, 1978), 33; Mitchell, *Blake's Composite Art*, 35; Paley, *Energy and the Imagination*, 143, 200.
42 See e.g. Thomas R. Frosch, *The Awakening of Albion: The Renovation of the Body in the Poetry of William Blake* (Ithaca, NY: Cornell Univ. Press, 1974); Leopold Damrosch, *Symbol and Truth in Blake's Myth* (Princeton, NJ: Princeton Univ. Press, 1980); Steven Shaviro, '"Striving with Systems": Blake and the Politics of Difference', *boundary 2*, 10 (1982), 229-50.
43 Paul de Mann, 'Intentional Structure of the Romantic Image', in Harold Bloom (ed.), *Romanticism and Consciousness: Essays in Criticism* (New York: W. W. Norton, 1970), 69.
44 Frye, *Fearful Symmetry*, 21.
45 Ibid. 14-15.
46 John Locke, *An Essay Concerning Human Understanding*, ed. Alexander Campbell Fraser (1894; repr. New York: Dover, 1959), i. 211-12.
47 Ibid. i. 121-2.

### 226  Notes to Introduction

48  Ibid. ii. 167.
49  Ibid. i. 164-5.
50  Alexander Koyré, *Newtonian Studies* (London: Chapman and Hall, 1965), 23.
51  Quoted by Arthur Johnson, ed., in Introduction to *The Advancement of Learning and New Atlantis*, by Francis Bacon (Oxford: Clarendon Press, 1974), vii.
52  Jacques Derrida, *Speech and Phenomena: And Other Essays on Husserl's Theory of Signs*, trans. David B. Allison (Evanston: Northwestern Univ. Press, 1973), 6.
53  Ibid. 6-7.
54  Ferdinand de Saussure, *Course in General Linguistics*, trans. Wade Baskin, ed. Charles Bally, Albert Sechehaye, and Albert Reidlinge (1959; rev. edn. Glasgow: Fontana, 1974), 120.
55  Michael Ryan, *Marxism and Deconstruction: A Critical Articulation* (Baltimore: Johns Hopkins Univ. Press, 1984), 14.
56  For a discussion of this term see Jacques Derrida, 'Différance', in *Speech and Phenomena*, 129-60.
57  Ibid. 104.
58  Ibid.
59  Ibid.
60  This ground should not be confused with the ground that Urizen searches for in *The Book of Urizen* and *The Four Zoas*. It is, of course, also very different from the first ground, or set of axioms, sought by philosophy.
61  See e.g. Abrahams, *William Blake's Four Fold Man*, 1 and 22; Hazard Adams, 'Blake, Jerusalem, and Symbolic Form', *Blake Studies*, 7 (1975), 166; Mark Bracher, *Being Form'd: Thinking Through Blake's 'Milton'* (Barrytown, NY: Station Hill Press, 1985), 1; Damrosch, *Symbol and Truth in Blake's Myth*, 30; Frosch, *The Awakening of Albion*, 27 and 106-7; James, *Written Within and Without*, 67; Mitchell, *Blake's Composite Art*, 217-18; Paley, *Energy and the Imagination*, 169 and 258.
62  Frye, *Fearful Symmetry*, 19.
63  Henry Crabb Robinson, *The Diary of Henry Crabb Robinson: An Abridgement*, ed. Derek Hudson (London: OUP, 1967), 87.
64  For a discussion of the differences between Hebraism and Classicism see Murray Roston, *Prophet and Poet: The Bible and the Growth of Romanticism* (London: Faber and Faber, 1965), 15-41.
65  Jacques Derrida, 'Violence and Metaphysics', in *Writing and Difference*, trans. Alan Bass (London: Routledge & Kegan Paul, 1978), 153.
66  Edward J. Rose, 'Los, Pilgrim of Eternity', in Stuart Curran and Joseph Anthony Wittreich, Jr. (eds.), *Blake's Sublime Allegory: Essays on 'The Four Zoas,' 'Milton' and 'Jerusalem'* (Madison, Wisconsin: Univ. of Wisconsin Press, 1973), 83-99, calls Los 'the watchman of man's mental night or winter, the visionary spirit abroad in the temporal world of mortal men' (p. 98). (Critics who

write about Los do not always direct their attention to the Los of the Lambeth prophecies as distinct from the Los of, for example *Jerusalem*. Nevertheless, in the following pages I have cited a number of critics whose discussion of the general character of Los, or of the poet/prophet as he appears in the later poems, is of interest to, or can be applied to, our present discussion).

67 Frosch, *The Awakening of Albion*, calls Los 'the power of human creativity' (p. 189 n.); Edward J. Rose, 'Los: Pilgrim of Eternity', writes that 'Los is the act of perceiving' (p. 83). See also: Deen, *Conversing in Paradise*, 20; Mitchell, *Blake's Composite Art*, 166.

68 See e.g. Christine Gallant, *Blake and the Assimilation of Chaos* (Princeton, NJ: Princeton Univ. Press, 1978), 17-18.

69 Erdman, in *Prophet Against Empire*, writes that Los's name is a pun on loss and that this name suggests man's need for a continual 'loss of self' (p. 253 n). See also: Deen, *Conversing in Paradise*, 71; Aaron Fogel, 'Pictures of Speech: On Blake's Poetic', *Studies in Romanticism*, 21 (1982), 224; Ronald L. Grimes, *The Divine Imagination: William Blake's Major Prophetic Visions* (Metuchen, NJ: The Scarecrow Press, and the American Theological Library Association, 1972), 95; Paley, *Energy and the Imagination*, 65.

70 Paley, *Energy and the Imagination*, 64-5. See also John Beer, *Blake's Visionary Universe* (Manchester: Manchester Univ. Press, 1969), 78; Edward J. Rose, 'The Spirit of the Bounding Line: Blake's Los', *Criticism*, 13 (1971), 54.
There are, of course, numerous other aetiologies that have been proposed for Los. Frye in 'Notes for a Commentary on *Milton*', in Vivian de Sola Pinto (ed.), *The Divine Vision: Studies in the Poetry and Art of William Blake* (London: Victor Gollancz, 1957) suggests that 'A Chaucerian synonym for fame, *los* or *loos*, may be the source of the name of Blake's great hero' (pp. 100-1). H. M. Margoliouth, *William Blake* (1961; repr. Hamden, Conn.: Archon Books, 1967), writes that Los 'may be a partial anagram of "soul"' (pp. 15-16); E. B. Murray, 'Jerusalem Reversed', *Blake Studies*, 7 (1974), 11-25, writes that at one point in *Jerusalem* Los is 'referred to by Blake as the giver of the "Space of Love" . . . where the initial letters perhaps too happily spell his name in reverse by, in fact, spelling "Sol"' (pp. 12-13). See also Daniel Stempel, 'Blake, Foucault, and the Classical Episteme', *PMLA*, 96 (1981), 395.

71 See e.g. S. Foster Damon, *William Blake: His Philosophy and Symbols* (Boston and New York: Houghton Mifflin, 1924), 379; Grimes, *The Divine Imagination*, 94.

72 Frye, *Fearful Symmetry*, 254.

73 Ibid. 252. See also Paley, *Energy and the Imagination*, 256. Erdman, *Prophet Against Empire*, notes that Los's role as blacksmith is 'an apt heroic symbol of his own position among the skilled trades' (pp. 330-1).

74 Paley, *Energy and the Imagination*, 256. The list of associations evoked by the name 'Los' could be greatly expanded. Morton

## 228   Notes to Introduction

Paley, although writing specifically about the Los of Jerusalem, gives a good catalogue of these associations in *The Continuing City* (Oxford: OUP, 1984), 234 (see also pp. 236, 267).

75  Damrosch, *Symbol and Truth*, 373-4.
76  Frye, *Fearful Symmetry*, 253.
77  Paul Ricoeur, *Freud and Philosophy*, 15-16.
78  In the following argument I use a distinction between the ontic and the ontological which is taken from Martin Heidegger, *Being and Time*, trans. John Macquarie and Edward Robinson (Oxford: Basil Blackwell, 1962). The word 'ontic' refers to the superficial, or external, dimension of beings. From this perspective the beings that one encounters in the world are merely objects. The term 'ontological', I use to refer to 'the state of Being that is constitutive for those entities that exist' (*Being and Time*, 33). William J. Richardson, SJ, in *Heidegger: Through Phenomenology to Thought*, Phaenomenologica, 13 (The Hague: Martinus Nijhoff, 1963), distinguishes between 'ontic' and 'ontological' knowing in the following way. Ontic knowing is the 'Natural knowing that clings to the superficial dimension of the beings it meets, taking them for beings and nothing more ... On the other hand, Knowing that gathers ... beings ... together in terms of what makes them to be such, therefore seizes them in their objectiveness, reality and actuality, sc. *as* what they are (in their Being)—this is "ontological" knowing' (p. 343).
79  A major exception to this stricture is Donald Ault's *Narrative Unbound*. See also my 'Final States, Finished Forms, and *The Four Zoas*', *Blake: An Illustrated Quarterly*, 20 (1987), 144-6.
80  Stuart Curran, 'The Structures of Jerusalem' in Curran and Wittreich (eds.), *Blake's Sublime Allegory*, 329.

CHAPTER 1

1  Alexandre Kojève, *An Introduction to the Reading of Hegel: Lectures on the 'Phenomenology of Spirit'*, trans. James H. Nichols, Jr., assembled by Raymond Queneau, ed. Allan Bloom (New York: Basic Books, 1969), 8.
2  James, *Written Within and Without*, 56. Raymond Dexter Havens gives a fascinating account of Milton's standing in, and influence on, the eighteenth century in *The Influence of Milton on English Poetry* (New York: Russell and Russell, 1961). Havens observes that 'between 1705 and 1800 *Paradise Lost* was published over a hundred times'. By contrast, the *Faerie Queene* 'appeared only seven times in the same period' and there were no more than fifty editions of Shakespeare's plays (pp. 4-5).
3  Joseph Anthony Wittreich, Jr., in *Angel of Apocalypse: Blake's Idea of Milton* (Madison, Wisconsin: Univ. of Wisconsin Press), makes this point. He writes that: 'As Blake looked back upon the Milton

## Notes to Chapter One 229

tradition, upon what Milton wrote and what subsequent generations made of it, he saw a poet who, rather than escaping the anxiety of influence, was doubly afflicted by it. Milton had spent an entire career breaking loose from convention, undermining orthodoxy, and revolutionizing forms to encompass his radically new vision. Now that vision had become bound down by the very system of aesthetics from which he tried to liberate the poet and by the very orthodoxies, political and religious, that he tried to subvert' (p. 73).

4  There are numerous accounts of Blake's relationship to, and criticisms of, Milton. See e.g. Bloom, *Blake's Apocalypse*, 79-82; S. Foster Damon, 'Blake and Milton', in de Sola Pinto (ed.), *The Divine Vision*, 89-96; Frye, *Fearful Symmetry*, 337-9, 352-5; John Howard, *Blake's 'Milton'* (London: Associated University Presses, 1976), 183-8; James, *Written Within and Without*, 67-72; Florence Sandler, 'The Iconoclastic Enterprise: Blake's Critique of 'Milton's Religion', *Blake Studies*, 5 (Fall 1972), 13-57; Denis Saurat, *Blake and Milton* (New York: Russell and Russell, 1965); Irene Taylor, 'Say First! What Mov'd Blake? Blake's Comus Designs and *Milton*', in Curran and Wittreich (eds.), *Blake's Sublime Allegory*, 233-58; Wittreich, *Angel of Apocalypse*; Wittreich, 'Opening the Seals: Blake's Epics and the Milton Tradition', in *Blake's Sublime Allegory*, 23-58.
5  Curran, 'The Structures of *Jerusalem*', in *Blake's Sublime Allegory*, 329.
6  Howard, *Blake's 'Milton'*, 265 n.
7  Frye, *Fearful Symmetry*, 332; 'Notes for a Commentary on *Milton*', in de Sola Pinto (ed.), *The Divine Vision*, 130.
8  James, *Written Within and Without*, 15; Susan Fox, *Poetic Form in Blake's 'Milton'* (Princeton, NJ: Princeton Univ. Press, 1976), 58. Yet Fox observes that 'although polite rearrangement can minimize the interruption, it cannot dispense with it altogether'.
9  James Rieger, 'The Hem of their Garments', in *Blake's Sublime Allegory*, 273.
10  Fox, *Poetic Form*, 34.
11  Some idea of the global nature of this fall can be gleaned from the Bard's characterization of it as an event which occurs in Albion's mountains and in his tents. This does not imply that the fall consists of two quite separate events, but that Albion's fall occurs throughout the entire extent of a giant form.
12  At this stage of the poem the reader could not, with any degree of certainty, identify these three figures with the Classes of the Elect, the Redeemed, and the Reprobate. A full reading of the Bard's Song would have to trace the series of recognitions by which the reader comes to this understanding. In the interests of brevity, I do not attempt such a task.
13  S. Foster Damon, *A Blake Dictionary: The Ideas and Symbols of William Blake* (1965; repr. London: Thames and Hudson, 1973), 413.

230  Notes to Chapter One

14  See e.g. James, *Written Within and Without*, 18; Frye, *Fearful Symmetry*, 336; Bracher, *Being Form'd*, 25-6. As I shall argue, the distinction between the visionary and society, the Reprobate and the Elect, are not quite as clear-cut as these critics suggest.
15  James, *Written Within and Without*, 23-4. James also notes that in Blake's œuvre the Cherubim can be either divine or Satanic (p. 24).
16  Bracher, in *Being Form'd*, reads 5: 3 as yet one more example of Satan's *quid pro quo* metaphysics. In fact, the act of embracing sin in order to be able to 'put it off' is quite clearly not isomorphic with 'the state in which all give an eye for an eye and a tooth for a tooth, in a system of brutal reciprocity' (p. 27).
17  Blake's distinction between male (active) and female (passive) powers is hardly original. Locke writes in *An Essay* that 'Power . . . is two-fold, viz. as able to make, or able to receive change. The one may be called *active*, and the other *passive* power' (i. 309). Locke's distinction is itself 'the Aristotelian distinction . . . according to which substances may be either efficacious in producing change, or susceptible of change' (Locke, *An Essay*, i. 309 n). Many religions use a parallel distinction as a metaphor for the relationship between God and his creation. The former is seen as a male, active power, while the latter is a female and passive power that is created, or formed, by God. In eternity the relationship between active and passive powers seems to be analogous to that of an individual to his/her body: we do not, in fact, move our bodies any more than they move us; active and passive powers are aspects of what Hume called 'entire power'. In the course of the Fall, however, this relationship is disrupted and the passive power forms the horizon of an isolated, enclosed world. In the following pages I have understood male and female to refer in the first instance to active and passive powers rather than to either men or women. This is not meant to imply that Blake is not sexist. Quite clearly there is a highly problematic relationship between the 'sexist' terms which are the raw material for some of Blake's most persistent metaphors and the implications of those metaphors. For a detailed discussion of Blake's 'sexism' see e.g. Susan Fox, 'The Female as Metaphor in William Blake's Poetry', *Critical Inquiry*, 3 (1976-7), 507-19; Alicia Ostriker, 'Desire Gratified and Ungratified: William Blake and Sexuality', *Blake: An Illustrated Quarterly*, 16 (Winter, 1982-3), 156-65.
18  James notes in *Written Within and Without* that it is unclear as to whether it is 'Milton or Charles who is to be "atoned"?' (p. 25). He also observes that Milton and Cromwell could both fit into the class of the Redeemed and into the class of the Reprobate; the fire in Golgonooza could be either the Great Fire (as Damon argues in *A Blake Dictionary*, 204) or the fire of Los's forge in Golgonooza.
19  See Howard, *Blake's 'Milton'*, 91.
20  Fox, *Poetic Form*, 31. Bracher, in *Being Form'd*, 28-9, makes a similar point.

## Notes to Chapter One 231

21 This line is often taken from its context in the poem and read as an allusion to Blake's relationship with Hayley. See e.g. Frye, *Fearful Symmetry*, 331.
22 Bracher, *Being Form'd*, 22.
23 Ibid. 24.
24 Ibid. 22.
25 I am indebted to Dr Michael J. Tolley for pointing out that we may see Satan's milling in the Eternal living Process as the organization of a living surface, and for detailing some of the complexities involved in Blake's presentation of the Plow and Harrow as instruments of Harvest.
26 Locke, *An Essay*, i. 212.
27 Eve Teitlebaum, 'Form as Meaning in Blake's *Milton*', *Blake Studies*, 2 (Fall 1969), 37-64. James writes in *Written Within and Without* that in this passage 'Los supplies a model of successful response to Satan's subterfuge' (p. 22).
28 I am indebted to Dr Michael J. Tolley for this analogy.
29 Erdman, *The Illuminated Blake*, 226.
30 Ibid.
31 Leutha's confession is sometimes seen as a turning point in the song (see e.g. Fox, *Poetic Form*, 50). In fact, by offering to take Satan's guilt upon her own shoulders, she quite clearly remains within the system of judgement that we have been discussing.
32 James, *Written Within and Without*, 17.
33 Howard, *Blake's 'Milton'*, 16-17.
34 Bracher, *Being Form'd*, 69.

CHAPTER 2

1 Fox, *Poetic Form*, 28.
2 See Paul Davies, *The Edge of Infinity: Naked Singularities and the Destruction of Spacetime* (London: J. M. Dent, 1981), 5.
3 For a more detailed description of Eden, Beulah, Generation, and Ulro see: Abrahams, *William Blake's Fourfold Man*, 64-104; Fox, *Poetic Form*, 195-212; Frye, 'Notes for a Commentary on *Milton*', in *The Divine Vision*, 105-29; Howard, *Blake's 'Milton'*, 33-41.
4 Augustinus Aurelius, *St Augustine's Confessions*, Eng. trans. William Watts (1631; rev. edn. London: William Heinemann; and New York: Macmillan, 1962), ii. 235-7.
5 This rather precise description of the Shadow's limits suggests the geography of *Paradise Lost*. Milton is following a path that resembles the one taken by the historical Milton's Satan. In Blake's poem Milton is attempting to reintegrate all of the portions of the self that were fragmented in *Paradise Lost*.
6 Mitchell, *Blake's Composite Art* (Princeton, NJ: Princeton Univ. Press, 1978), 70. Mitchell goes on to suggest that for Blake the third force is imagination.

The image of the vortex is discussed in: Adams, *Blake and Yeats*, 104–10; Donald Ault, *Visionary Physics: Blake's Response to Newton* (Chicago: Univ. of Chicago Press, 1974), 148–60; Kay Parkhurst Easson and Roger R. Easson (eds.), *'Milton', by William Blake* (London: Thames and Hudson, 1979), 151–2; Fox, *Poetic Form*, 71–2; Frosch, *The Awakening of Albion*, 70–81; Frye, *Fearful Symmetry*, 350.

7  Mitchell observes in *Blake's Composite Art* that in this passage there is a progression through four phases: 'The first phase is the recognition of the object as a world with its own unique laws ... the second phase is a recognition of the object as something that has relations with things outside itself ... the third phase is to see it as a "universe" ... In the fourth phase ... the object is seen ... as a human form ... (pp. 71–2).

8  Fox observes in *Poetic Form* that the 'vortex is a condition of fallen humanity' (p. 73).

9  Locke, *An Essay*, i. 277–8.

10  For an elaboration of this point see Edith Wyschogrod, *Emmanuel Levinas: The Problem of Ethical Metaphysics* (The Hague: Martinus Nijhoff, 1974), 89.

11  Rudolf Bultmann, 'A Reply to the Theses of J. Schniewind', in *Kerygma and Myth: A Theological Debate*, ed. Hans-Werner Bartsch, trans. Reginald H. Fuller (London: SPCK, 1972), 116.

12  Merleau-Ponty, *The Prose of the World*, 28.

13  Ibid. 11–12.

14  Ibid. 12.

15  The title-page of copies A and B of *Milton* describes the poem as 'a Poem in 2 Books'. In copies C and D we read that it is 'a Poem of 12 Books'.

16  Wittreich, *Angel of Apocalypse*, 11. See also, Frye, *Fearful Symmetry*, 322–3.

17  I am indebted to Dr Michael J. Tolley for pointing out to me the relationship in these lines between the tarsus, revelation, the 'black cloud', and Error.

18  Frye observes, in 'Notes for a Commentary on *Milton*', that this episode suggests 'Christ's healing the blind man with clay and spittle' (p. 134).

19  W. J. T. Mitchell, 'Blake's Radical Comedy: Dramatic Structure as Meaning in *Milton*', 297, in Stuart Curran and Joseph Anthony Wittreich (eds.), *Blake's Sublime Allegory* (Madison, Wisconsin: Univ. of Wisconsin Press, 1973).

20  Damon, *William Blake*, 179.

21  Harold Fisch, 'Blake's Miltonic Moment', in Alvin H. Rosenfeld (ed.), *William Blake: Essays for S. Foster Damon* (Providence, RI: Brown Univ. Press, 1969), 52; Frye, *Fearful Symmetry*, 337; James, *Written Within and Without*, 5; Mitchell, 'Blake's Radical Comedy', 307; Edward J. Rose, 'Blake's Milton: The Poet as Poem', *Blake Studies*, 1 (Fall 1968), 37.

### Notes to Chapter Two 233

22  Fox, *Poetic Form*, 18.
23  Frye, *Fearful Symmetry*, 316.
24  Michael J. Tolley, 'Blake's Songs of Spring', in Morton D. Paley and Michael Phillips (eds.), *William Blake: Essays in Honour of Sir Geoffrey Keynes* (Oxford: Clarendon Press, 1973), 126.
25  See e.g. Damrosch, *Symbol and Truth in Blake's Myth*.
26  Paul de Man, 'The Rhetoric of Temporality', in *Interpretation: Theory and Practice*, ed. Charles S. Singleton (Baltimore: Johns Hopkins Univ. Press, 1969), 173.
27  Ibid. 174.
28  Ibid. 177.
29  Ibid. 191.
30  James Rieger, 'The Hem of their Garments', in *Blake's Sublime Allegory*, 279.
31  James, *Written Within and Without*, 133.
32  See Paul Ricoeur, 'Towards a Hermeneutic of the Idea of Revelation', in Lewis S. Mudge (ed.), *Essays on Biblical Interpretation* (Philadelphia: Fortress Press, 1980), 117.

CHAPTER 3

1   Martin Heidegger, 'Hölderlin and the Essence of Poetry', in Werner Brock (ed.), *Existence and Being* (London: Vision Press, 1949), 313.
2   Sir Isaac Newton, *Mathematical Principles of Natural Philosophy and [the] System of the World*, trans. Andrew Motte (1729), trans. rev. Florian Cajori, ed. R. T. Crawford (Berkeley and Los Angeles: Univ. of California Press, 1962), i. 6.
3   Erdman, *The Illuminated Blake*, 281. Henry Lesnick, 'The Function of Perspective in Blake's *Jerusalem*', *Bulletin of the New York Public Library*, 73 (1969), 49–55, agrees that the wind is blowing from the right and that it 'appears to be blowing both his long hair and his coat back toward the left' (p. 50).
4   Stuart Curran, 'The Structures of *Jerusalem*', in *Blake's Sublime Allegory*, 329.
5   Damon, *William Blake*, 185.
6   Ibid. 195.
7   Joseph Wicksteed, *William Blake's Jerusalem* (Boissia, Clairvaux, Jura: Trianon Press, 1953), 5.
8   See, e.g. W. H. Stevenson, 'Blake's *Jerusalem*', *Essays in Criticism*, 9 (1959), 259; Mitchell, *Blake's Composite Art*, 170; Mollyanne Marks, 'Self-Sacrifice: Theme and Image in *Jerusalem*', *Blake Studies*, 7 (1974), 48.
9   Damon, *A Blake Dictionary*, 210.
10  Erdman, *Prophet Against Empire*, 462.
11  Marks, 'Self Sacrifice', 28.

12 Karl Kiralis, 'The Theme and Structure of William Blake's *Jerusalem*', *ELH* 23 (1956), 131-2.
13 Mellor, *Blake's Human Form Divine*, 287; Joanne Witke, 'Jerusalem: A Synoptic Poem', *Comparative Literature*, 22 (1970), 266; Edward J. Rose, 'The Structure of Blake's *Jerusalem*', *Bucknell Review*, 11 (1963), 35-54; Bloom, *Blake's Apocalypse*, 405, and 'The Bard of Sensibility and the Form of Prophecy', *Eighteenth-Century Studies*, 4 (1970), 6-20; Wittreich, 'Opening the Seals', 48-52. For an account of the relationship between *Milton* and *Paradise Regained* see Stuart Curran, 'The Mental Pinnacle: *Paradise Regained* and the Romantic Four-Book epic', in Joseph Anthony Wittreich Jr. (ed.), *Calm of Mind* (Cleveland and London: Case Western Reserve Univ. Press, 1971), 133-62.
14 Morton Paley, *The Continuing City* (Oxford: OUP, 1984), 284.
15 Mitchell, *Blake's Composite Art*, 174.
16 Curran, 'The Structures of *Jerusalem*', 339.
17 Paley, *The Continuing City*, 303.
18 Doskow, *William Blake's 'Jerusalem'*, 15. For a discussion of the organizing role of the prose prefaces in *Jerusalem* see James Ferguson, 'Prefaces to *Jerusalem*', in Michael Phillips (ed.), *Interpreting Blake* (Cambridge: CUP, 1978), 164-95; Mitchell, *Blake's Composite Art*, 185-9; Witke, 'Jerusalem: A Synoptic Poem', 275.
19 Mitchell, *Blake's Composite Art*, 189, 192.
20 Bloom, *Blake's Apocalypse*, 422; George Mills Harper, 'The Odyssey of the Soul in Blake's *Jerusalem*', *Blake Studies*, 5 (1972), 78; Karl Kiralis, 'A Guide to the Intellectual Symbolism of William Blake's Later Prophetic Writings', *Criticism*, 1 (1959), 200; Marks, 'Self-Sacrifice', 40.
21 Henry Lesnick, 'Narrative Structure and the Antithetical Vision of *Jerusalem*', in *Blake's Visionary Forms Dramatic*, ed. David V. Erdman and John E. Grant (Princeton, NJ: Princeton Univ. Press, 1970), 391.
22 Paley, *The Continuing City*, 302.
23 Ibid. 290.
24 Augustinus, Aurelius, *St Augustine's Confessions*, ii. 253.
25 Locke, *An Essay*, i. 239.
26 Ibid. 256.
27 George Berkeley, *Principles of Human Knowledge*, ed. G. J. Warnock (Glasgow: Fontana, 1962), 113-14.
28 Locke, *An Essay*, 239.
29 W. H. Auden, 'For the Time Being', in *Collected Poems*, ed. Edward Mendelson (London: Faber and Faber, 1976), 297.
30 David Hume, *An Inquiry Concerning Human Understanding*, in *On Human Nature and the Understanding*, ed. Antony Flew (London: Collier Macmillan, 1962), 65.
31 See e.g. Doskow, *William Blake's 'Jerusalem'*, 15.
32 It is possible that the 'theme' refers to *The Four Zoas* and *Milton*. The subject of *The Four Zoas* is quite clearly a vision or theme

which is heard in sleep, for it is a *dream* of nine Nights. Moreover, its theme is precisely the one outlined in the opening lines of *Jerusalem* for it tells us of the Fall that brought existence into 'the sleep of Ulro' (Nights one to three), 'the passage through' the 'Eternal Death' of fallen history (Nights four to six), and of the awakening to Eternal Life (Nights seven to nine). The process of awakening that is glimpsed in *The Four Zoas* is, of course, fully elaborated in *Milton*. In both poems awakening results in a vision of the Saviour, the engagement in which *Jerusalem* can be heard.

33  Frye, *Fearful Symmetry*, 359.
34  Reproduced on p. 304 of Damrosch, *Symbol and Truth*.
35  Even after several readings *Jerusalem* can be experienced as a force which threatens the constituted world of the self. See e.g. D. J. Sloss and J. P. R. Wallis, *The Prophetic Writings of William Blake* (Oxford: The Clarendon Press, 1926), ii. 107; Algernon Charles Swinburne, in *William Blake: A Critical Essay* (2nd edn., London: John Camden Hotten, 1868), 307; Brenda S. Webster, *Blake's Prophetic Psychology* (London: Macmillan, 1983), 272.
36  Paul Ricoeur, *The Symbolism of Evil*, trans. Emerson Buchanan (Boston: Beacon, 1967), 348.
37  Morton Paley, in 'Cowper as Blake's Spectre', *Eighteenth-Century Studies*, i (1968), 236-52, finds a model for the Spectre in the life of William Cowper. See also Paley, *The Continuing City*, 246-50.
38  Damon, *William Blake*, 190. Kiralis extends this characterization in 'A Guide', 201-4. Erdman explains the importance at this time of Erin (Ireland) in Blake's symbolism by linking her with 'the renewal of the struggle for Ireland's independence' (see *Prophet Against Empire*, 482). This association underlines that it is in the spaces of Erin that the possibility of freedom and vision are preserved. See also, Paley, *The Continuing City*, 266.
39  Frye, *Fearful Symmetry*, 372-4.
40  Damon, *A Blake Dictionary*, 130.
41  Erdman, *Prophet Against Empire*, 474.
42  Damon, *A Blake Dictionary*, 458.
43  Paley, *The Continuing City*, 314.
44  Paley writes in *The Continuing City*, that the 'death of Albion and the ensuing fragmentation of humanity in *Jerusalem* is presented as the disastrous result of a primordial sexual encounter' (p. 167). This is a widely held view and I do not wish to quarrel with it, except to argue that this encounter occurs at a point which is already quite some distance along the path of the Fall. In discussing the Fall the first thing that must be established is why there are sexes at all. Los, for example, tells Enitharmon that 'Sexes must vanish & cease | To be, when Albion arises from his dread repose' (92: 13-14, E252). This is not to suggest that there is no sexual activity in Eternity (see e.g. 61: 51, E212; 69: 43-4, E223); however, as these passages attest, it is very different from that which takes place in the fallen world. The 'primordial sexual encounter' which

236   *Notes to Chapter Three*

   is the subject of 19: 40-7 and 20: 30-41 must therefore itself be the
   result of a prior activity. Paley recognizes that *Jerusalem* recounts
   events which occur prior to Albion's sexual encounter with Vala.
   This 'anterior myth' is, he argues on p. 173 of *The Continuing City*,
   'a *psychomachia* describing man's repression of his sexual passion
   and its destructive consequences'. This is, however, to advance as
   an explanation the very thing that needs to be explained. It is, as I
   have argued, withdrawal from relationship, by Albion and Luvah,
   that fragments the self and sets the scene for the 'Torments of love
   and jealousy in Albion'.
45 A full discussion of this passage would have to relate it in detail to
   the illumination on plate 28. For a discussion of this illumination
   see Erdman, *The Illuminated Blake*, 307; John E. Grant, 'Two
   Flowers in the Garden of Experience', in *William Blake: Essays for
   S. Foster Damon*, 355-62; Paley, *The Continuing City*, 169-72.
46 Frosch writes in *The Awakening of Albion* that 'Vala is the outline
   of our desires projected onto a pedestal outside ourselves and
   seized, possessed, or worshipped there, while the inner desires
   continue to go their own way' (p. 189). E. B. Murray suggests in
   'Jerusalem Reversed', *Blake Studies*, 7 (1974), 11-25, that Vala's
   name 'is a syllabic reversal of Luvah's' (p. 13). See also, Paley, *The
   Continuing City*, 189-96.
47 Jean H. Hagstrum, 'Babylon Revisited, or the Story of Luvah and
   Vala', in *Blake's Sublime Allegory*, 103.


CHAPTER 4

1 Michel Foucault, *The Order of Things: An Archaeology of the
  Human Sciences* (1971; repr. New York: Vintage Books, 1973),
  217-18.
2 See e.g.: Gertrude D. Conway, 'Wittgenstein on Foundations',
  *Philosophy Today*, 26 (Winter 1982), 332-44; John Dewey, *The
  Quest for Certainty: A Study of the Relation of Knowledge and
  Action* (New York: Anchor, 1929).
3 T. S. Eliot, *Collected Poems: 1909-1962* (London: Faber and Faber,
  1963), 206.
4 Heidegger, *Existence and Being*, 302.
5 Damon, *A Blake Dictionary*, 347. See also Frye, *Fearful Symmetry*,
  360-71; Kiralis, 'A Guide', 197-201; Paley, *The Continuing City*,
  270-2; Edward J. Rose, 'Blake's Metaphorical States', *Blake
  Studies*, 4 (1971), 27.
6 Damon, *A Blake Dictionary*, 37, 389.
7 Kiralis, 'A Guide', 197.
8 Damon writes in *William Blake* that 'Merlin is the Prophet (or Poet)
  submitted to the Feminine Will. According to the old legends,
  Merlin was seduced by *Nimue*, the Lady of the Lake (Matter), who

enclosed him forever in a rocky tomb, though he could never wholly die' (p. 449).
9 Frye, *Fearful Symmetry*, 367-8.
10 Kiralis, 'A Guide', 199.
11 Erdman draws a connection between Bath and the whig, Richard Warner. See, *Prophet Against Empire*, 476-8. For a discussion of the twenty-eight cathedral cities see Damon, *William Blake*, 186, 450, and *A Blake Dictionary*, 71-4.
12 Morton Paley discusses the alternative arrangements of the second chapter of *Jerusalem* in *The Continuing City*, 295-302, and reaches a very different conclusion from the one that I advance in this chapter. He writes that *Jerusalem*'s 'two great central myths carry with them a sense of plot, but that plot is a relatively simple one underlying complexly elaborated episodes. The episodes are developed in blocs or segments. Their thematic connection with the controlling myths is usually evident, but their narrative connection with one another is often less so . . . There is a story in *Jerusalem*, consisting of many episodes, but this diachronic aspect of the work is for the most part subordinated to its synchronic aspect: the interrelationship of themes as manifested in its 'spatial form.' The organizational container reinforces the expectation of a strong narrative line, an expectation which is subverted time after time in the work itself' (pp. 302, 303). The immediate difficulty with this view of the poem is, first, as I have argued in the previous chapter, that the synchronic aspect of the poem cannot (in this analysis) be distinguished from the 'Mathematical Form' that is held by the reasoning memory. On p. 307 of *The Continuing City* Paley anticipates this difficulty. He writes that: 'In giving a list of such events as examples of synchronism, I am far from wishing to suppose any Mathematical Form as governing the work. On the contrary, such a list will show that *Jerusalem* cannot be reduced to a diagram but follows its own internally generated course of development.' This admission would suggest that the 'synchronic aspect' of the poem is itself 'subverted time after time in the work itself'. More specifically, the points that Paley brings forward to indicate the 'non-sequentiality', or relative unimportance, of the narrative order of the second chapter are unconvincing. He writes that 'what narrative line there is distinct in the majority order and broken up in the minority order' (p. 302), but the arguments that he advances to support this contention are not persuasive. He writes on p. 301, for example, that in the minority order 'the Friends are made to reach their lowest point in 42 *before* they attempt to save Albion' and that from this position 'it is scarcely credible that the Friends should try to bear Albion back through Los's gate to Eden or that Oxford should take Bath's leaves from the Tree of life'. It is possible to argue, however, that in the minority ordering it is Los who rouses them from their state of

sleep, induces them to assume their waking personalities once more (against the whole tide of the Fall) and so make one more effort to call Albion. In this ordering, however, the narrative is not non-sequential, it is, if anything, more dramatic. Similarly, Paley argues on the same page that: 'The dramatic appearance of the Divine Vision like a silent sun is ... more appropriate after the collapse of the Friends' efforts than it is following 28 in the minority arrangement', and that: 'Most important, perhaps, moving E to second place among the segments puts Albion *hors de combat* before he makes major speeches on 29, 30, 35, and 42.' Both of these sequences are, however, appropriate if it is remembered that Albion's withdrawal involves both the entry into a state of loss and a journey in this realm. As I have argued, in terms of ontological time the Divine Sun has set and Albion has fallen at the very beginning of the chapter. The remainder of the chapter therefore traces the movement of Albion within this space and time. On the other hand, from the perspective of sequential time the space of withdrawal is finally reached only when the attempts of others to recall Albion end in failure. These two narratives are, as I have argued, intimately related to each other. It is important to remember that in the second chapter of *Jerusalem* we are not dealing with a host of different orderings, but with two, and that in the first, third and fourth chapters the plates exist in invariable order. Moreover, in the final copy of the poem the order of the second chapter of the poem reverts to that of the first, a move which suggests that we should consider carefully Blake's claim that: 'Every word and every letter is studied and put into its fit place' (E146). One can therefore argue that the sequential ordering of the poem is of paramount importance.

13 Discussion of plates 43 and 44 [29 and 30] is complicated by Blake's conflation of two myths: the messengers of Job's disasters and the return of the dove to Noah. In the interests of brevity I will, however, not discuss subsidiary issues such as this.

14 This rather complex example is supported by a host of minute particulars. As Los ventures into Albion's interior he hears a conversation between Vala and Jerusalem which brings us back to similar passages at the end of the first and the beginning of the second chapter. Similarly, at the very end of this chapter, 'an Aged pensive Woman' takes

> A Moment of Time, drawing it out with many tears & afflictions
> And many sorrows: oblique across the Atlantic Vale
> Which is the Vale of Rephaim dreadful from East to West,
> Where the Human Harvest waves abundant in the beams of Eden
> Into a Rainbow of jewels and gold, a mild Reflection from
> Albions dread Tomb. Eight thousand and five hundred years
> In its extension.
>
> (48: 31-7, E197)

## CHAPTER 5

1. Martin Heidegger, *On Time and Being*, trans. Joan Stambaugh (New York: Harper and Row, 1972), 11.
2. Bergson observes the same phenomenon with regard to music. See Henri Bergson, *Time and Free Will: An Essay on the Immediate Data of Consciousness*, trans. F. L. Pogson (London: George Allen & Unwin; and New York: Humanities Press, 1910), 100-1.
3. Erdman, *The Illuminated Blake*, 332.
4. Mitchell writes in *Blake's Composite Art*, 189, that 'there are signs that the order of the two middle chapters reflects a vision of the historical development of consciousness as a movement from masculine to feminine dominance.'
5. Damon, *William Blake*, 456.
6. The syntax is somewhat ambiguous. Harold Bloom, for example, argues that it is the Cities and not the Atlantic Ocean who speak lines 8-11 (E940).
7. Erdman, *The Illuminated Blake*, 336.
8. Bandy, *Mind Forged Manacles*, 160.
9. In Eternity, Enitharmon is the ground for a movement towards others. Los is here the radiant sun and Enitharmon the expansive form of this sun. This expansion, however, exists in relationship with its contrary, for during the winter of Eternity's life Enitharmon is a seed who encloses Los. It is only in spring/summer that this closed form is fractured and Enitharmon and Los become expansive once more. In winter, therefore, Enitharmon can be described as a 'looking-Glass' which reflects back to Los, as a reversed image, the shape of his own being. The one is in this way changed into the many (63: 20-2, E214) and the closure of sleep contains the possibility of the more extreme closure of death and withdrawal. This capacity of Enitharmon to reflect back to Los the shape of his own world is the most obvious explanation for the events that Los witnesses: he thought 'it a Poetic Vision of the Atmospheres' (63: 40, E215).
10. Basil Willey, *The Eighteenth Century Background: Studies on the Idea of Nature in the Thought of the Period* (London: Chatto and Windus, 1949), 2.
11. Ibid. 205-52.
12. *Chambers Encyclopaedia*, 1955 edn., v. 368.
13. Willey, *The Eighteenth Century Background*, 2.
14. Frye, *Fearful Symmetry*, 377, associates Hand with the three Hunt brothers. Erdman, *Prophet Against Empire*, 459, derives him from 'the accusing "indicator" or printer's fist of Leigh Hunt's editorial signature'. Edward J. Rose, 'Blake's Hand: Symbol and Design in Jerusalem', *Texas Studies in Literature and Language*, 6 (1964), 50, usefully describes him as a 'kind of anti-Los' who 'absorbs *all* his brethren'.

## CHAPTER 6

1. W. H. Auden, 'For the Time Being', in *Collected Poems*, 275.
2. Paley notes in the *Continuing City* that the golden string 'is visually depicted as russet brown'. It is therefore made out of the same substance 'that is woven into our own bodies—and that is also shaped into the text of *Jerusalem*' (p. 93). See also, E. B. Murray, 'Jerusalem Reversed', *Blake Studies*, 7 (1974), 12.
3. In the first chapter of *Jerusalem* we learn that the fallen world is on the east side of Eden. Therefore, to get to Jerusalem, as well as Eden, we 'by backward steps [must] move'.
4. Erdman sees this figure as 'Hand, with "ravening" beak ... and a cock's comb—a signal of the morning' (*The Illuminated Blake*, 357). Mitchell suggests that this figure is an 'eagle-man' who 'unites the iconography of St. John ... with the pose of Dürer's *Melencolia I* to produce an emblem of the apocalyptic prophet as melancholy artist' (*Blake's Composite Art*, 211).
5. Bloom, *Blake's Apocalypse*, 421.
6. Morton Paley finds a source for Gwendolen's attempt to reduce Hyle to an infant in Joanna Southcott's claims to be 'the virgin who was to give birth to the new Messiah, Shiloh'. See 'William Blake, The Prince of the Hebrews, and the Woman Clothed with the Sun', in Morton D. Paley and Michael Phillips (eds.), *William Blake: Essays in Honour of Sir Geoffrey Keynes*, 260-93, 280-93.
7. Rainer Maria Rilke, 'You, neighbour God, if sometimes in the night', in *Poems from the Book of Hours*, trans. Babette Deutsch (1941; repr. New York: New Directions, 1975), 13.
8. Frye, *Fearful Symmetry*, 357-8.
9. Mitchell, *Blake's Composite Art*, 184. See also W. H. Stevenson, 'Blake's Jerusalem', *Essays in Criticism*, 9 (1959), 259.
10. Jurgen Moltman, *Theology of Hope: On the Ground and the Implications of a Christian Eschatology*, trans. James W. Leitch (London: SCM Press, 1967), 15.
11. For a discussion of the use of 'Kingdom of God' in Luke 17: 20-37, see Norman Perrin, *Jesus and the Language of the Kingdom: Symbol and Metaphor in New Testament Interpretation* (1976; repr. Philadelphia: Fortress Press, 1980), 57-60.
12. Ibid. 40.
13. Moltman, *Theology of Hope*, 32.
14. Ibid.
15. Erdman, *The Illuminated Blake*, 379.
16. Ibid.

## CHAPTER 7

1. This is the strategy adopted by Deen in *Conversing in Paradise*.

# Index

Abrahams, Cecil Anthony 225 n., 226 n., 231 n., 235 n.
active and passive powers 47, 65, 68-9, 75, 112, 133, 165, 195, 230 n.
Adams, Hazard 9, 226 n., 231-2 n.
Albion:
  awakening of 212-15
  and Brittannia 212
  and *différance* 21-2, 42, 89
  and the fallen world 89, 161-2, 212
  as humanity 42
  and Jerusalem 133-6, 161, 205
  and loss 203
  remembering the body of 203-9
  and his Spectre 134-5, 161-2
  and Vala 133-6
  withdrawal of 15-16, 110-13 *passim*, 142-57 *passim*, 229 n., 235-6 n.
  see also Enitharmon, and Albion; Jesus, and Albion; Los, and Albion
allegory 37, 95-6
'Allegory addressed to the Intellectual Powers' 129, 152, 155
America 205
apocalypse 19, 24, 79, 86, 124, 213-17
Apollo 25, 26
Auden, W. H. 107, 191
Augustine 66, 106, 138
Ault, Donald 10-11, 228 n., 232 n.

Bachelard, Gaston 30
Bacon, Francis 16, 18-19
Bandy, Melanie F. 10, 173
Beer, John 227 n.
Bergson, Henri 106, 239 n.
Berkeley, George 8, 13, 106
Beulah 65-7, 231 n.
Blake, William 7, 19, 21-2, 73, 78, 93
  see also Los, and Blake; Milton, and Blake; Ololon, and Blake
Bloom, Harold 9, 48, 75, 105, 166, 183, 194, 200, 229 n., 234 n., 239 n.
*Book of Los, The* 205
*Book of Urizen, The* 11, 27, 30, 43, 65, 86, 116, 118, 183, 208
Bracher, Mark 50, 51, 52, 62, 226 n., 230 n.
Brittannia 133, 212
Brothers, Richard 73
Bultmann, Rudolf 7, 71
Burke, Edmund 83
Butts, Thomas (Blake's letters to) 114

Calvin, Jean 46
Cambel 199-200
Charles I 48
Christ, see Jesus
Classicism, see Hebraism and Classicism
Coleridge, Samuel Taylor 7-8, 96
Collins, Anthony 183
Conway, Gertrude D. 236 n.
Cromwell, Oliver 48-9, 230 n.
Cunningham, Allan 1
Curran, Stuart 32, 40, 102, 104, 234 n.

Daedalus 26-7
Damon, S. Foster 1, 2, 7, 46, 79, 102, 104, 120, 121, 143, 166, 229 n., 230 n., 236-7 n.
Damrosch, Leopold 28, 225 n., 226 n., 227 n., 233 n.
Daughters of Albion 47, 107-8, 166, 168, 177, 195-203 *passim*
Daughters of Los 168, 202-3
Davies, Paul 231 n.
Deen, Leonard W. 10, 227 n.
De Man, Paul 11, 95-6, 224 n.
Derrida, Jacques 3, 19-21, 24-7
*Descriptive Catalogue* 113
Deuteronomy 158
Dewey, John 236 n.
*différance* 19-20, 21, 22, 25, 26, 226 n.
Doskow, Minna 10, 104, 234 n.

Easson, Kay Parkhurst and Roger R. 231-2 n.
Eaves, Morris 10
Eden 65, 123, 124, 231 n.
Elect, Reprobate, and Redeemed 41-54, 56, 60, 79, 81, 86, 229 n., 230 n.
Eliade, Mircea 7
Eliot, T. S. 138
embrace:
  of his body by Milton 67-8
  of Enitharmon by Los 149, 155-6
  of fallen world 79, 84, 86-7, 95, 155-7
  of Milton and Ololon 92-5
  of his Spectre by Los 67, 149
  and transformation 24
Enitharmon:
  aetiology 155-6
  and Albion 119, 204, 207
  division from Los 118, 119, 216, 208
  in Eternity 29-30, 239 n.
  'Looking-Glass of' 177

Enitharmon (cont.)
  and Spectre of Los 76, 119, 216-17
  struggle with Los 206-8
  and Vala 135
  see also Los, and Enitharmon
Erdman, David 2, 7, 102, 104, 227 n., 235 n., 236 n., 237 n., 240 n.
Erin 120, 186, 235 n.
Error, consolidation of 4, 120, 125-6, 144, 207, 213, 215, 220
Eternity:
  and Blake's poetry 6-7
  and the Fall 162-4
  the geography of 64-6
  and Locke 17-18, 106-7
  prophet's role in 28-9
  Reuben's role in 118
  Spectre's role in 118
  and vortexes 68-9
Europe 19, 63-4, 81, 205
'Everlasting Gospel' 64

female power, see active and passive powers; sexism in Blake
Ferguson, James 234 n.
Fisch, Harold 79
Fogel, Aaron 227 n.
Foucault, Michel 137
Four Zoas, The 18, 29, 32, 67, 81, 87, 116, 117, 125, 137, 170-1, 208, 210, 219, 220
Fox, Susan 41, 42, 49, 79, 229 n., 230 n., 231 n., 232 n.
Freud, Sigmund 3, 7, 69, 81
Frosch, Thomas R. 133-4, 225 n., 226 n., 227 n., 232 n., 236 n.
Frye, Northrop 2, 7, 8-14, 22-3, 28, 29, 40-1, 79, 112, 121, 145, 214, 227 n., 229 n., 230 n., 231 n., 232 n., 236 n., 239 n.

Gadamer, Hans Georg 3-4
Galant, Christine 227 n.
Gates of Paradise 25
Generation 65-7, 168, 182, 203, 231 n.
Ginzberg, Louis 143
Gleckner, Robert F. 9
Golgonooza 79-83, 120-6, 202
Grant, John E. 236 n.
Grimes, Ronald L. 227 n.
Gwendolen 196, 197-9, 200-3 passim, 240 n.

Hand 184-5, 239 n., 240 n.
Harper, George Mills 105, 223 n.
Havens, Raymond Dexter 228 n.
Hayley, William 231 n.
Hebraism and Classicism 26-7, 226 n.
Heidegger, Martin 101, 106, 138, 158, 228 n.

hermeneutics:
  of belief 7, 223 n.
  of suspicion 3, 7, 223 n.
Hilton, Nelson 224 n.
Howard, John 40, 61, 229 n., 230 n., 231 n.
'How sweet I Roam'd' 5-6
Hume, David 25, 108, 230 n.
Husserl, Edmund 82
Hyle 197-9

Icarus 20, 25-7
Imagination 7-11, 12, 97, 106-8, 221, 223 n., 224 n.
  see also Jesus, the Imagination
infinity 68-70, 232 n.

James II 48
James, David E. 10, 41, 46, 61, 79, 97, 226 n., 229 n., 230 n., 231 n.
Jerusalem:
  alternate ordering 153-7, 237-8 n.
  commentary: [1-25]: 101-36; [26-50]: 137-57; [51-75]: 158-90; [76-100]: 191-217
  critique of Locke in 17-18
  ending 213-17, 218-19
  form of and narrative in 104-6, 233 n., 234 n.
  and the golden string 108-9, 191-2, 240 n.
  illustrations discussed: [1] frontispiece: 101-2, 233 n.; [6]: 117; [22]: 159; [28]: 236 n.; [53]: 160; [54]: 65, 161-2; [55-6]: 164-5; [57]: 168; [62-3, 65-9, 71]: 176; [78]: 192; [100]: 216-17
  reading experience 102, 112-14, 235 n.
  and temporality 105-8, 128-9, 189
  theme 14-16, 109-10, 234-5 n.
  see also Milton, and Jerusalem; narrative, in Jerusalem
Jerusalem 15, 140, 172, 174, 193, 205
  and Vala 132-4, 135-6
  see also Albion, and Jerusalem; Jesus, and Jerusalem
Jesus:
  and Albion 15-16, 21-2, 110-11, 130-1, 212-15 passim
  body of 189, 209-10
  child of Vala 209-10
  and encounter 74, 91, 92, 95, 206
  as Holy Ghost 173
  as iconoclast 189, 219
  the Imagination 11-12, 14-16, 18, 220, 221
  and Jerusalem 172-5, 210
  and relationship 72, 110, 218-20
  Seventh Eye of God 164
  as transgressor 45, 220-1
  and vision of Jerusalem 109-13
  see also Los, and Jesus
judgement 46-7, 55-61 passim, 94

## Index

Kant, Immanuel 106
Kiralis, Karl 104, 105, 145, 235 n., 236 n.
Kittel, Harald A. 10
Kojève, Alexandre 37
Koyré, Alexander 18

Lesnick, Henry 105, 233 n.
Leutha 52, 231 n.
Lister, Raymond 223 n.
Living Form 52
Locke, John 16-19, 24, 53, 63-4, 66, 69, 72, 83, 92, 106, 111, 116, 117, 134, 195, 211, 230 n.
  see also time, Lockean
Los:
  and Albion 42, 90, 94, 115-17, 119-20, 142-50 passim, 189, 209-11
  as arbitrator 44, 55, 57, 231 n.
  and Blake 27, 73, 126-31 passim
  described 27-31, 218, 227 n., 227-8 n., 240 n.
  and Enitharmon 29-30, 44, 118-19, 155-6, 204, 239 n.
  and fallen world 27, 30, 31, 43, 44, 90, 116
  and form of Blake's poetry 32
  and Golgonooza 120-6 passim
  as ground of the present 185-8
  and Jesus 28, 217, 218-21, 225 n.
  as loss 27, 30, 83, 227 n.
  Printing Press of 83
  as Prophet 27, 28-31, 83-6 passim, 115-16, 119-20, 218, 240 n.
  and Rahab 159-61, 167
  Song of 204-5
  and his Spectre 29, 30, 44, 117-20, 155, 211-12
  and the Three Classes 41-5, 49
  and Urizen 30, 43, 169, 170
  and Urthona 30, 155-6
  and Vala 119, 135
  as Watchman 27, 148, 166, 226 n.
  see also Enitharmon, division from Los; Milton, and Los
Luvah 133-4, 178-82 passim, 194

McGann, Jerome 224 n.
male power, see active and passive powers; sexism in Blake
Malory, Sir Thomas 144
Man, Paul de 11, 95-6, 224 n.
Margoliouth, H. M. 227 n.
Marks, Mollyanne 104, 105, 233 n.
Marx, Karl 3, 7, 81
Mathematical Form 52-3
Mellor, Anne K. 10, 234 n.
'Mental Traveller' 23
Merleau-Ponty, Maurice 4, 72, 73
Merlin 144, 236 n.
Milton:
  commentary: (1) Preface: 37-8; (2-13)

Bard's Song: 6, 24, 29, 32, 40-62, 66, 79; (14-29): 63-90; (30-43): 91-7
illustrations discussed: (i) title-page 38-40, 232 n.; (6) 4-5; (10) 58-60; (32) 72-3
and Jerusalem 110, 234-5 n.
vision of time and space in 87-9
see also narrative, in Bard's Song
Milton:
  and the Bard 63, 73
  and Blake 71-5, 77, 93, 228-9 n.
  descent 63-8, 70-5, 231 n., 232 n.
  and Los 78
  and Ololon 92-5
  Shadow 67, 68
  on title-page 38-40
  and Urizen 75-6
Milton, John 38, 48, 66, 75, 228 n., 228-9 n., 230 n., 231 n., 234 n.
Mitchell, W. J. T. 10, 68, 77, 79, 104, 105, 214, 225 n., 226 n., 227 n., 231 n., 232 n., 233 n., 240 n.
Murray, E. B. 227 n., 236 n.,239 n., 240 n.

Narcissus 18
narrative:
  in Bard's Song 40-1, 45, 229 n.
  in Jerusalem 104-6, 127, 128
  in Milton 87
  and vision 149-53
Newton, Sir Isaac 16, 18-19, 82, 101, 158, 202
Nietzsche, Friedrich 3, 7
Ololon:
  and Blake 93
  descent 90-5
  see also Milton, and Ololon
ontic 228 n.
  see also time, ontic
ontological 80, 228 n.
  see also time, ontological
Oothoon 78, 91
Ostriker, Alicia 230 n.
Other 78, 91
Otto, Peter 228 n.

Paine, Thomas 83
Palamabron 50-61 passim
Paley, Morton 10, 104, 105, 128, 225 n., 226 n., 227 n., 227-8 n., 235 n., 235-6 n., 236 n., 237-8 n., 240 n.
passive power, see active and passive powers; sexism in Blake
Paul, St 74
perception, role in Blake's art 8, 13, 22-4, 69, 81, 226 n.
Perrin, Norman 215, 240 n.
prophetic art 6, 7, 21, 24, 29, 83, 126, 130, 220
  see also visionary art; visionary deconstruction

# 244 Index

Rahab 20, 75, 76, 159-61, 182, 196-7, 201
Raine, Kathleen 1-2, 7
Redeemed, *see* Elect, Reprobate, and Redeemed; Jesus, as transgressor
regeneration 19, 24, 31, 82, 189-90, 212-14, 216
Reprobate, *see* Elect, Reprobate, and Redeemed; Jesus, as transgressor
Reuben 143-5, 204, 236 n.
Richardson, William J. 228 n.
Ricoeur, Paul 2, 30, 115, 233 n.
Rieger, James 41
Rilke, Rainer Maria 209
Rintrah 50-61 *passim*
Robinson, Crabb 25
Rose, Edward J. 9, 79, 224 n., 226 n., 227 n., 234 n., 239 n.
Rossetti, William Michael 1
Roston, Murray 226 n.
Rudd, Margaret 1

Sandler, Florence 229 n.
Satan 44, 50, 51-61 *passim*, 70, 79, 97, 142, 230 n., 231 n.
Saurat, Denis 229 n.
Saussure, Ferdinand de 2, 19
sedimented language 4, 6, 40
self 223 n.
sexism in Blake 32-3, 230 n.
  *see also* active and passive powers
Shadowy Female 75, 76
Shaviro, Steven 225 n.
Sloss, D. J., and J. P. R. Wallis 235 n.
*Song of Los, The* 29-31 *passim*, 205
Sons of Albion 133, 178-80, 183-4, 195
Southcott, Joanna 240 n.
Southey, Robert 1
Spectre of Los 29-30, 44, 116-18, 155-7, 210-12, 216, 235 n.
speech 4, 6, 40
Stempel, Daniel 10, 227 n.
Stevenson, W. H. 233 n., 240 n.
Swinburne, Algernon Charles 235 n.
symbol 37, 95-6, 233 n.

Taylor, Irene 229 n.
Teitlebaum, Eve 55
Tharmas 81
Thel 9, 66
Thornton, R. J., *The Lord's Prayer*, Blake's annotations to 173
Three Classes, *see* Elect, Reprobate, and Redeemed
time:
  as body of Albion 66
  of Embodiment 81-2, 86-9, 94, 111, 120
  relation to Eternity 7, 9, 11, 31-2, 130, 138
  Lockean 107, 128, 137, 153, 158

Newtonian 82, 101, 158
ontic 128, 204, 215
ontological 30, 101-36, 137-43 *passim*, 149-57 *passim*
  present 158-90, 239 n.
  productions of 7, 33
  sequential 102, 120, 137-43 *passim*, 149-53 *passim*
  *see also* Jerusalem, and temporality; Milton, vision of time and space in
Tindal, Matthew 183
Tirzah 75, 76, 182, 196
Toland, John 183
Tolley, Michael J. 91, 231 n., 232 n.
Trusler, John (Blake's letter to) 13, 23-4

Ulro 14, 65-7 *passim*, 81, 231 n.
Urizen 9, 11, 15, 20, 44, 75, 81, 116, 138, 170, 226 n.
  *see also* Los, and Urizen
Urthona 11, 29, 30, 156
  *see also* Los, and Urthona

Vala 20, 119, 131-6, 150-1, 160, 177-85 *passim*, 193-7, 236 n.
vision 13, 14, 62, 96-7 (defined), 109-15, 126-33, 151-4 *passim*, 171-6, 188-90, 192-3, 203-5, 210-16 *passim*
  *see also* narrative, and vision
'Vision, A' 114
visionary art 6, 7, 21, 26-7
  *see also* prophetic art
visionary construction 26, 32-3, 97, 108, 128, 221
visionary deconstruction 6, 26-7, 32-3, 37-62, 97, 221
*Vision of the Last Judgment* 11-13, 110, 138
*Visions of the Daughters of Albion* 24, 78, 91
Vogler, Thomas A. 224 n.
Voltaire 1
Vortex 68-71, 231-2 n., 232 n.

Wallis, J. P. R., *see* Sloss, D. J., and J. P. R. Wallis
Warner, Richard 237 n.
Watson, Robert, *Apology for the Bible*, Blake's annotations to 28
Webster, Brenda 235 n.
Wicksteed, Joseph 102
Willey, Basil 182-3
William III 48
withdrawal from relationship 9, 15-19, 21, 31, 64-5
Witke, Joanne 234 n.
Wittreich, Joseph Anthony 73, 228-9 n., 229 n., 234 n.
Wyschogrod, Edith 232 n.